UNDERSTANDING
THE COST OF WELFARE

UNDERSTANDING THE COST OF WELFARE

Third Edition

Howard Glennerster

Third edition published in Great Britain in 2017 by

Policy Press
University of Bristol
1-9 Old Park Hill
Bristol
BS2 8BB
UK
t: +44 (0)117 954 5940
pp-info@bristol.ac.uk
www.policypress.co.uk

North America office:
Policy Press
c/o The University of Chicago Press
1427 East 60th Street
Chicago, IL 60637, USA
t: +1 773 702 7700
f: +1 773-702-9756
sales@press.uchicago.edu
www.press.uchicago.edu

© The Policy Press and the Social Policy Association 2017

British Library Cataloguing in Publication Data
A catalogue record for this book is available from the British Library

Library of Congress Cataloging-in-Publication Data
A catalog record for this book has been requested

ISBN 978-1-4473-3404-0 paperback
ISBN 978-1-4473-3403-3 hardcover
ISBN 978-1-4473-3405-7 ePub
ISBN 978-1-4473-3406-4 Mobi
ISBN 978-1-4473-3407-1 ePdf

Cover design by Qube Design Associates, Bristol
Front cover image: www.alamy

Contents

Detailed contents

List of tables and figures

Tables

Figures

About the author

Howard Glennerster is Professor Emeritus of Social Policy at the London School of Economics and Political Science, UK. He has been an advisor to Her Majesty's Treasury and to the Secretary of State for Health. He is a Fellow of the British Academy, a Fellow of the Royal Society of Arts and an Academician of the Social Sciences section of the Learned Societies.

Acknowledgements

I would like to express thanks for permission to publish the following diagrams from other publications:

- The Controller of Her Majesty's Stationery Office for the following item, which is Crown copyright: **Figure 8.2**.
- **Figure 1.2** is reproduced from Burchardt, T. and Obolenskaya, P. (2016) 'Public and private welfare', in R. Lupton, T. Burchardt, J. Hills, K. Stewart and P. Vizard (eds) *Social policy in a cold climate: Policies and their consequences since the crisis*, Bristol: Policy Press. Reproduced by permission of Policy Press.
- **Figure 7.1** is adapted from a diagram on the King's Fund website.
- **Figure 8.1** is reproduced from William Laing, 'Strategic commissioning of long term care for older people: Can we get more for less?' (September 2014). Reproduced by permission of Laing Buisson.
- **Figure 9.1** is reproduced from C. Belfield and L. Sibieta (2016) 'Long run trends in school spending', Institute for Fiscal Studies. Reproduced by permission of the Institute for Fiscal Studies.
- **Figure 9.2** is reproduced from C. Belfield and L. Sibieta, 'English schools will feel the pinch over the next five years', *Observations*, 21 October 2015, Institute for Fiscal Studies. Reproduced by permission of the Institute for Fiscal Studies.

Colleagues at the London School of Economics (LSE) in the Centre for Analysis of Social Exclusion (CASE) have again been remarkably generous with their time, notably, Bert Provan for his major contribution to Chapter Eleven. Nic Barr has been invaluable commenting on chapters close to his work, but in many ways, over many years. We gave parallel lecture courses in the 1980s from which our two books sprang. We each went to and commented on each other's lectures, hence the frequent cross-references. Emily Jones helped me with material for the Osborne family example in Chapter One. My thanks are to John Hills for helping me do that, but in many other ways too. We have worked together for so many years, in so many ways, that it is difficult to disentangle attributions. All the errors are mine. Chris Deeming gave many useful comments, not least on social policy north of the border.

I owe a great deal to the secretarial, administrative and computing staff of STICERD (Suntory and Toyota Centres for Economics and Related Disciplines), of which I was once chairman. I have never worked with nicer or more helpful colleagues.

Catherine Gray, commissioning editor of Policy Press, has given steady encouragement and support and persuaded me to update this edition for one more time.

My more personal thanks go to Ann, who has put up with my scribbling since we wrote a Fabian pamphlet together in 1962 and has always been a helpful critic.

Just after I had finished the first draft of this book Ann suffered a brain haemorrhage at breakfast one morning. Our lives changed. I ceased to be a cared-for, critiqued and maths-advised academic and became a full-time carer. Ann became the recipient of first-class National Health Service attention and both of us received support from a wide range of friends and family. That could not have better illustrated the theme of this text.

Howard Glennerster
London School of Economics and Political Science
February 2017

Glossary

NB: Cross-references to other glossary terms are denoted by **bold text**.

Academies
Schools funded directly by the central government in England that are largely independent of the **local education authority** in their area.

Average tax rate
The percentage of total income taken in tax.

Chains
These are organisations set up to provide common services, like specialist advice, to schools that are no longer receiving support from their **local education authorities**.

Child Tax Credit
A payment made to those with children on low incomes. Being subsumed within **Universal Credit**.

Comprehensive Spending Review
An in-depth review of public spending by government departments undertaken at regular intervals.

Defined-benefit pensions
Schemes that give benefits specified in advance in relation to some proportion of final salary or time spent in that employment, not directly to the level of contributions paid in.

Defined-contribution pensions
Schemes that set contribution rates with benefits dependent on the total of contributions made and on the investment returns made on the funds invested.

Devolution
Powers to administer services and legislate on them made over to regional parliaments or assemblies in the UK.

Direct taxes
Taxes levied on individuals' or corporations' income.

Externalities
Where an activity like producing a product or driving a car may impose costs on others or give general benefits that are not captured in the price of the product or in the costs that face individuals' actions.

Formula funding
The use of mathematical formulae to allocate funds to local areas or service providers.

Funded pensions
Schemes that build up reserves that, when invested, are supposed to be sufficient to pay for future pension commitments.

Gross domestic product (GDP)
The total output or income of a country.

Housing benefit
A payment made to those on low incomes to cover specified housing costs but subject to limits and penalties. To be subsumed in **Universal Credit**.

Human capital
An analogy with physical capital or machinery. Investing in an individual's education may make her more productive in her lifetime.

Incidence of taxation
Where the cost ultimately falls – a firm may pass on a tax to a consumer.

Indirect taxes
Taxes on expenditure – Value Added Tax (VAT), duties on alcohol or fuel.

Income support
Means-tested cash assistance provided by central government to poor people in the UK.

Information failure
Markets need good information available to consumers and producers for that market to work properly. There are systematic reasons why that information may not exist in certain kinds of market.

Local education authorities (LEAs)
Elected local authorities who oversaw and funded all state schools in their area. They are now having their powers removed and passed to the governing bodies of **academies** and local inter-school '**chains**'.

Life cycle
The sequence of circumstances through which a person passes from birth, childhood and parenthood, to old age and death.

Mandated spending
Governments require citizens to take out private insurance, for example for health-care cover.

Marginal tax rate
The percentage taken on the last pound earned.

Monopoly
When one firm or public institution is the sole provider of a good or service.

National Institute for Health and Care Excellence (NICE)
Advises the secretary of state and local health and social care providers on the clinical, professional and cost effectiveness of health and social care interventions. It advises for England and Wales authorities and has its counterpart in Scotland.

New Labour
An attempt to redefine Labour Party policy including in a way that was more favourable to a mixed economy of welfare, seeing virtues in competition between providers.

Neo-liberal
A body of political thought that has become internationally influential. It advocates a minimal role for the state.

Nudging
Governments seek to influence individual behaviour in ways that are, in governments' view, in individuals' long-term interests. For example, contributing to a pension.

Pay as you go
Pension schemes that are financed by the state, collecting just as much in each year as is necessary to pay for the costs of benefits that year.

Private Finance Initiative (PFI)
Relying on a private company to build and maintain a facility or rail network in return for annual payments.

Privatisation
To convert a publicly owned body into private ownership or to change the funding of an organisation from dependence on public funds (taxation) to private income (fees).

Progressive taxes
Taxes that take a lower percentage of low incomes than of higher ones.

Public goods
A range of goods and services that it is not in the interests of a firm in a competitive market to provide but from which the community at large benefits.

Real terms
An expenditure series in which spending over time is calculated as if prices had not changed. Actual prices or spending in any one year are inflated or deflated to put them on a common basis.

Regressive taxes
The reverse of progressive taxes – they take a higher percentage of the incomes of the poor than the rich.

Tax allowance
The amount of income that is exempted from tax.

Tax credit
A deduction from an individual's tax liability. A non-refundable tax credit can only be claimed up to the limit of one's tax liability. A refundable tax credit can be claimed in full even if it is more than your tax liability.

Tax expenditure
The value of **tax allowances** and non-refundable **tax credits** as they appear in the public accounts.

Tax relief
The amount of expenditure (eg on a private or occupational pension) that can be deducted from income before tax is paid.

Treasury control

The set of constitutional rules that puts Her Majesty's Treasury at the heart of public spending decisions in the UK.

Universal Credit

Six benefits are being combined into one under this title – income-based Job Seekers Allowance, Housing Benefit, Child Tax Credit, Working Tax Credit, income-related Employment and Support Allowance, and Income Support.

How to use this text

This book is primarily intended for students of social policy who need to understand what economists say about social policy without delving into the depths of economic theorems. I give references to texts that do that throughout the book. It begins with four chapters that try to set out as simply as possible the basic economic principles that analyse and justify the way 'welfare' services are paid for which are then discussed in more detail in Part Two.

In the first chapter I explain how it is possible to adopt a range of different strategies to secure families' wellbeing over a lifetime. We might try to rely on private insurance markets or our own savings strategies but in most countries families largely depend on governments to fund, regulate and often provide such services. That balance varies between countries.

Chapter Two explores why governments have come to play such a large role. There are important general ways in which markets fail to work well for the kinds of services discussed in Part Two. Then, for each chapter in Part Two, I pick up these general theories and relate them to each service under the heading 'Some economic theory'. But services often do not evolve in ways economic theory might suggest is ideal! Politics plays its part. So each chapter in Part Two begins with a brief history of how services came to be funded in the way they did in the United Kingdom (UK) and ends with some illustrations of different ways it has evolved elsewhere.

Part One concludes with two chapters that explore the economics and politics of taxation and then of public spending allocations – what I call 'rationing'.

Since 'devolution' in the UK much social service spending, and now some more taxing powers, have passed to the legislatures in Scotland, Wales and Northern Ireland. I try to show how these devolved powers differ in each part of the UK.

If a student or other reader is only interested in finding out about the funding of health care or schools she can read the relevant chapter in Part Two but would be well advised to read Part One as well!

Finally, in Chapter Twelve, I try to draw conclusions and distinguish diverse but politically feasible ways to resolve the serious funding issues UK public services face. I have summarised and given references to a range of viewpoints. However, I found from my experience of teaching LSE students that you could not entirely hide behind the formula 'on the one hand, ... and on the other, ...'. 'No, but what do *you* think?' they would say. 'Well, you do not have to agree,' I would reply, 'but this is what I think'. The same applies for readers of this book.

Part One
Principles

one

The cost of welfare

Summary

I define 'welfare' as to remain in good health and 'sufficiency'. Some individuals may be able to achieve that at their own cost for much of their lives but even they will cease to be able to do so in times of unemployment and illness or in old age. Private insurance against many of these risks does not work for many people.

State welfare policies are therefore designed to ensure that all individuals' basic needs are met, whatever misfortune affects them and whatever their age. Most families receive back from the welfare state as much as they pay in taxes towards it over a lifetime. Even a higher-income family will get back the great majority of what they paid in. It is important to distinguish who *pays* from who *provides* a service. This balance has been shifting in recent years.

Governments finance services directly from taxes but also:

- reduce tax demands if individuals spend money to provide for their own welfare, for example, buying their own house or taking out a pension – this is sometimes called 'fiscal welfare';
- require individuals to save for their retirement or take out private health insurance – 'mandatory spending';
- require employers to pay minimum wages and provide pensions or health insurance; and
- 'nudge' or encourage individuals to provide for their long-term needs.

Welfare

It is necessary to begin by defining and defending what I mean by 'welfare'. In 1985, having just returned from a stay in the US, I began a book entitled *Paying for welfare* by observing: 'To the American on the sidewalk welfare means cash handouts to hoodlums' (Glennerster, 1985, p 3). In the subsequent 30 years, there has been a steady and deliberate attempt to devalue the English use of the word, to taint it with its American stigma.

This book keeps unrepentantly to the use of the term in the *English* language. How is government to ensure that its citizens 'fare well', or remain in good health and 'sufficiency' as the Concise Oxford Dictionary puts it? They must be able to live at peace, in safety from foreign or terrorist attack, from local disorder or personal assault. For centuries, these have been considered a collective responsibility, the state's duty.

Families take responsibility for ensuring their own welfare through work and saving, caring for their children, and being careful about their health. However, life is full of risks and uncertainty. As later chapters explain, there are now well-understood reasons why people may not fully understand or take account of these risks or simply not be in a position to do anything about them because private insurance markets do not operate efficiently, or, in some cases, at all.

In his recent study *Good times, bad times*, John Hills (2015) charts in detail, and for different households, how much they rely on the welfare state to soften the blows to their well-being that chance adversity and simple ageing can bring. Even parenthood brings its risks, as well as its joys. We pay in and largely draw out from this common pot at different stages in our lives when we need to. Simplifying the rich personal detail in his study, Hills (2015, p 73) concludes:

> By the time a typical family reaches its late fifties it could have received cash benefits equivalent to half the value of a house, and services from health and education equivalent to a whole house. But it would have paid in more than two houses' worth of taxes. If it survived into its mid-eighties [Now likely!] the lifetime taxes would have reached the equivalent of three houses, but this would be balanced by one-and-a-half houses' worth of benefits and state pensions and the same again in health care and education.

However, Hills' better-off family might have chosen not to rely on the state. In a neoliberal future, they might well have to do without its help altogether. An appropriate starting point for this text is to therefore undertake a thought experiment. Let us assume that a future state plays no part in sustaining people's welfare apart from maintaining their physical security through the armed forces and police – or, at the very least, it only intervenes in rare cases of extreme hardship. What would that cost an ordinary, reasonably well-off family?

Let us take as our example the younger generation of the Osborne family whom Hills uses as one of his examples – Henry, now 35, and Clare, now 33. They have two children – Lucy, aged eight, and Edward, aged three. They are certainly a reasonably well-off family, owner-occupiers living in Stockport with a joint income of over £60,000 a year. They are better off than four fifths of the population.

Clare is working three days a week and Edward's grandmother is providing some childcare. However, the family pays for 25 hours of childcare and early education provision each week at an average cost for a child in the North West of England (£101). It would be half as much again in London! The annual total of 570 hours that they buy is broadly in line with what the state now provides for three to four year olds. Its cost comes to £2,300 a year. (Figures from the Family and Child Care Trust, but they are complicated by the cross-subsidisation of the costs met by local authorities and so should be taken as rough estimates of the costs that might hold if this were a pure market.)

Lucy goes to school. She is only eight but fees will rise as she gets older. Boarding is out of the question or attending a top fee-paying school but an average termly day school fee in the North of England is £3,422 (in 2016; figure from the Independent Schools Council). It would be more in Greater London (£5,233).

Henry and Clare are concerned that their two children should eventually be able to go to university. Universities are now charging a full economic fee to cover tuition – what they used to charge only overseas students. That enables some cross-subsidisation of poor students but they will not qualify. The couple have ambitions that their two children might want to study in London – to the London School of Economics or Imperial College – and take either life sciences, computing or economics. They examine the fees that these colleges are charging and take a rough average. They assume that their offspring will only want to take a three-year undergraduate course, so they go to their friendly local bank manager and ask how much they will have to save each year to achieve the sum needed. He points out that they must assume that university tuition fees will go on rising – at least at 2% per annum. It seems that the sum they will need for both children might amount to about £180,000. Then they will have to support their children's living expenses at college. That would be £11–12,000 a year if they went to London, friends told them, but rather less if their children went to Manchester. Those costs would rise, too, perhaps by 2% a year in normal times. In total, he says, it is difficult to see them needing to find less than a quarter of a million pounds in 10 to 15 years' time if they really want their children to go to London. However, even a provincial university will require them to save perhaps £200,000.

What concerns the couple more immediately is that they have to take out adequate cover to meet any health-care costs. They are fortunately in good health and do not smoke. One insurer offers them cover at £2,650 a year for the family and another suggests £2,900, given their postcode. This sum covers dental and optician care, but in every case, they need a GP referral to trigger such cover. There is no cover offered for GP visits. The insurance company says that if they did that, people would be continuously going to their GP for reassurance. That could change, but if it did, their health insurance premiums would surely rise. As it is, GPs in the area are charging £90 for a 15-minute consultation. Moreover, they are told that if they are found to have a pre-existing condition, the costs of treatment will not be covered. There seems no way to get cover if they turn out to be really ill for a very long period with a long-term condition. Talking to Henry's parents made it clear that the costs of health cover would rise as they got older. One insurer was charging their parents over £4,000 annually for cover.

This leads them to think about what happens when they become really old. Henry recalls reading something by an economist called Professor Dilnot, who said that 'a quarter of people aged 65 will need to spend very little on care … half can expect costs of up to £20,000 but one in ten can expect costs of over £100,000'. That was said some time ago. Henry thought that it would be a good idea to see if you could insure against that possibility. However, he found that private long-term care insurance was no longer available in the UK. It would be possible to take out an Immediate Needs Annuity when he retired (see: www. moneyadviceservice.org.uk). These annuities are designed to cover the difference between regular pension income and the costs of likely care. However, it looked expensive. In 2011, a study by the Personal Social Services Unit at the London School of Economics (LSE) had calculated that the average down payment for such an annuity was about £70,000 per person.

Relying on running down the capital in their house to pay for care looked the best thing to do – 'equity release'. Taking into account the value of their house, they should be able to pay for five years of care. That was true for 70% of people aged 50 he read (Mayhew et al, 2016). However, there had been expensive scams in such schemes in the past. It could mean that not much capital would be available to hand on to their children. It was rather worrying.

Then they had to think about their pensions. Henry was lucky to still be a member of a defined benefit scheme run by his employer. Like the average member of such schemes, they were contributing 5% of his salary; his employer was contributing 16%. The scheme was closed to younger colleagues.

The (hypothetical) new government was suggesting that it would not in the long term even pay a flat-rate state pension; it would be means-tested. They would have to make very sure that their pension was adequate to live on without suffering a large fall in their standard of living when they retired. Pension experts told him that *his* contribution ought to be much higher to get a more generous pension.

Finally, they were at least buying their own house. That meant not just mortgage payments, but the costs of heating it and keeping it properly repaired. Like the average British family, that was taking just less than a third of their income.

Adding all this up, it looked as if they were paying about half their income keeping themselves properly covered and housed. If they had been living in London, that would have been much more. However, this was without taking into account the large dose of savings that they would have to make to see their children through college or due to the threat of a declining state pension. They realised that they were relatively fortunate. Many of the outgoings would be the same for a poorer family. Indeed, with a less good health record, a poorer family might find their private health insurance premium was higher than theirs. All these flat-rate insurance costs would have to come out of a much lower income. How were they coping?

Of course, they were paying less tax than their parents had, but not that much less. There still was a health service of sorts. It looked after the long-term sick, the long-term mentally ill and disabled and most old people. That took about half the sum the old universal National Health Service (NHS) had cost. The state was still supporting older people who had not been forced to save for their long-term care. Poorer parents were still receiving free schooling. So, their taxes had only been cut by about a third. They were paying out more than they had gained. Moreover, that all depended on not getting seriously ill or Henry losing his job or either of them having a serious accident. Such a hypothetical world is not yet with us. However, to focus on the costs of *public* welfare and ignore the costs of its alternative is to badly distort the picture.

Why welfare works best through collective action

In his founding essay on social policy, Richard Titmuss argued:

> All collectively provided services are deliberately designed to meet certain socially recognised 'needs': they are manifestations, first, of society's will to survive as an organic whole and, secondly of the expressed will of all the people to assist the survival of some people. (Titmuss, 1958, quoted in Alcock et al, 2001, p 62)

Titmuss never elaborated a fully worked-out theory of need (Glennerster, 2014). However, others have tried with more success. Doyal and Gough (1991) argued that all, or virtually all, political and moral theories start from the presumption that individuals ought to be able to survive and live healthy autonomous lives in which their basic needs are realised. Other authors have tackled these issues using a different framework. Sen (1985, 1993) has elaborated a set of 'capabilities' – a set of 'valuable things that people can do and be'. Cut off from being able to access them, they lose their identity and the freedoms that make them fully human. A human rights framework extends Sen's approach (Vizard, 2006; Dean, 2010). This text moves the discussion on to ask: if so, what is the cost, who pays and how?

When Titmuss was writing that essay, collective social service provision was taking not much more than a tenth of the UK's Gross Domestic Product (GDP) or the total of the nation's income. By the mid-1980s, it was taking over 20%, and by 2016, it was taking more than a quarter after reaching its peak in the days of the economic crisis in 2008–10 (see **Figure 1.1**).

Figure 1.1: *Collective welfare spending* in the UK, 1900 to 2016*

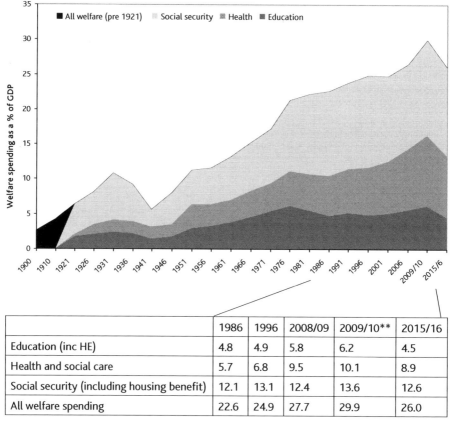

	1986	1996	2008/09	2009/10**	2015/16
Education (inc HE)	4.8	4.9	5.8	6.2	4.5
Health and social care	5.7	6.8	9.5	10.1	8.9
Social security (including housing benefit)	12.1	13.1	12.4	13.6	12.6
All welfare spending	22.6	24.9	27.7	29.9	26.0

* This includes the old Poor Law, modern social security, housing benefit and its predecessors. From 1987 some small items are included from agencies like the criminal justice system. They formed 0.5% of GDP in 1987. Social care spending has been removed from the official figures on social protection and added to health care for consistency with previous figures. Housing capital is excluded. Education includes public spending on higher education but excludes fee income.

**Maximum recession impact year.

Sources: Glennerster (2007); HM Treasury annual Public Expenditure Statistical Analyses (2016 and previous editions).

It would be wrong to see social policy as only a means of redistributing income over the life course or to the poor. It can also help to increase a nation's output and hence its capacity to fund welfare services as well as enhancing individuals' wellbeing. Parents may be unable to invest adequately in their children's education without support. Education brings individual and collective rewards. A more healthy labour force is a more productive one. This 'social investment perspective' is a new term for an old set of ideas (Smyth and Deeming, 2016).

Choice, agency and 'privatisation'

Burchardt et al (1999) sought to capture the extent of choice and agency available to service users both within and outside public services. They have repeated that exercise on several occasions. It is therefore possible to track how far services have become more 'privately provided' or 'privately funded'. It also enables us to unpick the rather confused statements that are sometimes made about 'privatisation'. This analysis does not try to incorporate a measure of state 'regulation' (Powell and Miller, 2014). However, is does clarify what has been happening to the balance between public and private funding and public and private provision. *Figure 1.2* is reproduced from the authors' latest analysis (Burchardt and Obolenskaya, 2016).

The quartered circle distinguishes between *public* provision and *public* finance, and shows where they overlap. An NHS hospital funded by the state providing NHS care is one kind of pure case – a 'pure public service' (the pure white segment). Users may have choice between those publicly provided hospitals – a 'quasi-market'. That can be distinguished from *private* provision with public *finance* – a private hospital contracted to take NHS patients or an old person's home paid to take local authority clients (the bottom-right outer segment).

It shows *public* provision and *private* finance – a private-pay bed in an NHS hospital paid for by the user (top-left inner circle). It also distinguishes *private* provision and *private* finance (bottom-left outer circle), in other words, the pure market – paying fees to a Harley Street specialist or private patients going to a private hospital and paying their own fees, or parents paying for a private school.

Burchardt and colleagues go on to distinguish between the extent of agency and choice involved in different arrangements. The top right-hand segment of public provision and finance would include an inner element (labelled 1), where patients mostly go to the local hospital or children to the nearest school. However, there is also an outer part of the segment where parents can choose which school to attend by presenting a voucher and where patients are given a free choice of public or private hospital. In the real world, these choices are constrained. In England, as will be explained later in the book, users have *some* choice of school and hospital. The bottom left-hand segment distinguishes the full free market provision on the outside from one where an institution provides services for a local authority but the user pays an agreed or set fee – the inner segment. In the right–hand diagram, the authors distinguish the forms of 'privatisation' to which this analysis gives rise. They have done so on a comparative basis back to 1979/80. In that year, total public *and* private spending on those items amounted to 26% of GDP. By 2013/14, that sum had risen *five times* in absolute terms to be equivalent to nearly 40% of GDP (see *Table 1.1*).

Total spending can then be allocated between each of the quadrants in *Figure 1.2*. It is therefore possible to see how far the share of spending on 'pure' publicly administered and publicly funded services has fared compared to pure private services.

Figure 1.2: Wheels of welfare

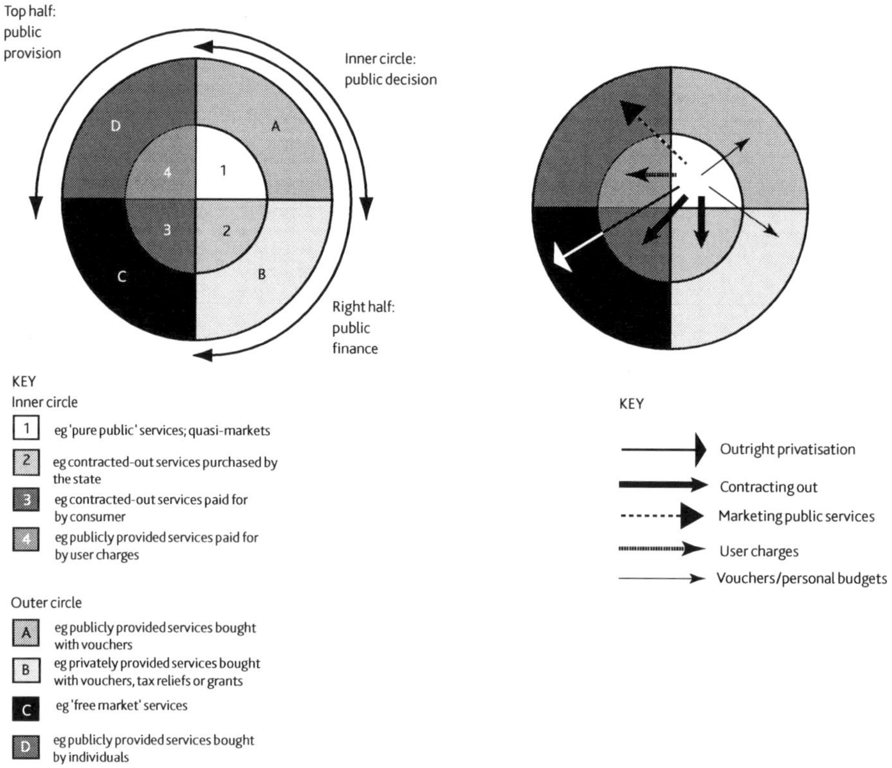

Top half:
public
provision

Inner circle:
public decision

Right half:
public
finance

KEY
Inner circle

1 eg 'pure public' services; quasi-markets

2 eg contracted-out services purchased by the state

3 eg contracted-out services paid for by consumer

4 eg publicly provided services paid for by user charges

Outer circle

A eg publicly provided services bought with vouchers

B eg privately provided services bought with vouchers, tax reliefs or grants

C eg 'free market' services

D eg publicly provided services bought by individuals

KEY

Outright privatisation

Contracting out

Marketing public services

User charges

Vouchers/personal budgets

Source: Burchardt and Obolenskaya (2016)

In 1979/80, rather more than half (54%) of all welfare spending could be classed as falling into the 'public finance and public provision' segment. That is what some have called 'hard-core traditional' or 'classic' welfare state spending. This figure, though, reinforces our original contention that even in its pre-Thatcher form, the 'classic welfare state' was never a good way to understand how welfare services were funded and organised. Even then, private housing and private pension spending, together with private schools and private health provision, made up about a fifth of the total welfare activity.

Tax-subsidised private pensions and owner-occupied housing (see later), as well as publicly funded but privately provided services in health and education, together made up another quarter of the activity.

By 2013/14, a slow but steady transformation is evident. By then, only 38% of the 'welfare economy' was both publicly funded *and* publicly provided. An identical share was privately funded and privately provided. Just over a fifth of total spending occupied the several categories of mixed funding and provision.

Table 1.1: *Total public and private spending on welfare services in the UK, 1979/80–2013/14 (£billion, real terms 2013/14 prices and as a percentage of GDP)*

	1979/80	1995/96	1999/2000	2007/08	2013/14
Health	33.3	63.6	77.3	115.2	120.6
Social care	6.7	21.9	25.4	35.7	37.3
Education	29.8	45.0	46.0	73.1	79.5
Income maintenance	106.9	155.2	162.8	234.3	250.2
Housing	48.2	85.4	108.4	158.4	206.9
Total as % of GDP	26.1	30.4	30.4	35.6	39.6

Source: Obolenskaya and Burchardt (2016).

A new 'social division of welfare'

Titmuss drew attention to the range of ways in which the government can shape the funding and provision of welfare – what he called 'the social division of welfare' (Titmuss, 1958; Alcock et al, 2001). Governments could use the tax system to encourage individuals to save for their retirement or use private health care – 'fiscal welfare'. Employers could also be encouraged to provide for their employees – 'occupational welfare'. Titmuss did not approve; the rich benefited disproportionately, he argued.

More recently, economists have come to recognise the importance of such mechanisms and suggest ways to extend them (Tanzi, 2011). Governments can supplement 'taxing and spending' as a way to achieve social goals. If taxes are difficult to raise, governments should require people to insure themselves or encourage them to do so. This debate is reflected in later chapters. Outlined in the following is a range of ways in which the state can try to ensure that resources are devoted to goals it thinks desirable without formally taxing individuals and providing government services.

Regulation and 'quasi-taxation'

Examples of this approach already exist:

- Car owners must, by law, take out private third-party insurance against claims that may be made against them if they injure someone while driving the car.
- Employers with more than a given wage bill will have to pay a levy of 0.5% on their 'pay role' (wage and salary bill) to cover the costs of training. This will be converted into a training voucher for their workforce and others.
- The law now requires employers to pay a minimum hourly wage. The Blair government introduced a national minimum wage in the UK for the first time in 1998. The 2015 Conservative government promised to raise its level significantly, suggesting that this was a better way to ensure higher incomes for the low-paid than subsidising their wages through tax credits.
- Recent UK pension law requires employers, over a given size, to offer a pension scheme to their employees. If their employees join, the employer must contribute to the scheme up to a set limit. The effect is not that different from levying a social security tax on employers.
- A similar example is the requirement laid on employees to take out health insurance up to a given level. That was the basis of Obama Care and other systems discussed in Chapter Seven.

However, the UK Office of Budget Responsibility (OBR, 2015) has commented: 'These [measures] are economically equivalent to pay roll taxes'. The OECD calls such measures and others like them 'mandatory social expenditure'.

Falling somewhat short of such compulsion is a strategy to which this book will return –'nudging'. It is a concept popularised by two American economists (Thaler and Sunstein, 2008). It involves presenting individuals with choices in such a way that they are more likely to respond by acting in their best long-term interest, at least as seen by the government! It is a form of 'libertarian paternalism'.

Different ways of doing things internationally

Different societies have evolved varied ways of paying for welfare. **Table 1.2** sets out an international comparison of the scale of economic activity devoted to

Table 1.2: International welfare expenditure: public and private, 2013 (percentage of GDP)

	Australia	Belgium	Canada	Denmark	France	Germany	Ireland	Italy	Netherlands	Norway	Spain	Sweden	USA	UK
Net current public social expenditure (sick leave, health, unemployment, pensions	17.8	25.7	16.5	22.5	28.0	23.0	18.6	24.1	20.1	18.0	23.5	22.9	19.8	20.5
Private 'mandated' expenditure on same+	1.7	0	0	2.5	0.2	1.4	0	0.6	0.7	1.2	0	0.4	0.3	0.9
Private voluntary expenditure	0.9	0.8	4.4	2.0	3.2	1.9	2.0	0.7	7.1	1.0	0.4	3.1	11.1	5.0
Public expenditure on education	3.9	5.6	4.6	6.1	4.5	4.7	5.0	3.7	4.7	6.2	3.6	5.2	4.2	5.2
Private expenditure on education#	1.7	0.2	1.4	0.2	0.5	0.6	0.2	0.3	0.8	0.1	0.7	0.2	2.0	1.5
Total education spending	5.6	5.8	6.0	6.4	5.0	5.3	5.2	4.0	5.5	6.3	4.3	5.4	6.2	6.7
Total net 'welfare' spending (Public and private)	26.0	34.0	27.5	34.0	36.7	31.6	25.9	29.4	33.4	26.5	28.2	30.7	37.4	33.1
Tax relief on private pensions	*1.9*	*0.2*	*1.5*	*0*	*0*	*0.9*	*1.1*	*0*	*2.1*	*0.5*	*0.2*	*0*	*0.8*	*1.5*

Notes: + private insurance required by law. # including higher education

Source: OECD (2016a); Adema, Fron and Ladaique (2011); OECD (2016b).

'social spending'. This is a rather odd Organisation for Economic Co-operation and Development (OECD) term that includes state cash benefits for those who are sick, unemployed or unable to work. However, it also includes both public and private spending on health care and pensions. Pensions are not included in a fully comparable way because of the complexity of the way tax systems deal with them. Some countries tax their social benefits; others do not. This table shows net spending on benefits after taxation. It includes private and public education spending but not housing costs. This combined spending is expressed as a percentage of GDP, essentially the scale of each country's economic activity. It may come as a surprise to find that the US devotes somewhat more resources to these purposes than the UK or most other advanced economies in Europe. The US finances them in different ways.

State funding plays a large part in every society. The means by which that is undertaken varies widely. The sources of funding may be through social insurance contributions, general national taxation, taxes tied to particular purposes or local taxation. Services receive their money in different ways. Part Two of this book analyses the way that is done for each service area.

It is important to make a distinction between who *finances* a service and who *provides* it. In Germany, most of the money raised to pay for health care comes from social insurance contributions. However, the sick funds, which receive the money, frequently buy health care for their patients from private hospitals and clinics; many are not-for-profit private hospitals run by a religious foundation. Public finance is not the same thing as public provision.

Overview

To conclude, human welfare, broadly defined, can be achieved and paid for in a variety of ways. It can be provided by varied agencies, public and private, and by formal and informal means. The mix varies across countries.

Families in all societies are subject to a variety of risks over a lifetime but the costs of insuring against them privately can be large. No private market may exist at all. Government funding plays a large part in redistributing incomes from periods of work to those when work is impossible. But it also helps to make individuals and the wider economy more productive. It has a 'social investment function' and hence is an indirect way of enhancing welfare and wellbeing.

There are ways in which government can require or encourage people to provide for their own welfare and employers can be made to pay. Though not formal 'taxation' these measures have tax-like effects.

Questions for discussion

1. In how many different ways can governments finance, provide or cajole individuals and firms into paying for welfare?
2. How far can and do families take responsibility for their own welfare?
3. How has the provision and finance of welfare services changed over time in the UK or any other economy that you know?
4. Consider the pros and cons of different ways to encourage service provision other than 'taxing and spending'.

Further reading

For those who wish to follow up on the discussion of human need, **Doyal and Gough (1991)** is a classic beginning. Our companion volume **(Dean, 2010)** reviews more recent conceptual developments.

A powerful rejection of the welfare 'myth of them and us' and an account of the way in which the state redistributes from periods of relative plenty to periods of relative need is to be found in **Hills (2015; 2nd edn, 2017)**.

Recent changes to the relative scale of the state's activity compared to the private market are outlined by **Burchardt and Obolenskaya (2016)**.

The possibilities of a 'nudge strategy' are discussed in **Thaler and Sunstein (2008)**.

Market failure and government failure

Summary

This chapter seeks to explain in simple terms why standard economic theory holds that market exchange is an efficient way to allocate most goods and services. However, economics also recognises that there are major limits to the efficiency of market exchange and that they apply in important ways to the services discussed in Part Two of this book. On the other hand, economists also argue, organisations run by governments pose systematic problems too:

- Market exchange between many purchasers and providers where both have good information produces efficient outcomes. However, in many situations, these assumptions do not hold. They are called market failures.
- Yet, governments may find it difficult to ascertain voters' preferences, and services may be delivered by state monopolies that are not responsive to consumers.
- Not-for-profit organisations exist, in part, to counteract these deficiencies, but they have limits of their own.
- Social policy has tried to balance the advantages and disadvantages of each.

Why markets work – sometimes

Standard classical economic theory, certainly since Adam Smith (1974 [1776]), has been founded on the claim that, for most purposes, efficient economic outcomes result from self-interested exchanges between many individuals:

> Give me that which I want, and you shall have this that you want.... It is in this manner that we obtain from one another the far greater part of those good offices which we stand in need of. It is not from the beneficence of the butcher, the brewer, or the baker that we expect our dinner, but from their regard to their own interest. We address ourselves not to their humanity but to their self-love and never talk to them of our own necessities but of their advantages.... [All our wants are supplied] by treaty, by barter and by purchase. (Smith, 1974 [1776], pp 118–19)

The seeds of much modern economic theory are embedded in this famous extract:

- *Self-interest is more consistent and reliable than good will.* We can never be sure that a neighbour, even less a stranger, will help out when we are in need and certainly not over a long period (Bulmer, 1986). We can usually be sure that a tradesman will deliver if we have the money to pay. Nor will we have any feeling of future obligation or shame, which may come with taking a neighbour's help. However, are we so sure that human self-interest is always the best driving force that we can rely on? May not the love and care that a mother (Or father!) has for her child be more sustainable than a paid professional's willingness to care for the child? As it is a cash relationship, the carer has the undoubted right, written into her (or his) contract of employment, to stop work at some hour and to move on to another job. The mother has no such 'right' in accepted social practice. Yet, as we move away from such intense personal ties, Smith's proposition gains force. Even internal family decisions – who works and whether to marry or have children – are susceptible to economic market analysis (Becker, 1976). Some see this as deeply offensive, but it makes sense of some of the personal decisions that we make.
- *Dynamic efficiency and the profit motive.* The promise of profit encourages new entrants to the marketplace to keep thinking of new ways to meet consumers' needs and wants. Is there a market niche that they could fill? As a result, economists argue, a market economy will show *dynamic efficiency*. The failure of centralised socialist monopolies in Eastern Europe to foster such a climate of innovation arguably led to the demise of the whole system. However, the recent history of the Internet, the i-phone and many other key inventions point to a different conclusion (Mazzucato, 2013). Much innovation has derived

from publicly funded basic research. Its exploitation has followed the market model, but its origins have not. Both models interact with and are necessary to one another. Moreover, there are barriers to new firms entering the market. Existing players may be too big, too entrenched with high consumer trust or too politically powerful – the costs of market entry may be too high for any or all of these reasons.

- *Consumer sovereignty.* In theory, where individuals have cash in their pockets, they can encourage firms to respond to their preferences. If enough consumers want organic foods, the supermarkets and the farmers will, in the end, respond. If enough consumers want free-range eggs and are prepared to pay a little more for them, supermarkets will stock them. If consumer preferences are met, the economy will exhibit *allocative efficiency.* Resources will be allocated in a way that is required to produce what consumers want. Supermarkets may be too powerful and exploit farmers but the answer to that is to improve competition so that farmers are not so reliant on a few big companies.
- *Productive efficiency.* Free markets also ensure, the theory goes, that firms produce what consumers want at the lowest price consistent with their survival. The market will minimise *X-inefficiency* – unnecessarily high cost output.

This set of propositions leads economists to argue that, in most cases, where there are multiple providers and many consumers, and where consumers have perfect, or sufficiently good, information, free markets will be the *most efficient* form of organisation in every sense of the term discussed earlier.

That does not mean that such an outcome will be fair or *equitable.* Economists do not deal in equity. That is especially true in a free market for labour. There is no reason why employers should pay their employees more if they have children or pay what society may think is a 'living wage'. A rival employer will always be able to outcompete the more generous one by pushing wages down to a level nearer that which single or childless couples will accept, especially if there are many of those in a local community. (Remember that there are relatively few families with dependent children at any one time compared to the population as a whole.) As we saw in Chapter One, governments may intervene in various ways to change that – requiring a living wage to be paid or subsidising the wages of those with children. However, every time that the government interferes in this way, there is an efficiency cost. The process is like a 'leaky bucket' (Okun, 1975).

Despite caveats the reader may have about the force of these arguments, it is widely accepted, at least by economists, that for much economic activity, markets work rather well. At the least, no one has invented a wholly superior system. However, economists also recognise that their ideal world of free competitive markets with perfect information rarely, if ever, exists. One firm, or a few firms, may come to dominate a market – one *monopoly* firm or several *oligopolies* may dominate. This leads to *imperfect competition*, on which there is a whole literature. Firms may find it difficult to enter a market. There may be systematic reasons why a free market is difficult to achieve, hence the legislation in the US or the UK to prevent price fixing or single firm dominance.

All these limits to markets have been well recognised by economists for many years. Indeed, recently, they have come to understand them much better. Economists have developed a body of theory which suggests that markets do not work well, or at all, in a wide range of circumstances that are of particular importance for social policy. Much of this theory has been formalised since the 1970s. Some of the insights have their origins in the work of Adam Smith himself.

Limits to markets

Public goods

Adam Smith first elaborated one limit to market exchange. Public activity was necessary where profit could never be reaped by one individual or a small number of individuals yet the wider public would gain from their provision – 'roads, bridges and harbours' were his examples (Smith, 1974 [1776], p 78). In the 1950s, this insight came to be elaborated more fully:

- For a market to work properly, a product has to benefit the people who buy it. It will not be produced or not sufficiently produced if it merely confers some general benefit on the public at large. Clean air is costly to achieve. No one individual can buy it and keep the benefits to themselves. Policing is another example; so, too, is education. Everyone benefits from a more educated population – the quality of public debate affects the kinds of services that are provided in a neighbourhood. *Excludability* means that I can be prevented from consuming something until I have paid for it. This does not hold with clean air or the benefits of an educated population. *Non-excludability* is the opposite and is a characteristic of a public good.
- Public goods are also *non-rejectable*. I may object to being 'protected' by the armed forces or a nuclear deterrent. However, I cannot avoid being subject to their benefits or dangers unless I leave the country, and perhaps not even then. The benefits of clean water and measures to minimise public health hazards are something that we all benefit from and cannot escape without going abroad to a country with none.
- People may club together voluntarily for the whole neighbourhood to be policed, but even here, there is a problem. Some people will be tempted not to contribute and still benefit from the policed neighbourhood. They will *free ride*. The solution is to force everyone to pay a *tax* to finance both the police and courts to enforce the law.

- Another characteristic of a public good is *non-rivalry*. If someone drives along an uncrowded road, they are not preventing others from doing so. Driving along the road should therefore be free. If the road becomes congested, each is slowing down the others by their presence. They impose a cost on others and should pay – the case for congestion charging.

Goods and services that have all these characteristics are called *pure public goods*. They require some kind of public action to be delivered at all. However, few social services are pure public goods in that sense; however, some are, like public health and the benefits of basic academic research.

Merit goods

There is a category of government activity that cannot be justified by this kind of logic. It may be that an individual is poorly informed, for example, about the benefits of education for her child, or parents may be so poor that they desperately need their child's income or for them to be married off very young. Parents may gain financially if they make their daughter available to the sex trade. In this situation, the state has chosen to override individual preferences.

There may be situations where resources are so scarce that leaving the market to operate could lead to starvation, for example, during a famine or in wartime. The state steps in to ration food and other necessities. This is not a popular line of argument in a consumer society or one that mistrusts 'elites', but it has led governments to ban child labour, require children to go to school, put limits on hours of work and ban slavery – once a legitimate economic activity.

Externalities

As we have seen, pure public goods are not that common. However, there is a class of products and services that are more common and share some of the same characteristics. It may be perfectly practical to produce a product that is bought by an individual – a car for example – but the process of manufacture may harm others, and so may my driving it. Either may produce carbon emissions and exhaust fumes that kill. Economists call this effect a *negative externality*. The price charged in an ordinary market does not reflect the costs imposed on others. Only when it does would the exchange be efficient in its full sense.

At the other extreme, a product or service may confer benefits on others, not just the purchaser – a *positive externality*. If I choose to educate my daughter and to pay her school fees, I am benefiting others by doing so – those she can talk to, her husband, her children, her employer, the wider community. A society that relied only on parents to buy schooling could end up with too little education because the benefits would reach far beyond the immediate family and not be factored into the judgement.

Much public policy derives from the existence of some kind of externality. The following are some examples of the varied ways in which we temper the effects of pure market exchange:

- The cars we buy are causing damage to the world that our grandchildren will inhabit. The price we pay for cars and the fuel they use should reflect the costs of that damage. Hence, there is a case for *taxes* which do that.
- Smoke from coal fires and the resulting smog killed large numbers of people in large cities in the UK until the mid-1950s. The Clean Air Act 1956 banned the burning of coal and other polluting substances – *regulation*.
- The danger of infectious disease leads governments to *detain, isolate and treat* victims of diseases like Ebola.
- Public transport attracts *subsidies* and car travel in congested areas carries a *charge* because of the costs that congestion imposes on the wider community.
- Charity or giving may be something that we wish to encourage for the wider good of society. Such activity attracts *tax relief.*

Income externalities and giving

If we all acted as if we were unaffected by those around us, a pure market model might work. In fact, we are social animals. If the free market in labour produces large numbers of poor people unable to feed their children, that affects not just those families, but those of us who are greatly disturbed by seeing starving children on the streets or on our televisions. We may go to the suburbs or gated communities to forget them but even that has its costs. In short, our happiness may depend not just on our income and well-being, but on others'. The classic formulation of this problem was advanced by Hochman and Rodgers (1969). In a two-person world, the problem of seeing a poor person on the street can be met by one person sharing her income until such a point that she is no longer disturbed by the poor person's plight. Even then there are problems. Money received as charity may not be as acceptable as money earned or gained as a right. My utility as a poor person may not be enhanced; it could be worsened by shame.

The problem becomes more complex in a world with more than two people. Others may also dislike seeing poor people on the street. However, they can free ride on the generosity of others. That may mean that poor people are less well treated than everyone wants. So, poverty relief becomes something that we agree to do together on a community-wide basis. We tax people to pay for social security or income support. (Some may still free ride by avoiding tax.)

Not all voters agree, however. They may believe that other voters are being too generous. Too much is going to immigrants who are not really 'us'. Voters may feel as if, in the view of one American philosopher, Robert Nozick (1974), they are being put in a labour camp and forced to work to sustain the 'work-shy'. Hence, how collectively generous we choose to be is contested.

Another difficulty with both private and public giving, which has worried many through the ages, is that it might make people 'dependent'. The poor learn to rely on charity, or state benefits, and lose their desire to work. Others argued that it was easier for the state to regulate such perverse incentives than it was for private charity. We see a modern version of this debate in the attempt to impose conditions on benefit recipients (see Chapter Six).

In the 1970s, another class of market failures began to be identified. They can usefully be grouped under the heading of 'information failure'

Information failure

For a market to work effectively, there has to be perfect knowledge, or at least good enough knowledge, about the product. If there are a lot of people buying a particular model of a new car, they may not be car mechanics, but they may know someone who is. The magazine *Which* may have done a survey. Other users will have experience of the model. Word of mouth spreads. The amount of technical knowledge available to the consumer may not be perfect, but it is generally 'good enough' to be able to make a sensible judgement. Nor does the car seller need to know much about the buyer except that she can pay. In some markets, neither condition holds.

Consumer information weaknesses

- Individuals going to a doctor are unsure what is really wrong with them. The patient is not demanding a particular treatment. She is asking the doctor to act as her proxy demander, to refer her to hospital if necessary, or to reassure her – this is a common reaction to something she has eaten. It is not serious. The capacity to judge the quality of eventual treatment is also restricted. Someone may go to a local garage frequently. They may try several garages and compare the results. In any medical system, this is more difficult. That is not to say that patients cannot make informed judgements, especially with the help of a GP. However, the consumer is at an information disadvantage.
- Choosing a school carries different kinds of difficulty. Parents think they know more than they do. Simple exam results tell us more about who is attending the school than how well it is likely to perform for any one child. League tables, unless they adjust for the social backgrounds of the children, or how able the children were when they entered the school, can be misleading. So can local gossip on 'what I saw in that playground last week'. None of this invalidates

choice in public services, but it makes it more complicated than 'choice' in a local supermarket.

In short, services where the quality is difficult to measure pose problems for simple market solutions.

Seller and buyer imbalances in information

The lack of information may not be confined to the consumer. The reverse situation can also pose a difficulty for market exchange. Sellers of health insurance and long-term care may find, or suspect, that their clients know a lot more about their potential to use such services than they do. This was a problem discussed over 40 years ago by an American economist, George Akerlof (1970):

- If you are selling your car second-hand, you will know all its defects. You have driven it for years. The car has all kinds of bad traits. It was part of a bad batch coming off the production line. You are a particularly bad driver and have damaged it in ways that are not obvious to discern in a trial run. The car is a bad buy – a 'lemon' in American slang. There is an incentive for owners of such cars to sell them and not be open about their defects. In such a market, everyone knows that and trade will take place at a level that is suboptimal. Prices may be too, even though you are not a cheat.
- Akerlof pointed out that this phenomenon was not confined to second-hand cars. It is particularly to be found in health care and long-term care insurance. People, and especially older people, have a lifetime of knowledge about their bodies and their eating, drinking and smoking habits. They have no incentive to be honest about them. The worse their record, and the greater the likelihood they will need care, the more likely they are to seek long-term care or health cover. An insurance company will be wary of taking an older person onto its books or it may charge a very high premium, suspecting that they are being approached by a 'lemon'. The average medical condition of intending insurance buyers worsens as the price rises. This affects both those who are and are not expensive risks. The insurer finds it hard to tell the difference. It may be that this cycle goes on until no insurance is sold. This is now the case in the UK with long-term care (for a discussion of this, see the report of the Dilnot Commission [2011], Burchardt et al [1999] and Chapter Eight). One way to give the market some chance of working is for the state to take on the 'catastrophic cases' – the cases that would be very costly for the private market to cope with. That was Dilnot's suggested remedy. This general kind of phenomenon is called *adverse selection*. The insurance company's likely response – to try hard to identify and exclude bad risks – is called *cream skimming*.

- There is also a contrasting problem – *moral hazard*. If someone takes out insurance against theft, she may be less careful about protecting her property – hence the rules that insurance companies make to ensure that she does so. Insurers do not know whether you will respond like this or are naturally cautious. They will tend to assume the worst and they will charge high premiums. (For an early treatment of this issue, see Pauly, 1974.) The phenomenon is not confined to private insurance. A generous level of state sickness benefit may mean that people take longer off work.

Uncertainty

- Markets do not like uncertainty. Uncertainty means that an insurer cannot predict from past human behaviour what is likely to be the future pattern of events or risks. We have good information on people's past life expectancy and trends in it. We can make predictions about future trends and correct them if we get them wrong. A whole profession of actuaries exists to advise on such probabilities. What we cannot cope with in this way is uncertainty – unpredictable events about which there is no way of assigning a probability to the event occurring. Inflation is one example. Private pension providers will be reluctant to give full inflation protection to future pensioners.
- An additional problem is that many uncertainties are linked. If the event happens to one person, it is probably happening to many more. Unemployment is an example. If the economy is facing difficulties, many people will be affected. My chance of being unemployed is not just random and unconnected to your chance of being unemployed. This is a disastrous combination for private insurers. They will not insure against unemployment except to a very limited degree, for example, a mortgage holder may be able to put off repayment for a limited period.
- There are examples of uncertain *and* linked futures. What will be the nature of long-term care for older people in the next four decades? What will it cost? How many people will need it? Private insurance companies are thus very reluctant to offer long-term care products for this reason too.

Human behaviour

A new branch of economics – behavioural economics – has examined the way in which individuals actually make decisions and use information. It shows that people find financial information about the future difficult to understand, and even if they do understand it, they find it difficult to act on. People who know very well that they ought to sign up for a pension plan or save in other ways fail to do so. However, if their employer offers them a pension scheme but gives them a chance to opt out, they mostly do not opt out. The Pensions Commission drew on this work in making its recommendations, as will be discussed in Chapter Five (Pensions Commission, 2004, p 208; 2005, pp 68–9). In short, there is now a rich literature on the ways in which individuals do not act as strictly rational economic beings.

A powerful efficiency case for a welfare state

It is not possible to say that any particular social welfare policy is wholly justified by any one of these arguments. Many come into play, with different weight put on some, or many, of these theories. Welfare interventions are justified by a combination of public good issues, externality problems and information deficiencies. However, taken together, this range of market failures helps to explain why there is a powerful economic *efficiency* case for public funding, provision and regulation, particularly where human welfare is affected. That is quite distinct from any arguments that derive from social justice. As Nic Barr (2012a) put it, and I am summarising, there is no case for a welfare state where we have:

- perfect competition, perfect information, rational behaviour, complete markets and no distortional behaviour; or
- no concerns about fairness or social justice arising from the market distribution of income or wealth.

Neither holds in the real world. However, that is not the end of the argument. Some economists have grave doubts about the efficiency of public sector organisations and the political process. These doubts have been formalised in a set of arguments that we may call, by analogy with the foregoing, 'a theory of government failure' (Le Grand, 1991).

Government failure

Big government is a danger

A body of work developed after the Second World War that resisted the conclusions that critics of the market were advancing. It had its origins in the 1920s but seriously took off in the 1940s with the publication of Hayek's (1944) *The road to serfdom*. It began to make the case against both Keynesian economics and the rise of post-war welfare states. This body of work has been called 'neoliberal economics'.

It is not to be seen as just a body of ideas that emerged by chance. It derived from an organised network of individuals who promoted their ideas in a systematic way, not least through 'think tanks', to promote a particular strain of economic thought. Friedrich Hayek, Milton Friedman, Henry Simons and Ludwig von

Mises were major figures (Plant, 2012; Stedman Jones, 2012). Different members set different limits that they wanted to impose on state power. However, all wished to minimise it.

State power was to be feared if it went beyond defending and policing society. Much of the force of these convictions derived from the writers' experience of Nazi Germany in the 1930s. They believed that once given excuses for intervention, state power would grow until it took over all aspects of life. Some were prepared to accept a small role for the state to address extreme poverty or to educate children but only in ways that minimised state *provision*. Within this broad range of writing, there are arguments that have to be addressed about how state services work even if we believe that governments are not essentially evil or destined to result in totalitarianism.

You cannot please everyone all the time

The trouble with public goods, particularly those produced at a national level, is that different people interpret the 'public good' in different ways. Take national defence as one example. Some people are pacifists; some may want to invade other countries to ensure national safety. Others want a small but mobile army capable of peacekeeping operations. There is no way that they can agree on one defence policy. This is a rather simplified example of the kind of problem with which economists have struggled for a long time (Arrow, 1951). Coalitions may emerge that swing from one compromise to another but no one solution dominates all others. We might be right in saying that national defence has to be carried out by government but that is only the beginning of the problem. The political market for public goods can never produce a 'perfect' solution. However, the market cannot produce one at all.

Where the public good is confined to a local area – a local park, say – there is a partial solution. Voters can move, or some can, to places with more parks. If a voter wants a lot of local road space, or very good schools, parks and high taxes, she can, in theory, move to an area where most other voters share the same preferences. This theory was first advanced in a formal way by Charles Tiebout (1956). It assumes that people can move freely. To the extent that some cannot, and they will mostly be the poor, this is not a realistic model, but there is some force in the Tiebout argument. However, it has grave limits when it comes to cash benefits. Any local jurisdiction that offers generous welfare benefits is likely to attract poor residents. As I argue in Chapter Three, the UK has developed one of the most centralised ways of funding its welfare state of any country in the world. This has some advantages – fewer 'postcode lotteries' determining service access – but also a lot of disadvantages.

Self-interested and 'median' voters

An optimistic view about the way in which politics works might assume that once a case has been made for giving support to sick or poor people, concerned voters will vote for the tax funds to make this possible. A much more sceptical tradition of writing takes as its starting point the assumption that although there are some altruists, the dominant motive of voters is self-interest, not social justice (Tullock, 1976). People vote for the National Health Service (NHS) because it gives them a good deal compared to relying on private health insurance. However, people also have an interest in not paying taxes. People do seem prepared to pay taxes to help some categories of poor people, notably, the old, but less so for unemployed people. Given that the 'middle class' is large, influential in the media and critical in marginal seats, we might expect them to be the main beneficiaries of social policy. Where a state service ceases to be of much help to the average voter, political support for paying taxes may erode. People may leave in order to use the private sector equivalent, and the remaining service for 'poor people becomes a poor quality service', as Titmuss put it (Alcock et al, 2001, p 121).

Thinking of the voter as a self-interested player is therefore important not just in designing services, but also in explaining to the average voter what the welfare state actually does for them over a lifetime, as I tried to do in Chapter One. The difficulty is that voters may not only be self-interested, but also have short time horizons (for an extended discussion of these issues, see Goodin and Le Grand, 1987).

Political scientists have given particular attention to the power of the 'median' voter. If we imagine the electorate holding a set of views spread out between right-wing minimal government and minimal taxes and right across to those favouring high taxes and interventionist government, it is logical to expect politicians to gear their policies to capture the votes of those who will just tip the majority in their favour. The presumption that the 'middle' or median voter along this spectrum is the key to winning elections has been challenged – perhaps not least in a post-2016 world! It depends on there being a 'single peak' or cluster of voters in the middle and on a single dominant spread of opinion. However, politics is not a simple left–right continuum. There may be extremist clusters. Abstentions from voting by particular groups can be decisive. The results can be manipulated by voting rules. It takes no account of the differential power and influence that some groups have on political outcomes. The rich can dominate the media and the political process. Democracies do sometimes collapse into dictatorships (Acemoglu and Robinson, 2006).

Self-interested bureaucrats

It is not only voters who may seek to maximise their own immediate interests:

> Bureaucrats are like other men. This proposition sounds very simple and straight-forward, but the consequences are a radical departure from orthodox economic theory. If bureaucrats are ordinary men, they will make most of (not all) their decisions in terms of what benefits them not society as a whole. Like other men, they may occasionally sacrifice their own well-being for the wider good, but we should expect this to be exceptional behaviour. (Tullock, 1976, quoted in Hill, 1993, p 110)

This argument came to dominate much Conservative and, indeed, some New Labour thinking in the 1990s. Two strands in this literature are evident. One saw all or most claims for additional public spending as a mere reflection of public servants' desire to grow their organisations – to be budget maximisers. The other strand concentrated on the fact that public services were usually monopolies and hence had the power to exploit their users.

Budget maximisers?

The classic book that began this debate was written by an economist who had been employed in the US equivalent of the UK Treasury, the Bureau of the Budget (Niskanen, 1971). Congress decided on big spending programmes in collusion with big agencies, like the Social Security Administration and the Department of Defense. From his searing experience as a budget controller, he developed a whole theory of government spending. Bureaucrats benefited financially in direct proportion to the size of the programmes that they administered, he claimed. Hence, they were always seeking to increase the size of their budgets. They had particular power because they knew more about their programmes than anyone else. They could 'hoodwink' legislators into believing that there was a need to expand that agency.

Niskanen's line of reasoning is not to be completely dismissed. It is helpful in understanding local budget battles between health and social service agencies, for example (Glennerster, 1983). However, there are better ways to analyse these conflicts than pure monetary gain:

- It is a one-sided account. There are powerful pressures working against spending departments internally and externally. In the UK, a powerful Treasury (see Chapter Four) plays a central role in setting limits to public spending. Powerful economic interests resist higher taxes on companies. Politicians worry about raising taxes on their voters.

- It also gives a narrow and misleading description of what motivates public servants. Large budgets do not regularly bring those involved large salaries, and even if they do, they also bring larger headaches. Dunleavy (1991) presents a detailed critique of the theory. He does not dismiss the idea that civil servants and social service providers use their power for their own ends some of the time, but even when they do, it manifests itself in other ways. They 'shape the bureau' – their organisation – in their own interests rather than the clients'. The lack of collaboration between health and social care agencies is one example to which we shall return.

X-inefficiency

Another American economist, Leibenstein (1966), coined the term 'X-inefficiency'. By this, he meant the tendency of firms in a non-competitive situation to be less than wholly efficient in the way in which they produce their product. Working practices might be slack; responses to customers might be slow or rude. 'Monopoly profit' may be reaped not only by the shareholders, but by the workers in a service, who are not as responsive and effective as they should be. That is the kind of inefficiency that many critics argue besets public services.

Public servants as knaves or knights?

It is not necessary to see all public servants as wicked to see the force of this argument. Someone in a social service agency is doing a stressful or, indeed, a boring job. She wants to get home to her family, or she goes for a night's drinking and calls in sick and gets away with it.

It is also more difficult to see what is going on in the classroom or old person's home than on a production line. Social service personal – 'street-level bureaucrats' – may be more able to simply 'get through the day' (Lipsky, 1980) without challenge. On the other hand, critics responded, a public service agency may be more motivated by high professional standards. People 'go the extra mile' or work beyond their contractual hours. In Julian Le Grand's (2003) terms, some may be 'knights' and others 'knaves', and most of us may be a mix of both. How does government structure an organisation to maximise knightly behaviour?

Exit, voice and loyalty

One of the most influential accounts of these tensions is that by Hirschman (1970), in his book *Exit, voice and loyalty*. He argues that there are two kinds of sanction that consumers have over organisations that serve them:

- One is to take their custom elsewhere. He calls this *exit*. However, there are often reasons why it is difficult for users to exit. The choice to take a child to another school may be impractical or costly. It may be that a patient has been with a doctor or surgery for a long time and has a sense of *loyalty*. This may therefore temper the effectiveness of exit.
- Another way to influence a service is through *voice*. A parent may belong to a parents' association or get elected to the school's governing body. There is more scope for voice in public services. However, this may not work. If you have no chance to move your child – to exit – why should anyone listen? Voice is also costly in time and effort. It may come more easily to middle-class parents.

Where neither voice nor exit work well and loyalty to the institution is high, standards may decline.

Countering government failure

Neoliberals saw the arguments outlined earlier as sufficient reason to push back the boundaries of the state. However, some who were anxious to sustain public services thought that these deficiencies had to be corrected. If not, public services would lose public support and decline, as Hirschman predicted (Glennerster and Le Grand, 1995).

Reformers' strategies can be grouped under three headings: greater competition (more exit power for consumers); more open performance measurement (more information to guide possible exit); and more voice guided by more information and local accountability. Each reinforced the other.

More competition between providers

The early moves came from American neoliberals. Savas (1977, 1982) argued that where local refuse collection and other local services had been contracted out to competitive tendering, the efficiency of services had improved and costs had been cut. This claim was taken up enthusiastically by Mrs Thatcher's administration in the 1980s. Let local services continue to be provided free by local councils but put their provision out to tender. Invite private agencies to compete to provide them under contract. Indeed, force local councils to do this. Compulsory Competitive Tendering (CCT) resulted. There was not much 'voice' here.

Then, under the NHS and Community Care Act 1991, social services departments were required to spend the special community care money they received buying services from private agencies (see Chapter Eight). The NHS was required to put services like hospital cleaning out to tender (see Chapter Seven).

More performance measurement

This had a dual rationale. One of the problems inherent in free unpriced service provision is that those providing the service have no 'market signals'. If children have to come to your school and you have no parent feedback, how do you know if you are doing a good job? Hence, there was a case for giving schools such information through the regular testing of pupil achievement in standard nationwide exams. Second, and quite distinct, was using testing and regular progress reports as a more objective feedback for teachers. These approaches were and are controversial. It is important to see them in the broader theoretical arguments about government failure.

Moral limits to both the market and the state

So far, discussion has been confined to the efficiency limits to markets and the state. However, there is whole other dimension to the debate. Are there moral limits to the market? Buying people as slaves was made illegal in this country two centuries ago. Most people find that buying sex crosses some moral boundary. Sandel (2012), in a book called *What money cannot buy: The moral limits of markets*, discusses the moral boundaries that societies set to market exchange. He covers some of the same territory as Titmuss (1970) but goes much wider.

However, as there are moral limits to markets, so there are to state action. Would we be right to ban all religious schools? How far should the state invade a family's actions in the home – marital rape and abuse, yes – but where do we stop? If conditional benefits induce complete dependency on the state is that morally acceptable (Curchin, 2016)? This all takes us well beyond the economic focus of this book but not beyond what students should consider.

Neither state nor market – the voluntary sector

Why a voluntary sector?

The voluntary sector, or not-for-profit sector, as Americans call it, presents a problem for economists. There is a clear theoretical case for a profit-making market and for state intervention. However, why do *not-for-profit* organisations exist? The standard argument that economists have advanced is that where *both* markets *and* the state fail, not-for-profits fill the gap (Weisbrod, 1986). However, what gap and why are not-for-profits the solution?

Weisbrod couches his argument in terms of the collective choice problem discussed earlier. If people are voting to decide how much of a public good government should provide, many will be disappointed. Some may object to any support for abortion clinics, or they may feel that too little is being done for

AIDS sufferers. There is little that a citizen can do but protest if the state is doing too much, but if it is doing *less* than she would like, she can give money to an organisation that will fill the gap. The example of support to an AIDS charity is not a *pure* public good, but the argument holds. The function is one that the market is unlikely to take up.

Hansmann (1980, 1987) adds other explanations. Individuals are unlikely to give money to a profit-making organisation. They fear that the money will merely go into the owner's pocket. Voluntary organisations compete to be more *trustworthy* than others. They emphasise their altruistic virtues.

This does not mean that voluntary organisations are perfect either. They may not have profit-maximising owners, but they may give their staff too lavish offices or expense accounts. They may spend too much on overheads and fundraising. Salamon (1987) calls such behaviour 'voluntary failure'.

Billis and Glennerster (1998) have argued that these theories are only partially convincing. Previous authors had concentrated on the demand side – why other organisations fail – not on the positive virtues of voluntary organisations – what voluntary organisations can do better. We argued that while the state may be good at providing services that the average voter cares about and has regular experience of – schools or primary care – it is much less good at providing services for smaller and more stigmatised groups. This may be true of some minority ethnic groups, lesbians or gay men – or the condition may be very rare. Here, the average voter may be ignorant. Little state funding may be made available. Here, voluntary organisations, perhaps set up by the parents or partners of sufferers, may come into play and do a better job.

Quite distinct from their cash-raising power, these organisations may be *organisationally* quite different. They operate in more informal ways – perhaps having sufferers or their relatives on the governing committee. They may use volunteers related to those they serve. They are better able to keep the organisation in tune with the needs of the users. The comparative advantage of such organisations may come from their smaller size, less formal and less rigid structures, and the use of volunteers.

Local communities are throwing up experiments that include community shops, time banks, food banks and self-help build schemes that are inheritors of the old mutual aid societies that flourished centuries ago (Christie and Leadbeater, 1998). Others have argued that existing state-run services, like hospitals, should be converted into not-for-profit or 'mutual' organisations. Employees share in their ownership and success in rather ill-defined ways. The Cameron government explored and encouraged this idea. A unit within the Cabinet Office was created to help organisations that wished to move in this direction – to become much more like John Lewis, as the publicity put it. Critics claimed that this was no more than a device to privatise by the backdoor (Molloy, 2014).

These conflicting theories and many innovations over time have left modern welfare provision best described as a 'mixed economy'. There are many different kinds of providers and the boundary lines between them are shifting. This is the case not just in the UK, but in most other economies too, as we shall see in Part Two. Recessions are not good for giving or for the charitable sector. After the 2008 crash charitable sector growth was negative for six consecutive years (Clifford, 2017).

Overview

In conclusion, markets have their advantages: they promote innovation; they hold producers to account; and, at their best, they respond to consumer preferences. However:

- Modern economic theory has elaborated a range of market failures that apply particularly to the range of services covered in this book.
- There are also ways in which large-scale public monopolies fail – government failure.
- Social policy has to balance these failures. A range of strategies – more consumer choice, personal budgets and better service performance information – have been adopted to counter government failure. How successfully this has happened in individual services will be discussed in Part Two.

There is also a role for not-for-profit voluntary organisations to fill gaps that may be politically unpopular or simply neglected. Such organisations may perform better for some client groups than large public agencies.

Questions for discussion

1. Why do economists think markets are a good way to allocate resources?
2. What are the most important market failures that affect social welfare?
3. What is meant by 'government failure'? What are some ways to mitigate it?
4. What case can be made for not-for-profit organisations?

Further reading

For those who want to follow up theories of market failure as they apply to welfare services, the best source is **Barr (2012a)**.

A lucid critical account of neoliberal ideas is given by **Plant (2012)**.

Le Grand (1991) is a succinct presentation of the view that some 'government failure' is real and remediable. His ideas were expanded on in **Le Grand (2003)**.

Explanations for the existence of a not-for-profit sector are discussed in **Billis and Glennerster (1998)**. For a view of its future, see **Alcock (2013)**. A wider discussion of the 'mixed economy' of welfare is to be found in **Powell (2007)**.

three

What to tax?
Who to tax?
How much to tax?

Summary

If it is the case that governments need to intervene in cases where markets do not work, as I argued in Chapter Two, they may do so by passing laws that require individuals or employers to act in certain ways – to pay employees a minimum wage, for example. However, for the most part, welfare policy involves government providing services or benefits and raising taxes to pay for them. There are different ways to do this:

- Individuals' income *and* the products and services that they buy can be taxed.
- Companies can be taxed on their profits and on the number of people they employ – their pay roles.
- Part of individuals' stock of wealth can be taxed away. Wealth has been neglected as a source of revenue in the UK and elsewhere, though it was once more heavily taxed.
- The UK tax system is highly centralised, though some devolution of taxing powers is now taking place.
- Most advanced economies have not risen to the challenge of paying for the welfare states to which they say that they are committed. To do so will take political courage as the cost of these services is rising, not least because of demographic change.

What to tax?

Some history

Throughout the 19th century, British governments of all parties sought to keep tax demands to a minimum. Moreover, they sought to ensure that no one section of the population could complain that it was 'overtaxed'. A wide range of relatively small levies were imposed by the national government and small-scale welfare services – the Poor Law, public health and, later, schools – were mostly financed locally. As one historian of taxation, Martin Daunton (2001, 2002), put it: 'The underlying assumption was that taxes should not alter the shape of society and that they should follow the principle of proportionality, that is extracting more or less the same proportion of total income from everyone' (Daunton, 2002, p 8).

Two world wars and the subsequent coming of the 'welfare state' required much more revenue. That could only come from those with higher incomes and, to a lesser extent, wealth. 'Proportionality' came to be replaced by 'progressivity' – if you had a higher income, you could afford to pay a higher share of it. Nicholas Kaldor, Professor of Economics at Cambridge and tax advisor to successive Labour governments, argued that tax liability should depend on an individual's 'capacity to pay' (Kaldor, 1955). He advanced this view most clearly in his Memorandum of Dissent from the Royal Commission on Taxation in 1955:

> In our view the taxable capacity of an individual consists in his power to satisfy his own material needs, ie to attain a particular living standard. We know of no alternative definition that is capable of satisfying society's prevailing sense of fairness and equity. (Quoted in Titmuss, 1962, p 33)

For Kaldor, 'capacity to pay' extended beyond an individual's income or spending power to the wealth and the capital gains enjoyed in any period. His advice to introduce a capital gains tax was accepted by the Labour government in 1965. However, his advice to introduce a wealth tax did not have a successful outcome (Glennerster, 2012).

In 1900, taxes on income and wealth provided less than 40% of all government revenue. By 1947, including National Insurance, that figure had risen to over 60%. Following the two world wars, electorates became used to paying higher rates of tax. Far more families were drawn into the income tax net. In 1938, only 4 million families paid any income tax; by the end of the Second World War, that figure was 14.5 million. After both world wars, but especially after the Second World War, governments were able to reduce the high rates of tax charged during the war but not to pre-war levels. It was therefore possible to introduce a new welfare state *and* lower taxes (Peacock and Wiseman, 1961).

However, that did not last. Collective welfare costs rose faster than national income, as was shown in Chapter One. So, income tax came to be levied further and further down the income scale. Wives, as well as husbands, came to pay tax as they began to enter the labour market in larger numbers. By 1968, the number of families paying income tax had risen to 21 million. The government gave up making tax returns a family affair. Everyone above a threshold income became an individual taxpayer. By 2000, there were 27 million income taxpayers – a far cry from the 4 million households 60 years earlier.

Much the same happened with National Insurance Contributions – a payment made by most workers and their employers towards the costs of National Insurance benefits. Introduced at a very low flat rate, they gradually grew relative to incomes and became proportionate to income over a band of earnings up to a ceiling. At first, married men's contributions could earn their wives the right to benefits. From the 1970s, all women had to pay their contributions.

The state has always taxed spending in some way – first, luxuries on imported goods, and then most goods and services. There is now a Value Added Tax (VAT) that does this. There are also separate taxes on alcohol and tobacco – 'bad things' to be discouraged, at least so long as they do not hinder raising tax revenue too much!

While these forms of national tax were growing in importance, others were declining. At the beginning of the 20th century, *local taxes* provided a third of all the state's revenue. By the late 1940s, this share had fallen to about 7%. By the end of the 20th century, it had fallen to between 3% and 4%.

Taxation of inherited *wealth*, begun at the end of the 19th century, provided a useful 5% of total revenue in the late 1940s. By the 1990s, that had fallen to about 0.5% and is still at about that level.

The shape of modern taxation in the UK

Thus, the UK has a tax structure that, at least until 2016, has been very centralised and directly felt by all households. *Table 3.1* lists UK taxes and their expected revenue in 2015/16. It begins with income tax and National Insurance Contributions, described previously. 'Gross of tax credits' means the total taxes individuals would pay before government steps in to reduce them because of poverty and family circumstances. The list then spells out the range of 'indirect taxes' – paid by individuals as part of the price they pay for a product. There are also taxes on capital, or wealth, and taxes levied on companies.

Table 3.1: Sources of government revenue, 2015/16 forecasts

	Revenue (£ billion)	Percentage of total receipts
Direct taxes		
Income tax (gross of tax credits)	170.2	25.3
National Insurance Contributions	114.8	17.1
Indirect taxes		
Value Added Tax[a]	115.9	17.2
Fuel duties	27.1	4.0
Alcohol duties	10.7	1.6
Betting and gaming duties	2.6	0.4
Vehicle excise duty	5.6	0.8
Air passenger duty	3.1	0.5
Insurance premium tax	3.5	0.5
Landfill Tax[b]	1.0	0.1
Climate change levy	2.3	0.3
Aggregates levy	0.3	0.0
Customs duties	3.0	0.4
Capital taxes		
Capital gains tax	6.4	1.0
Inheritance tax	4.2	0.6
Stamp Duty Land Tax[c]	11.5	1.7
Stamp duty on shares	3.2	0.5
Company taxes		
Corporation tax (net of tax credits)	42.3	6.3
Petroleum revenue tax	0.0	0.0
Business rates	28.0	4.2
Bank levy	3.7	0.6
Local taxes		
Council tax	28.4	4.2
Other taxes and royalties	30.7	4.6
Net taxes and National Insurance contributions	**627.6**	**93.4**
Interest and dividends	5.8	0.9
Gross operating surplus rent, other receipts and adjustments	38.9	5.8
Current receipts	**672.3**	**100.0**

Notes: [a] Net of (ie after deducting) VAT refunds paid to other parts of government. [b] For England, Wales and Northern Ireland. Land and buildings transaction tax operates instead of stamp duty land tax in Scotland, while landfill tax is devolved to Scotland. [c] See note b.
Source: Grace, Pope and Roantree (2015).

A number of features stand out:

- First, only a quarter of total revenue takes the form of income tax. It is the major 'progressive tax': higher earners pay proportionately more than poorer earners – the Kaldor principle of capacity to pay.
- The other big earners, VAT and National Insurance, are not progressive. National Insurance is essentially regressive – it bears more heavily on lower-income groups. It begins to be paid below the threshold for income tax. It is then a percentage tax that is capped at the 'upper earnings limit'. This is discussed later.
- Council tax is levied on the value of property but has a very low ceiling at which it ceases to rise with the value of property.

Table 3.2 shows how households are affected by this structure. Those on the bottom fifth (quintile) of the income range have 38% of their income taxed away. The top tenth pay 35% of their income in tax.

Table 3.2: *Taxes as a percentage of gross income for all households by quintile groups, financial year ending 2014, UK*

Percentages of gross income paid in tax	Quintiles of all households				
	Bottom	2nd	3rd	4th	Top
Direct taxes	9.7	11.0	15.6	19.2	23.5
Indirect taxes	28.1	19.1	17.8	15.3	11.3
All taxes	**37.8**	**30.2**	33.3	34.5	34.8

Source: ONS (2015a).

Table 3.2 is derived from an annual Office of National Statistics (ONS) publication in 2015. The table is excluded in this form from the 2016 release.

Council tax is the only local tax in the UK. Recently, the business rates on commercial property have been mostly allocated back to local government in the area in which it is collected. However, both taxes are still strictly controlled by central government. Scotland and Wales will gain some capacity to vary some of these taxes, as well as to keep and allocate the proceeds, as is discussed in Chapter Four, but the UK will remain a highly centralised tax state.

So far, we have described what governments have chosen to tax. That has been driven, understandably, by a political strategy – 'tax what you can get away with'. Economists would like governments to consider more carefully the question 'What is a good tax?' or, at least, 'What is the least bad tax?'.

Good and bad taxes

The Institute for Fiscal Studies (IFS) convened a group of economists chaired by the Nobel Prize-winner Sir James Mirrlees to consider just those questions. Its report (Mirrlees Review, 2011) is the best overview of the UK tax system to date and contains a wide range of policy recommendations. Put simply, the economic advice is: do not badly *distort* the choices consumers would otherwise make; do not *deter* people from doing things the economy needs, notably, to work and save; and *minimise complexity*. Society should not give scope to accountants to spend a lot of effort getting people and companies to arrange their affairs in ways that minimise tax payments and waste resources in the process. Taxing different sources of income at different rates is a bad idea. People spend a lot of effort redirecting their income in ways that minimises their taxes.

However, taxes can also help to make markets work better. Taxes can be used to bring home the economic costs of pollution by facing consumers with the costs they impose on others. 'Progressivity' – taxing those who have the most capacity to pay the most – is legitimate but this has to be done by designing the system carefully to minimise the costs associated with progressivity. That means thinking in terms of lifetime incomes not just a one-off snapshot. VAT – a tax on the sale of products and services – looks regressive when considered at one point in time because the rich save more of their income – they are not spending and hence pay less VAT. However, over a lifetime, that is far less true. The rich spend down their assets in old age. Then, they pay more VAT.

Finally, and here this author is less inclined to agree, the report argued that taxes should never be earmarked for particular purposes. All taxes should go into a common pot. Claiming that taxes go to pay for particular purposes, without a binding constraint to make sure that happens, is just political rhetoric. This is largely true but you might want to make some exceptions. This topic is discussed later in this chapter, in the health and long-term care chapters and in the final chapter. The Mirrlees Review came up with a range of critiques of current tax policy and recommendations for change. Some examples are cited in *Table 3.3*.

How does the UK differ?

As can be seen from *Table 3.4*, some countries put a heavier reliance on social security taxes levied on employees and their employers to fund pension and health-care costs. France raises nearly a half of its revenue that way, as does the Netherlands. Norway and Denmark raise nothing through that route. Germany, Belgium and Italy raise nearer a third of their revenue that way. The UK raises a fifth of its revenue through National Insurance Contributions.

Table 3.3: A good tax system compared to the present UK system

A good tax system	The current UK system
Taxes on earnings	
A progressive income tax with a transparent and coherent rate structure	An opaque jumble of different effective rates and a separate National Insurance system
A single integrated benefit for those with low income/high needs	A highly complex array of benefits – but moving towards a more uniform tax credit system. Complexities remain
A schedule of effective tax rates that reflects evidence on behavioural responses	A rate structure that reduces employment and earnings more than necessary
Indirect taxes	
A largely uniform VAT (same rate for all purchases except items where a good efficiency case can be made)	VAT with extensive zero-rating, reduced rates and exemptions. Financial services and housing mostly exempt
No transactions taxes	Stamp duties, recently increased, on property and land
Additional taxes on alcohol and tobacco (and other 'bads')	Alcohol and tobacco taxed
Environmental taxes	
Consistent price on carbon emissions	Arbitrary and inconsistent pricing
Well-targeted tax on road congestion	London congestion tax. Ill-targeted tax on fuel consumption
Taxation of savings and wealth	
No tax on 'normal' return to savings – some incentive to save for retirement	Broadly a muddle
A lifetime wealth transfer tax – a tax on wealth recipients	A largely avoided inheritance tax

Source: Adapted from Mirrlees Review (2011, Table 20.1).

Other countries raise more of their revenue through local or regional taxes – regional governments include the Lander in Germany, provinces in Canada or state governments in the US. In Germany and France, social security funds are in the hands of organisations at one remove from the government, with employer and trade union representatives, constrained by government rules.

In the UK, social security contributions go directly to the central government. The pros and cons of such an approach are treated in later chapters. However, it is worth noting here that in 2015, employees began paying National Insurance at about £8,000 a year of earned income. The income tax threshold was £10,600. About 1.5 million low earners had been taken out of income tax but were still paying National Insurance. That rate was 12% of earnings between £155 and £815 a week in 2015. On income beyond that, the contribution rate fell to 2% – not a progressive approach.

Countries differ in the progressivity of their tax systems. They also differ in how much they tax spending. The US has low sales taxes, which vary by state. In the European Union, all countries have to charge VAT, with a minimum standard rate of 15%. Some variations are permitted for some items, notably, food. There is no top limit, but several Nordic countries charge at a standard rate of 25%, with less on food. The UK raised its standard rate from 17.5% to 20% in the wake of the financial crisis and has kept it there.

Who to tax?

The brief history section at the beginning of this chapter showed how most people are now drawn into the income tax system. Both the Coalition and the present Conservative governments have sought to raise the threshold at which individuals have to pay income tax. In 2016, this had risen to an annual income

Table 3.4: *Tax revenue in different countries by percentage of gross domestic product, 2014*

Country	Total	Federal/central	Regional	Local	Social security
Belgium	44.7	25.7	2.4	2.1	14.2
Canada	30.8	13.0	12.1	2.8	2.9
Denmark	50.9	38.1		12.6	0
Finland	43.9	20.8		10.3	12.7
France	45.2	14.7		5.9	24.5
Germany	36.1	11.4	8.1	2.5	14.0
Greece	35.9	24.2		1.4	10.3
Ireland	29.9	24.6		0.8	4.3
Italy	43.6	23.5		6.9	13.1
Netherlands[a]	36.7	20.0		1.4	15.0
Norway	39.1	33.7		5.4	0
Spain	33.2	14.1	4.5	3.3	11.2
Sweden	42.7	21.3		15.8	5.5
UK	32.6	24.7		3.6	6.1
USA	26.0	11.2	5.0	3.9	6.2

Note: [a] 2013 some small items, for example, European Union levies, are not shown separately.

Source: OECD (2015a).

of £11,000 – an individual's 'personal allowance'. (It disappears for those with incomes over £122,000.) Government also chooses not to tax income that is spent on purposes it wishes to encourage. Until 2000, this included interest paid on mortgages for those buying their own houses, as is discussed in Chapter Eleven.

Money can be 'covenanted' or given away to 'discretionary trusts' over which an individual still has some influence. This has been a long-standing mechanism for avoiding tax, though constrained more recently. Titmuss (1962), with the help of his research assistant, Tony Lynes, traced the history of these mechanisms – why they were introduced and their scale. The National Audit Office (2015) undertook a review of tax reliefs across government and concluded that they cost the Treasury £335 billion in 2012/13.

When government chooses not to tax a band of an individual's income, the benefit to the individual clearly depends on how big that income is and what tax they would have otherwise paid. If government chooses to not tax the first £10,000 of someone's income, not the first £8,000, that person is £400 a year better off. If she were earning below £8,000 a year, it is of no value to her. The same holds higher up the income range. Relief from not paying a 45% tax is worth more than relief at the 20% rate. We return later to describe and discuss particularly import tax reliefs – those on pensions and housing – in later chapters.

Who taxes?

The UK has had one of the most centralised tax systems of any major democracy (Travers, 2015). Westminster has limited local authorities' power to tax by putting 'caps' on the amount that local councils can raise from the taxes that they can levy. It also decides what taxes local government can levy. There has been a succession of local taxes invented by national government – the rates, the poll tax and now the council tax. None have raised much money. Currently, the council tax provides only 4% of all national revenue.

The Westminster Parliament has absolute power to determine who has tax-raising powers. In the US, the states determine what taxes they raise. In the UK, Westminster has decided what powers to give the Scottish Parliament and the Welsh Assembly. It has granted Scotland more tax-raising powers in the Scotland Act 2016.

The Scottish Parliament always had the power to vary the standard rate of income tax by three pence but did not use those powers. Now it will receive the revenue generated from Scottish taxpayers by 10 pence in the pound out of the standard rate of 20 pence. The other 10 pence goes to Westminster. The Scottish Parliament can vary its 10 pence levy up or down. However, if it does so, it has to apply that equally to upper bands too. It cannot add to the top rate of tax and not to the standard rate. This limits the redistributive powers available to it. It can vary the thresholds at which its tax rates begin. These powers only apply to non–interest and non– dividend income.

The Scottish Parliament will also receive half of the revenue generated from VAT in Scotland. Previously, it had been given the power to replace Stamp Duty with a Land and Buildings Transaction Tax. It has no power to set the VAT rate or National Insurance Contribution rates. The widened powers to raise taxes will result in a lower grant from Westminster, as is discussed in Chapter Four. From 2018, the Welsh government will take over administration of the Landfill Tax and will replace the Stamp Duty by a Welsh Land Transaction Tax, as in Scotland.

What is not taxed?

Although personal incomes and consumer expenditure have been increasingly taxed in the past half–century, wealth has not been. That is despite the fact that wealth has grown faster than income and is highly unequal. In 1980, the total stock of wealth held by UK individuals was equivalent to about three times the total national income in any one year. By 2005, that ratio had increased to five to one. Countries that once had wealth taxes have abandoned them. In the Organisation for Economic Co-operation and Development (OECD) as a whole, taxes on property and wealth raise only 2% of all revenue.

In the UK, the share of tax revenue collected from inheritances fell from 1.5% in the 1940s to 0.2% today. Taxes on net wealth, property, inheritance and gifts amount to less than 1% of total national wealth (Glennerster, 2015a). If we exclude council tax, as not being a tax on capital, but a regressive tax on users, wealth taxes now take about 0.25% of personal wealth each year. In the 1940s, the figure was about 0.7%.

How much to tax?

How much can government tax without damaging the economy? If an activity is taxed, that will produce some behavioural response. People will act differently. If government taxes whisky very heavily, people may switch to other drinks, smuggle it, buy it illicitly or have their own private stills.

If government taxes what people earn, they may react by working *more* to restore their hoped–for living standards. Economists call this the 'income effect'. However, they may work *less*, thinking the extra they earn working at a boring job is not worth it. Economists call this the 'substitution effect'. Just what works for whom and how much are matters of empirical dispute.

Tax rates do not merely operate through things called taxes. If we give benefits to people and then withdraw them as their incomes rise, that has precisely the same effect. Multiple means tests can produce very high 'implicit' tax rates – the rate at which people fail to benefit from their higher earnings. Social policy analysts call this the 'poverty trap'. The new 'Universal Credit' is, in part, meant to address this problem and is discussed in Chapter Six.

Such income and substitution effects not only apply to income tax. An indirect tax like VAT has the same effect. VAT at 20% means that a worker can buy 20% less for every pound she earns. Both income and substitution effects follow.

This might, in theory, be minimised by imposing taxes that have few such effects. One is a lump sum, or poll tax, which applies equally to everyone and cannot result in behaviour designed to avoid it – short of rioting or not registering to vote. A poll tax does, however, offend the 'capacity to pay' principle discussed earlier and is seen by most people to be grossly unfair. There was an empirical test of that when Mrs Thatcher tried to introduce a poll tax after 1989. Less controversially, taxes on land, which cannot easily be created or hidden, are less prone to behavioural responses.

We are driven back to the question: how big are these behavioural effects? There are basically two ways in which economists have tried to answer this question. One is to look back at tax changes that have occurred in the past and measure how people responded in one country – say, the UK. The other is to look across countries. Do those countries with high tax rates do better or worse economically than others? Neither approach produces a decisive answer, but both do give some clues.

The Mirrlees Review (2011, p 29) concluded that 'most empirical work suggests that it is the substitution effect that dominates'. In short, most people do work less when faced with high taxes. Of course, that is not the end of the debate. Taxes do some economic good if they are spent wisely. There may be a small fall in the amount that we work but our children can be better educated. They will therefore be more productive and we may all be happier. Thus, the crunch question is: *at what point* does a rise in tax rates actually produce *less* revenue or cause major economic damage?

The whole framework for thinking about these issues was elaborated by Professor Mirrlees (1971) himself. It is called 'optimal tax theory'. It begins by seeking to clarify the objectives of government policy. It argues that a system that best achieves those objectives while satisfying or minimising the constraints is optimal. If we want to redistribute income to minimise poverty, we need to do so in a way that minimises deterrent effects on work, especially for the poor. We need to minimise complexity and administrative cost. Optimal tax theory is therefore a way to think, not an answer:

- Researchers at the IFS (Brewer et al, 2010) examined how far previous changes to the top rate of income tax on high earners in the UK (the top 1%) had affected the total revenue collected. How far did these earners reduce their work effort, change the way they were rewarded or use various methods to hide their income? Their conclusion was that when the top marginal tax rate rose above 56%, the government gained no more tax revenue. If you include *all* forms of tax charged on income (eg social security contributions), this implied that any increase in the top rate of *income* tax above 40% would not raise more revenue. Yet, the period they relied on for that conclusion was the late 1980s. People's capacity to avoid paying tax may have changed, as well as the general climate of opinion about tax. Mirrlees (Mirrlees Review, 2011, p 110) cautioned against putting too much reliance on a particular number and said of this piece of work that 'statistically there was only a two thirds chance that the revenue maximising rate was somewhere between 33% and 57%'. That leaves a wide range for judgement but it does caution against believing that high top rates of tax on the very rich will produce enough revenue to solve the big dilemma with which this book began. A case can be made that there could be *indirect* effects of raising the top tax rate. A feeling that the rich are 'playing their part' and that the whole system is fair may make it possible to raise more tax from the average voter.

• The other approach that economists have taken is to consider how well countries with higher marginal tax rates, or higher levels of taxation overall, have done economically. Is there evidence that those countries with high tax revenue do badly? A glance back at ***Table 3.4*** throws doubt on that, at least as regards tax levels somewhat higher than the UK. Germany, the Netherlands, Sweden and Denmark do not stand out as economic failures despite the fact that their taxes are higher.

• However, at some point, high taxes, especially on employing labour, are widely seen as counterproductive. An example is France. It is also the case that when Sweden's tax share rose above 60%, it *was* seen to be a problem. That country entered a banking and government deficit crisis in the early 1990s and its government took major steps to both reform its banking system and reduce its tax share by about 15% of gross domestic product (GDP) – since then, in the 40s rather than at 60% (Lindbom, 2014).

Perhaps the most thoughtful discussion of all these issues is to be found in a series of lectures that Tony Atkinson gave in Munich a number of years ago (Atkinson, 1999). He concluded:

> The studies of the aggregate relationship between economic performance and the size of the welfare state reviewed here do not yield conclusive evidence … some find that high spending on social transfers leads to lower growth, others find the reverse. The largest of the estimated effects – in either direction – do not seem believable. (Atkinson, 1999, p 184)

An American economist, Peter Lindert (2004), has traced the history of growing public expenditure since the 18th century across the now developed world. Again, he concludes that there is no clear evidence that countries that invested in welfare states did badly economically. They found ways to finance them without jeopardising economic growth. Indeed, they used public programmes to invest in human capital, science and transport, which added to their growth. What mattered was what they did with their public expenditure and the efficiency of their tax-raising capacity. It is a detailed and fascinating study, but it does not refute the conclusion of the comparative study with which we began this chapter. If you seek to sustain your welfare state and do not sufficiently raise the taxes needed to do so, the economic price can be high. That leads directly to the politics of taxation.

Voters' attitudes

There has been a sea change in British voters' views over the past 20 years, if the British Social Attitudes Survey is a good guide (see **Table 3.5**). At the beginning of the Blair period in office in 1998, roughly two thirds of those responding to the survey said that they would support an increase in taxes to pay for better health, education and social benefit spending. That fell to just over a third in 2010. That was not very different from what respondents said when Mrs Thatcher was prime minister and it stayed low until 2015, when there was an even split in the country between those favouring more spending and keeping spending the same. Those favouring less taxation and spending less has remained very low.

Table 3.5: *Public attitudes to taxation and social spending, UK, 1983–2015*

Question	% of respondents replying positively								
	1983	1986	1990	1998	2002	2005	2010	2014	2015
If the government had to choose it should:									
Reduce taxes and spend less on health, education and social benefits	9	5	3	3	3	6	8	7	4
Keep taxes and spending at the same level as now	54	44	37	32	31	43	56	52	48
Increase taxes and spend more	32	46	54	63	63	46	36	37	48

Source: British Social Attitudes (ESRC data archive).

Although New Labour in the Blair and Brown years did manage to increase spending on social policy, they both ran scared of making the case for higher taxation. They were afraid of being labelled 'the tax and spend party'. Only once did they explicitly make the case for more taxation to fund higher social spending. Following an internal review of the NHS by Adair Turner, Tony Blair concluded that the only way to significantly improve its performance was to move it from being one of the lowest-spending health-care systems in Europe to being at least on a par with other European nations (see Chapter Seven). It was paid for by an increase in National Insurance Contributions.

The case for more spending, and hence more revenue, *was* successfully made to the electorate, but it was never repeated. As social policy spending continued to rise before the banking crisis, revenue failed to keep pace. On the eve of that crisis, Labour was running a current spending deficit.

It would be wrong to single out the Blair and Brown Labour government for not raising enough tax to pay for its social policy promises. In 2000/01, that government was running a surplus. Conservative governments ran Current (non-investement) deficits too, and not only in times of recession (see **Table 3.6**).

Table 3.6: Total UK government revenue compared to total spending, 1980/81–2014/15: percentages of GDP

	Thatcher, Conservative			Blair, Labour		Crisis	Coalition
	1980/81	1990/91	1996/97	2000/01	2007/08	2009/10	2014/15
All public expenditure	46.0	37.7	38.2	36.2	40.2	45.7	40.7
Total government revenue	41.0	35.4	33.8	36.5	35.9	34.8	35.7
Public sector net investment	2.3	1.6	1.0	0.6	2.1	3.3	1.7

Source: HM Treasury's annual Public Expenditure Statistical Analyses and National Income Statistics ONS.

Is there anything that governments might do to improve the chances of raising more revenue to improve the standards of public services that voters, with the other side of their brains, seem to want? Is it possible to help people see what Richard Murphy (2015) calls *The joy of tax*?

Taxing differently and more effectively

Streeck and Mertens (2013) argue that throughout Europe, governments' capacity to tax sufficiently to meet growing welfare policy demands has been diminishing. Globalisation means that corporations can move their head offices and their tax liabilities to the lowest-taxed nations. Wealthy individuals can move their capital about internationally. The result, these authors argue, is that governments have taken the soft option – borrow the money to pay for their welfare states and hope that something will turn up. That seemed easy to do when large amounts of cheap credit were sloshing round the world looking for borrowers. However, this led to financial disaster in some countries and long-term unresolved problems everywhere. The authors question whether:

> Democratic states under capitalism, with their manifold public responsibilities, on the one hand, and severe restrictions on how they may raise the means needed to discharge them, on the other, will still be able to do what is required for the future viability of their increasingly unstable, fragile and disorganised societies. (Streeck and Mertens, 2013, p 56)

This line of argument led one of the authors to conclude subsequently that welfare states were, indeed, doomed (Streeck, 2016) – as, indeed, was democracy and capitalism.

This author is not prepared to accept that diagnosis – yet. There are ways to make tax collecting more effective that derive from the analysis in this chapter. Solutions vary between countries depending on their historical tax structures. In the following, we take the UK as a case study. A range of ideas has been advanced here that would make taxation both more effective and fairer. Globalisation does present constraints but they are not complete.

Raise the top rate of income tax

A lot of political attention is focused on this option. As discussed earlier, it is not likely to be a major direct contributor to higher revenue. However, it could create a political climate in which wider reforms and tax increases become possible. A higher top rate of tax may also be useful in sending a message to employers about what society thinks is a reasonable top limit for incomes but it is not, in itself, an effective revenue collection device. The very rich are too few in number, too mobile and too effectively tax advised to wait to be shorn. For more discussion of this, see the final chapter. However, a major attack on evasion and on the scale of tax reliefs *could* produce more revenue.

Tax evasion

Tax evasion 'illegally deprives Her Majesty's Revenue and Customs (HMRC) of revenue', as the National Audit Office has put it. People deliberately do not enter their full income on tax returns, or they operate in the hidden economy, do not make tax returns at all or are involved in criminal activity. On HMRC advice, the National Audit Office (2015) estimated that tax evasion lost the Exchequer £16 billion in 2014/15. It is impossible to estimate the scale of evasion accurately. Reducing it requires tougher sanctions, more assertive legal action and more staff in the Inland Revenue.

Tax avoidance

This is defined by the HMRC as where 'people bend the rules of the tax system to gain a tax advantage Parliament never intended'. The National Audit Office (2015) put this figure at £18 billion, making the total 'tax gap' £34 billion. Far greater losses arise from perfectly legal and intended tax reliefs that are widely used, though probably beyond the original expectations of legislators.

A root-and-branch reform of tax relief

There is a case for critically examining all forms of tax relief. Avoidance thrives because it has fertile ground in which to grow. That takes the form of extensive tax relief, notably, in the field of pensions. Chapter Six shows that even leading Conservative policy advisors doubt its wisdom or effectiveness in fostering pension saving.

Tax public 'bads'

Alcohol, tobacco and petrol are already taxed quite heavily but carbon and other emissions that gravely affect health are not. Nor are foods that cause obesity. Congestion charges to reduce pollution and traffic jams only effectively exist in Central London. There is a powerful case to be made for extending congestion charging nationally. Driving in a congested area increases costs to others and causes deaths to local residents. A charge to reflect those costs and to encourage people to use other forms of transport would be economically beneficial and raise revenue.

Tax wealth and property

We have shown that wealth is minimally taxed. Yet, there are a range of taxes that could be introduced that would be both efficient and equitable (Mirrlees Review, 2011; Hills and Glennerster, 2013; Glennerster, 2015a):

- Roughly half of all net wealth in the UK is in the form of property and land. The value of land and property is largely created and sustained by collective action – policing it, building roads and sewers, and supplying water. Without those collective actions, it would be valueless. Better schools raise the value of houses. Holding land that has planning permission to build but paying no tax on it does not encourage building. Hence, there is a powerful case to be made for a land or site value tax – a percentage tax on the value of the site. It would encourage development. Private developers would be charged on the value of the empty site they owned. As public investment in an area increased, the value of that land and local revenue would rise.
- The present council tax is levied on property values nearly 30 years out of date. Those years have seen property values rise massively, especially at the top. Those with high-value houses pay little more than those with moderately valued houses. As a minimum, the bands should be extended and then, in the long run, replaced by a site value tax and a local service tax (Mirlees Review, 2011).
- Inheritances are hardly taxed in practice and taxed in the wrong way. If government taxed the recipient of large gifts, it would encourage those with large holdings to spread them between recipients (Atkinson, 2015). This is sometimes called a 'lifetime accessions tax'. The period could be shorter than a lifetime – gifts spread over five years counted as income would be manageable.
- Thomas Piketty (2013) argues that there should be an international tax on wealth. This is a long-term aspiration rather than a practical immediate step.
- There has long been an argument for taxing international currency transactions at a tiny rate per pound. The idea originally came from an American economist, James Tobin (1978), hence its name, the Tobin tax. It would only work if it were done internationally. Tax reform in general is an international endeavour.

Hypothecate

Voters tend to see their taxes disappearing into some deep dark hole from which few benefits derive. They are encouraged to see things that way by the popular press. One way to mitigate this attitude is to tie particular spending to particular taxes. Some neoliberal economists have advocated such 'hypothecation' (Buchanan, 1975). They argue that it would mean a much more informed debate on tax at elections. The Left tend to think that it will encourage more taxation for things they care about, for example, the Fabian Commission on Taxation and Citizenship (2000) did so, as did a more recent contribution (Srblin, 2015). The King's Fund (2014) has argued for an increase in National Insurance to pay for improved health and long-term care spending. This is discussed further in Chapters Seven and Eight and the final chapter in this book. Orthodox economists are opposed.

The Mirrlees Review (2011) summarised the case against:

- There is no way, politically or practically, to ring-fence particular revenue for particular purposes. If there are floods or large-scale unemployment, political pressure to 'do something' will overwhelm paper budget lines. There are so many different purposes that government has and they cannot all have separate budgets separately financed. In practice, reformers only tend to favour such budgets for their own preferred items. Who is going to vote for money on prisons or the Inland Revenue? Voting for several scores of tax rates is not feasible.
- Nor is it clear that such a process would result in more revenue overall. Would people be prepared to vote more for social benefits other than pensions? British Social Attitudes Surveys suggest not.

Raise Value Added Tax

The great virtue of VAT is that it is difficult to avoid. It is not that regressive when seen over a lifetime. More welfare-generous Scandinavian economies have higher VAT rates. One beneficial lasting outcome of the banking crisis was that the UK raised VAT levels to 20%. That seems to have become accepted. A further rise above 20% may become necessary. Northern European countries have VAT levels at 21% and 25% for many services and goods. Nothing quite so large is necessary but some increase may well be.

Localise tax responsibility

Another way to help taxpayers see the benefits of their taxes might be to localise taxing powers to a greater degree. The outcome of higher spending on parks and rubbish collection can be appreciated or criticised. Tony Travers (2015) has argued that for a range of historical reasons, the UK tax regime has ended up 'a hyper-centralised anomaly'. What might be done?

- As a minimum, properties could be revalued to take account of the increased values since the early 1990s. Then, that could be done regularly. There is now much better computerised information on the prices at which houses change hands locally.

- New higher taxable bands could be added on the most expensive properties. Both measures would make the tax a little less regressive but probably even less popular!
- The revenue from business rates is being transferred to local councils.
- The post-2015 Conservative government has made a series of agreements with groups of local councils to devolve some spending and planning decisions to city/region mayors and other elected agencies. These arrangements are being made possible under new legislation – the Cities and Local Government Devolution Act 2016. The services covered are housing investment plans, transport, planning and policing powers. The first of these outline agreements was the Greater Manchester Agreement in 2015 (HM Treasury and the Greater Manchester Combined Authority, 2015). The budgets involved include health and social care, the Housing Investment Fund, transport funding and economic regeneration funds. This *does not* give these combined authorities access to significant additional public money, though. Various combinations of local authorities are also developing schemes – Sheffield, West Yorkshire, Cornwall and some others.
- The Scottish Parliament and Welsh Assembly are receiving additional taxing powers. I discuss this move in Chapter Four.
- The demands being put on welfare states are rising. The average age of their populations is growing and so is the cost of providing the same standards of service. People have come to expect higher standards. Incomes have been driven down by international forces beyond governments' control. The cost of compensating the losers is growing.
- The range of risks that electorates are asking the state to insure against is widening. The long-term care of their elderly parents is one example. The task of caring for children when both partners are at work is another instance where the state is extending its role in response to social change and political demand. Both these factors call for greater revenue raising capacity at a local level.

Overview

In short, in common with many other advanced welfare states, the UK needs to raise more in taxation to fund growing demands that arise from ageing, climate change and rising expectations or it must curtail what the welfare state is trying to do:

- The UK electorate's support for higher taxes has declined markedly in the past decade. There are good reasons for this. The basic tax structure is unfair to many middle and lower earners.
- There needs to be a root-and-branch reform of the tax system that funds modern social policy. An important element would involve a reduction in the scale of tax relief that mainly benefits the higher paid and a greater emphasis on taxing wealth.

- However, there is no escape from the need to persuade ordinary people that it is in their long-term interest to fund activities that insure against life's growing and changing risks.

Questions for discussion

1. What are the most important sources of revenue in the UK? How do they differ from those in other countries?
2. How is it that the UK has developed one of the most centralised patterns of taxation in the world? What might be done to change that?
3. How far is the UK's tax structure equitable?
4. Examine possible changes that might be made to improve the equity and the efficiency of taxes in the UK or any other country that interests you.

Further reading

The best simple descriptive account of the current UK tax system is **Grace, Pope and Roantree (2015)**, which the IFS revise at intervals.

The best critical account of UK taxation is to be found in the **Mirrlees Review (2011)**. It is often quite technical but the final chapter, 'Conclusions and recommendations for reform', is succinct and accessible.

The Chancellor's pre-Budget report each autumn and his annual Budget used to set out the government's tax plans (see: www.hm-treasury.gov.uk). These will now be merged into a single statement. The new and independent body set up to check and comment on the Chancellor's figures is the Office of Budget Responsibility (OBR). It publishes regular reviews of the UK's revenue prospects (see: www.budgetresponsibility.org.uk).

Opposing political views can be found in publications by the Adam Smith Institute and the Fabian Society. The former argue for tax havens as ways to stop excessive taxation, and an end to inheritance taxes. The Fabians want to 'reinvent taxation' **(Srblin, 2015)**. A case for more and fairer taxation is expounded in **Murphy (2015)**. The case for lower taxes is argued by the Taxpayers' Alliance. For a discussion of tax devolution see **House of Lords (2015)**.

four

Rationing – who gets what?

Summary

We have seen that the 'invisible hand of the market' often does not allocate resources efficiently or in ways that societies deem fair. If it does not do so, who does? The way societies have evolved to achieve this varies depending on their political structure – federal states or a centralised unitary state, for example. In this chapter, we primarily describe the way it works in the UK, which is evolving to a less centralised version, but the core dilemmas are the same.

- Social welfare rationing decisions range from *financial* rationing at the centre of politics to professional decisions taken at the point of *service delivery*.
- These can be seen as a hierarchy of rationing decisions that ultimately derive from the process of Treasury control of public expenditure.
- Mathematical formulae and other means are used to allocate money down to devolved administrations and local government. They aim to minimise political conflicts.
- Important steps are being taken in the UK to devolve rationing decisions, along with tax-raising powers. However, this process of decentralisation also raises issues of geographical equity in service provision.

Who decides?

In a market-driven economy, an individual buys what she or he can afford. However, for the reasons discussed in Chapter Two, societies have rejected the market as the sole arbiter of resource allocation. That leaves a different kind of problem – how do we collectively decide who gets what if the market is not doing so?

A key dilemma was put well by the German Marxist sociologist Claus Offe (1984). The market manages people's expectations. Someone may desire a Mercedes, but their capacity to afford it is determined by their worth in the labour market. They do not blame the government for their lack of a Mercedes, at least they mostly do not. Yet, in the case of health care or schools, the government *does* decide who gets what. It therefore tends to be blamed for the outcome. It can lose trust and legitimacy as a result.

There is no easy way to dampen expectations of high service standards in a political marketplace, even though voters are reluctant to approve higher taxes. This brings increasing frustration as expectations are dashed. There will, as a result, be growing disillusionment with the government and hence with the collective process of funding social welfare services. Perhaps that is what we are currently seeing.

A less pessimistic view is that, over time, we *have* evolved ways to reach political compromises about taxing and spending and collective means of 'rationing' social policy resources precisely because the alternative of the market is even more unattractive. This is a difficult process. The more open and explicit the choices are and the more directly voters are involved, the better voters may understand the constraints. The further away those choices are made, the less they are understood. If the cabinet in Whitehall decides that only minimal resources can be devoted to road improvements and it does not want to limit car usage, the result – that a particular child dies from a road accident – may appear as a random event, a pure accident. In fact, it derives, in part, from a first-order choice about the transport budget. It is the result of an unseen 'tragic choice' (Calabresi and Bobbit, 1978).

Managing scarcity

Some history

Levi-Strauss (1969), the French anthropologist, put the whole issue starkly in his discussion of scarcity in early societies. In the absence of socially accepted ways of allocating scarce resources, there will be conflict. Simple societies devise means of 'rationing' scarce resources – land for food and shelter and access to sexual relationships. These are the means of acquiring children, status and support in old age. Such scarce 'resources' are rationed – by taboo and stigma, tradition, and status.

More complex societies, he argued, evolved markets as ways of coping with the complexity of rules that would otherwise be involved, but there are still some resource allocation decisions that are deemed too problematic to leave to the market, and in times of danger and extreme scarcity, we resort to collective rationing.

In the Second World War, as the author remembers, each family was issued with a ration book each year. The family had to be registered with a particular butcher or grocer. That determined how much meat, eggs and butter they were sold. The book was marked. Points and coupons – little bits of paper – were cut out for extras, for example, sweets and clothes. They took the place of money and were allocated equally. Money ceased to be the main determinant of capacity to buy – unless you operated on the 'black market'. After the war, this tradition of need-based allocation came to be applied to health and education resources, as well as local authorities' capacity to provide other services, building on some earlier attempts at 'formula funding' (Glennerster et al, 2000, chs 2, 3).

Some economics

A traditional economics textbook will characterise 'rationing' in a negative way – a bureaucratic device that is inferior to the market. ***Figure 4.1*** is an adaptation of an undergraduate economics student's supply-and-demand curve. In a pure market, the higher the price of health care, the more health-care suppliers will be prepared to offer – the supply curve. The higher the price, the less consumers will demand. At some point, the two processes match – supply equals demand. However, that could leave many people without health care. The state then enters and the supply of health care is set by a *political* process. How much are we prepared to pay in taxes and devote to the National Health Service (NHS)? The supply is then the vertical line in the diagram. More people's needs are met than the market would have achieved. However, if the service is offered free, there is no price restraint on demand. There is no reason why the public should demand less than would be the case if private doctors offered their services free.

Unless the public is prepared to pay for the level of demand that arises from free health care, the supply will fall short of demand. A gap emerges between what people demand by turning up at the doctor or the casualty department and what the taxpayer is prepared to fund. Waiting lists and queuing emerge – waiting times in accident and emergency departments lengthen, as they have been doing.

This is an oversimplified account but has a core of truth. Not all health care has an elastic demand curve. People do not rush out to have their legs amputated when they find that it is free. They are inhibited about going to see 'the busy doctor'. They may be reluctant to accept that they are ill. However, such social limits to demand are being eroded, for example, cultural reticence about seeking psychiatric help is declining. Our willingness to pay more in taxes is not rising at the same rate, though, as we saw in Chapter Three. The economists are right: there is a growing rationing gap.

Figure 4.1: *The economic concept of rationing*

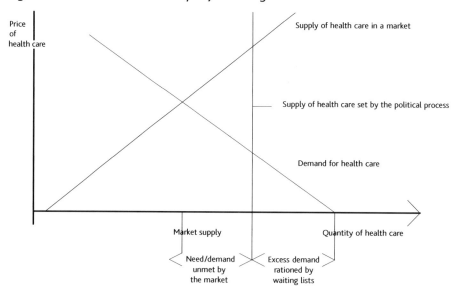

As a result, professionals are under increasing pressure and may find ways to divert patients, or to deter or delay them, even if they do not fully recognise what they are doing. Much 'rationing' takes place in unrecognised ways – how receptionists, medical staff or local bureaucrats respond to the demands made on them. Klein et al (1996) give a detailed case study of how this works in the NHS. However, all these actors are responding to a situation that originates in decisions made in Westminster or Edinburgh in response to politicians' judgements about how far they can tax.

A hierarchy of rationing

It is therefore possible to think of service rationing as a series of decisions that begin at the very centre of politics, in the negotiations that take place between Treasury ministers and their counterparts in the spending departments in Whitehall, Edinburgh, Cardiff and Belfast. The results then cascade down to local health and welfare services, parks, schools, and hospitals. The cascade continues until the local accident and emergency department has to cope with a large number of people arriving on a Saturday night and struggles to keep waiting times below four hours. Teachers have to decide how to allocate time in their lessons between those doing well and those falling behind. This 'cascade' is illustrated in ***Figure 4.2***.

Figure 4.2: Types of actual rationing

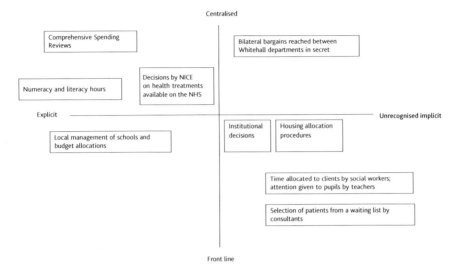

Note: NICE = National Institute for Health and Care Excellence.

The examples given illustrate where decisions are taken – some at cabinet level, some by the receptionist in the local surgery. However, these decisions also vary in another way – the explicitness and openness of the decision. Total public spending decisions and the resulting allocation of funds between departments are published in regular Comprehensive Spending Reviews, which are described later. It is possible, up to a point, to see who the gainers and the losers are with the help of bodies like the Institute for Fiscal Studies, but *how* these decisions were arrived at is obscure. What trade-offs were struck, what promises were made?

Figure 4.2 therefore has a second dimension – the explicitness of decisions to the left and unpublished implicit bargains to the right. Many decisions are unrecognised even by those making them. The instant decisions made by a teacher in front of a rowdy class may not be planned or explicitly thought out. Those boys are interrupting, deal with them. The teacher is not thinking: 'I plan to give less time to girls'.

Over time, professionals have become more aware of these issues. Decision processes *have* become more open and debated. One example discussed in Chapter Seven is the work of the National Institute for Health and Care Excellence (NICE). Instead of leaving clinicians entirely free to make decisions about what drugs to prescribe or procedures to adopt, this body gives advice on both the clinical efficacy and the cost effectiveness of treatments. Those that have been approved after an extremely thorough appraisal are likely to be funded by the local NHS. Those that are not so supported by evidence will probably not attract funding. The decision about what to do lies locally. Healthcare Improvement Scotland issues alerts to notify NHS Scotland about the publication of NICE guidance and advises on its applicability to Scotland. Single technology advice has no status in Scotland from August 2016. From April 2013, NICE has been responsible for advice on social care practice too.

Parliamentary control and audit

The power to vote for UK taxes and approve UK-wide spending lies with the Westminster Parliament – or, more precisely since 1911, with the House of Commons. In the case of functions not devolved to Scotland, Wales or Northern Ireland, the government department can only spend money with the approval of the House of Commons. The Public Accounts Committee and the officials in the National Audit Office have a duty to ensure that money is spent on purposes voted for by Parliament.

The official charged with overseeing this process, reporting to that committee and to the House of Commons, is the Comptroller and Auditor General. The post was created in 1314 and the title was retained despite the creation of the National Audit Office in 1983. The post-holder is an officer of the House of Commons, not a civil servant. The National Audit Office and the Public Accounts Committee are also charged with ensuring that the money is spent with due 'economy, efficiency and effectiveness'. The Committee is chaired by a member of the official opposition, though its membership is cross-party. It is Parliament's most powerful and respected committee (for an account of its work by its recent Chairwoman, see Hodge, 2016).

There used to be a separate body charged with auditing the accounts and practices of local government in England and Wales – the Audit Commission. This was abolished by the Coalition government. An independent company was created, incorporated by the Local Government Association, called Public Sector Audit Appointments Ltd. Some functions that used to be exercised by the Audit Commission were transferred to this new company in 2015. It is responsible for appointing private sector auditors for local government, the police and NHS bodies, as well as for setting audit fees. The National Audit Office decides the code of practice to be followed. This new set of arrangements only came into operation in April 2015 and it is too early to say what difference it has made.

Following the devolution of spending powers to Scotland and Wales, oversight has changed there too. In Scotland, the Auditor General scrutinises the accounts of the Scottish government and the Scottish NHS. The Accounts Commission for Scotland overseas local government spending, supported by Audit Scotland.

The Wales Audit Office is headed by the Auditor General for Wales, who audits the Welsh Assembly government and NHS Wales, appoints auditors for local government, and reports to the Welsh Assembly.

Northern Ireland has had its own Comptroller and Auditor General since its creation in 1921. This individual leads the Northern Ireland Audit Office, which audits local government and Northern Ireland government accounts, and reports to the Northern Ireland Assembly.

Treasury control

At the centre of the financial rationing process in the UK stands Her Majesty's Treasury. Its power derives from a series of constitutional conventions:

- No individual MP can put down a motion to spend public money. No proposal to authorise the spending of state money can be tabled without the signature of a Treasury minister. Similar rules apply in the Scottish Parliament (Heald and McLeod, 2003).
- No proposal involving additional spending can be discussed by cabinet or in a cabinet subcommittee unless it is accompanied by a Treasury paper outlining the cost and possible fiscal and economic consequences.
- No spending proposals may be developed within a department unless the Treasury is informed and asked to comment.
- No department can spend money, even if previously agreed, without specific and regular approval. A section of the Treasury is devoted to keeping a continuing oversight of each spending department.

Despite these apparently draconian powers, the Treasury has not always won its battles to contain public spending. Political imperatives can overrule even the Treasury, for a while. We have excellent documentary evidence of this from Lowe's (1989) account of the Treasury's attempt to cut back on social spending in a major way in the later 1950s. The Treasury failed. The whole Chancellor's team resigned and the spending went ahead. Afterwards, the Treasury fought back and argued that it had become procedurally unable to control public spending. An internal committee of enquiry was set up to consider the problem, chaired by Lord Plowden. His report (HM Treasury, 1961) has set the basic ground rules for Treasury expenditure control ever since. It argued:

- The pre-war consensus in favour of a small state had given way to a presumption of government spending to solve social problems. 'Natural restraint' was not enough.
- Individual ministers could approach cabinet with one-off proposals to spend money that convinced their colleagues of their individual merits. Most members

of cabinet would have their own pet plans. Such 'bubbling up' of incremental growth added up to unsustainable demands on the economy. Once politicians realised what the cumulative effect of their past decisions was going to mean for taxation at the next election, or in an economic crisis, public spending would be severely cut back. Such 'stop and go' was bad for services and the economy. What was needed was a long-term sustainable plan.

- Policies were embarked upon without testing their long-term implications for public spending and the economy. For example, a plan to expand places in teacher training colleges (as had just been agreed at that time) had long-term implications for spending on schools. This had not been considered.
- This whole process had to change.

Plowden's remedies followed:

- There should be regular comprehensive public spending plans agreed across Whitehall for both central and local government. No 'one-off' bright ideas for new spending should be considered at any other time. Every new item should be considered in competition with any other new programme that a ministry might want to put forward. They should be considered alongside long-standing policy commitments and their likely future cost. The spending time horizon should not be just one year ahead, but five years. Spending departments should be held to those limits. That would not only be better for the economy, but also give them the capacity to plan services over the medium term.
- Long-term spending plans should be considered alongside a judgement about the economy's capacity for growth and hence future revenue. Unless ministers were prepared to agree tax increases, spending should be kept within the economy's capacity to generate revenue. (For a review of the impact of Plowden's reforms on social policy departments, see Lowe, 1997a, 1997b.)

That logic and those 'remedies' have been applied ever since. The planning periods covered have varied. Sometimes three, sometimes four, years for such plans were chosen. Now, the control period is (theoretically) back to five years and the whole process is now called the Comprehensive Spending Review, a term introduced in Gordon Brown's term as Chancellor. The Treasury used to predict and publish future spending demands itself, assuming no policy change, over much longer periods – up to mid-century and beyond. The implied message is 'be careful, remember even if you do nothing, spending demands on current policies may grow'. The Treasury calculated how far demographic change, notably, the ageing population, would impact future spending on the NHS, social care, pensions and education.

However, the Treasury was considered too open to political pressure to manipulate these forecasts. A new independent body was created by the Coalition government in 2010 – the Office of Budget Responsibility (OBR). It has taken over the task of publishing long-term projections of spending and revenue. In 2016, it began to publish detailed analyses of long-term trends and the viability of particular areas of spending like pensions and health care, which we shall refer to in later chapters.

The constitutional change that introduced fixed five-year Parliaments made five years the logical period for planning once again – subject to the absence of major shocks. The vote to leave the European Union in 2016 was just such a shock. The new Conservative government's five-year plans were presented to Parliament in its first year by the then Chancellor George Osborne (HM Treasury, 2015b). They proposed eliminating the government's overall deficit – the amount it spent over what it gained in revenue – before the end of the Parliament. It then proposed to make a surplus: 'Putting money aside for the next bad times'.

This always looked highly ambitious. The OBR foresaw a fall in revenue that would arise from a slower growth of earnings, rising prices and lower consumer spending. As a result, the new Chancellor, Hammond, pushed the goal of reaching a surplus into the next Parliament and reset his spending priorities. A pre-publication process takes place in which the Treasury gives the OBR early notice of its figures and plans. The OBR staff respond and query until an agreed statistical position is arrived at. This whole process is fascinating and takes place behind very closed doors. Closed as they may be, this process sets the medium-term limits to the overall spending of each of the services with which we deal in this book.

(For many years, Chancellors gave what became effectively two Budget announcements a year. One trailed potential tax plans in the Autumn Statement and then the firm tax proposals in the Budget were announced just before the new tax year in April. From 2017, there will only be one statement a year, or so it is hoped!)

The spending plans set out in the autumn of 2015 would have reduced public spending as a share of economic activity to one of the lowest points since the Second World War – 36.4%. On only two previous occasions since the Second World War had the share of gross domestic product (GDP) devoted to public spending been as low. Between 1954 and 1957, the Conservative government held social service spending flat, introduced prescription charges and cut defence spending after the Korean War. It sustained the public spending share at about 36% for those three years. The share then grew steadily for the next 20 years (HM Treasury, 2015a).

The other period with a similarly low figure was during the first three years of Gordon Brown's Chancellorship (1997–2000). The Labour government had promised to keep to the previous Conservative expenditure plans until 2000 while the economy grew. As a result, by 1999/2000, total managed expenditure fell to

36% of GDP. There followed a steady rise of public expenditure as a share of GDP through in the early 2000s, reaching 45.7% in 2009/10 (Crawford et al, 2009).

Thus, in 21 out of the 44 years since 1972, public spending has taken somewhere between 40% and 45% of GDP. On nine occasions, it has been between 45% and 49%. On 14 occasions, it has been between 36% and 40%. Thus, the ambition to keep public spending at around the 36% level implied a much smaller state than has mostly ever been achieved since the Second World War.

In November 2016, Chancellor Hammond changed those ambitions but not by very much and only temporarily. Moreover, the extra money he was to borrow was to be devoted to 'infrastructure' spending, not social services. By infrastructure, he meant transport, roads, scientific research and some additional housing. The basic outline of the strategy can be seen in *Table 4.1*.

Table 4.1: Planned public expenditure and revenue, 2015/16–2020/21

	2015/16	2016/17	2017/18	2018/19	2019/20	2020/21	2021/22
Total managed expenditure (% of GDP)	40.1	39.9	39.8	39.1	38.0	38.0	37.8
Current receipts (% of GDP)	36.1	36.4	36.9	36.9	37.0	37.0	37.1
Public sector net debt (% of GDP)	84.2	88.3	90.2	89.7	88.0	84.0	81.6
GDP growth per annum	2.2	2.1	1.4	1.7	2.1	2.1	2.0
GDP growth per head	1.4	1.3	0.7	1.0	1.4	1.4	1.4

Source: HM Treasury (2016b).

Instead of a predicted growth rate in the economy of roughly 2.5% a year that Osborne had assumed in 2015, on the advice of the OBR after the vote to leave the European Union, public spending plans in 2016 were to be based on the assumption that growth would fall to 1.4% and then rise to about 2% by 2020. As the population was growing, too, that translated into a rise in real incomes (and output) per head of 1.4% a year, lower at some points.

However, to offset the impact of economic uncertainty, Hammond decided to increase government borrowing and let the total accumulated government debt rise to 90% of GDP by 2017. The share of public spending (total managed expenditure in *Table 4.1*) devoted to capital works was to rise from 10% in 2015/16 to 12% in 2021/22. However, public spending as a whole was set to *fall* as a percentage of the GDP from just over 41% in 2015/16 to 38% by the end of the Parliament. That was a higher share than Chancellor Osborne had be aiming for in 2020 (36.4%) but not that much more. A further fall in the next decade was suggested in the figures for 2021/22. So, it is reasonable to see the 2016 spending plans as a slight reduction in the speed of contraction, not a reversal of the trend that Conservative governments have been pursuing. It is still historically very low. This may be right or wrong depending on your political persuasion but the implications for social welfare services are serious.

Devolution

What has been described so far are negotiations between the Treasury and *English* spending departments. Since the devolution of spending powers to Scotland and Wales at the beginning of the 21st century, those administrations now decide how to allocate their budgets themselves. The Scotland Acts of 2012 and 2016 have devolved more major tax-raising powers to the Scottish Parliament. With that has gone Westminster's powers to ration. (For an introduction to the most recent devolution of social policy functions, see Part IV of Alcock et al, 2016.)

Each of the devolved administrations undertakes a similar process to that in Whitehall. However, the *total* allocation of money for each devolved administration has been determined by those English negotiations. In deciding how much money Westminster will give Scotland, for example, the Treasury calculates the percentage increases it has settled on for England for each of the devolved services. That overall rate of increase is the starting point for calculating what Scotland or Wales will get. A tough bargain for education and health in England will mean a tough overall outcome for Scotland. The same applies to the other parts of the UK. However, because increased tax powers are being devolved (see Chapter Three), the grant will now be smaller. The devolved administrations will have much more freedom to decide how much to tax and spend.

This grant-giving process has always been further complicated because it has to take account of the differential population growth that is occurring in the devolved countries. Scotland's population has been growing more slowly than England's, as has that in Wales. This has been going on for a long time and, as the Treasury sees it, it was not for many years reflected in Scotland's allocation. Thus, Scotland ended up getting more public money per head of population than England. That situation was, in the Treasury's view, being gradually put right by the 'Barnett Formula'. This is an allocation rule agreed in 1978 when the Labour Chief Secretary to the Treasury was Joel Barnett. It has no legal basis and is merely a 'convention', but one that politicians of all main parties have agreed to continue. (In fact, the idea of such a formula dates back to Lord Salisbury's Chancellor, George Goshen, in 1891 [see Thain and Wright, 1995]!)

The Barnett formula determines the 'increment', that is, the *extra* money each devolved Parliament should get in each expenditure round. Each country was given what it had gained in the last settlement plus a sum based on the *extra* that each English department got in the Westminster negotiations. However, that sum was then adjusted to reflect changes to the share of the UK population living in Scotland or other devolved parts of the UK.

The Barnett formula is as follows (for a more detailed account, see Christie and Swales, 2010):

> Baseline budget for the last period + Extra funding agreed in England × Proportion of population × Extent to which spending on devolved programmes differs

Thus, over time, the aim was to gradually move Scottish and Welsh allocations to equalise per capita spending across the UK. This was called the 'Barnett squeeze' – outside England! Those in the devolved jurisdictions complained that the calculations did not take full account of those countries' different needs. In 2009, a cross-party select committee of the House of Lords concluded that 'the Barnett Formula should no longer be used' to allocate funds to the devolved administrations and should be replaced by a formula based on 'relative need' (House of Lords, 2009). The devolution of taxing powers to these administrations that is now under way will change things considerably. As Scotland gains taxing powers to finance its devolved powers (see Chapter Three), so the Westminster grant will fall. *Table 4.2* shows spending per head of population in the various parts of the UK that resulted from the various allocation and rationing devices as they were in 2014/15.

While Scotland spends a tenth more on education and slightly more on health services, its housing expenditure is twice that in England (Chapter Eleven will explain why). Northern Ireland is a case on its own.

The control of local authority spending

From the days of the Plowden Report (HM Treasury, 1961), the aim of the Treasury was to control *all* UK public expenditure. This ambition extended not just to spending by central government, but also to that of local government. Practically no other finance ministry in the world attempts to do this.

Table 4.2: Identifiable expenditure per head on social services in England, Scotland, Wales and Northern Ireland compared to the UK average (2014/15 = 100)

England	
Education	98
Health	99
Housing	83
Social protection (mainly social security)	98
Scotland	
Education	110
Health	104
Housing	204
Social protection	107
Wales	
Education	102
Health	101
Housing	116
Social protection	115
Northern Ireland	
Education	121
Health	103
Housing	269
Social protection	119

Source: HM Treasury (2016a, Table 9.16).

Capital spending and the Private Finance Initiative

In the 19th century, the Treasury was afraid that the new democratically elected local authorities would be profligate in their borrowing. As they were public bodies, the Treasury feared that it would be landed with the job of taking over their debts if they got into difficulty. It was probably right.

The Treasury tried to ensure that it would never be put in that situation. Hence, it took on the responsibility of approving every local project that would involve borrowing – building a new school, for example. This process went on for more than a century. In the post-war period, central government used this power to shape school-building policy, housing policy and much else. Each individual project's plans, rationale, architects' proposals and building costs all had to be sent to the appropriate central spending department and the Treasury for approval.

After the Keynesian era, the Treasury added another argument. Controlling capital expenditure was an important lever in regulating overall demand in the economy. The Treasury needed to control that too.

More recently, governments have accepted that such detailed central control of each capital project was both unnecessary and inefficient. In 2003, Parliament introduced a 'prudential borrowing' regime that applied across the UK, though with slightly different rules in different devolved regions (the Local Government Act 2003 for England and Wales, the Local Government Scotland Act 2003 and Local Government Finance Act (Northern Ireland) 2011).

Local councils still have to seek approval for any borrowing from the appropriate devolved administration. There is an annual ceiling to the amount they can borrow. However, they do have a general power to borrow for any 'beneficial' capital project up to that limit. The sum borrowed has to be 'affordable' and in line with principles set out in a 'Prudential Code' endorsed by the Chartered Institute of Public Finance and Accountancy. Local councils receive national or sub-national government funding for some capital programmes, like schools, and can sell assets such as land or old buildings to help finance new building.

One way to avoid such harsh capital rationing has been the Private Finance Initiative (PFI). It began under a Conservative government in 1992. It handed over to a private company the task not only of building a hospital or a school, but also owning and maintaining it. That company would borrow the money to fund the scheme and then charge, for example, the local health authority for using the premises for a given period. The site would usually revert to the public sector, but in the interim, it was a private facility. This had appealed to the Conservative government in the 1990s but the Treasury maintained close control. Such schemes were only authorised under strict limits and if a case could be made.

To the incoming Labour Chancellor Gordon Brown, it had the great accounting advantage that this activity would not appear as public expenditure. It enabled the government to do more school and hospital building than would otherwise have been the case given the promise to contain public spending. In a review of the policy, the Commission on Public Private Partnerships (IPPR, 2001) concluded that there was some evidence that in the case of roads and prisons, there had been some economic benefit from PFI but not otherwise. Statutory bodies were not used to drawing up tight contracts. Private companies got better terms than they should have done. Probably too much capital spending was undertaken. These PFI projects left many statutory bodies with large and continuing financial commitments that are now coming home to roost.

Capping local revenue

The Rates Act 1984 gave central government the power to selectively 'cap' local rates charged by a local authority – the forerunner of today's Council Tax. This power was made general and transferred to the Council Tax in the 1990s. The Blair government then used these reserve powers with 36 authorities and threatened other local councils to keep their tax increases to a minimum. The Coalition government and the new Conservative government have set 'caps' to Council Tax rises in England that can only be overridden by a local referendum. Between 2012/13 and 2015/16, the government offered a 'freeze grant' to any authority that agreed not to increase its Council Tax. In 2016, a 2% cap on Council Tax increases was raised by another 2% for councils with social care powers. (To be precise, a referendum has to be called to approve a rise above these 'caps'.)

Nor has this approach been confined to England. In Scotland, the Council Tax was frozen in 2007. The Scottish government has compensated local governments with an additional grant but the constraint has become increasingly damaging to local initiative and accountability. To find an alternative, the Scottish government appointed a Commission on Local Tax Reform with cross-party representation. (The Conservative Party in Scotland did not nominate a member.) The Commission reported in December 2015 and the report is worth reading (see: www.localtaxcommission.scot).

It concluded that the Council Tax was unfair and ineffective as a means of raising local revenue. People in the most expensive band of property paid three times the tax of those in the lowest value band but the value of their properties was 15 times as great. Holding the tax down and not revaluing in perpetuity was unsustainable. It should be abolished. The Commission set out the pros and cons of a range of alternatives, modelling their likely effects, fairness and administrative difficulties and advantages. Three alternatives were explored:

- a reformed tax on property that was proportionate to regularly revalued property values;
- a land value tax; and
- a local income tax.

Each is discussed and their impacts are compared. No final recommendation is offered, but none is ruled out, with the suggestion that some mix of all three could work. From April 2017 the tax charged on properties in the top four bands will rise.

The Welsh government did attempt to add another band to the Council Tax in Wales in 2005, with a great deal of opposition and appeals against the valuations. Northern Ireland has kept household 'rates', the predecessor to the Council Tax. An individual property reassessment was carried out with 'transition arrangements' to smooth the process in 2007. Without some reform of local taxation any further moves to localise rationing is impossible.

Local rationing

Once the cabinet in Westminster, or the equivalents in the devolved parts of the UK, have allocated their budgets to spending departments, they have the job of allocating budgets to local authorities. This has come to be done through a series of formulae – a mathematical summary of the weight to be given to various factors. Local populations are weighted according to their need for service. One local authority may have a larger share of older people, or schoolchildren or children living in circumstances that are likely to demand specialist care.

A number of years ago, Glennerster et al (2000) traced the history of these various formulae. Those for health and schools will be discussed in more detail later. The general conclusion was that mathematical formulae had evolved in an attempt to minimise the political and administrative costs of handling special pleading from individual areas. Bleddyn Davies (1968) pioneered an approach that has become standard practice: measure the extent to which populations of different ages, with measurable characteristics like single parenthood or social deprivation, have different needs for local services – 'need-creating circumstances'.

Once a local council has received its funds, a comparable process to that undertaken in Whitehall follows. Each spending department makes its case to the local cabinet or group of senior councillors and the budget is allocated. Chapter Three showed how centralised the tax base is in the UK. This is now being decentralised to the devolved administrations. Within them, though, rationing continues.

Different kinds of rationing in different countries

We have seen that in a centralised state, rationing tends to be centralised too. In federal states and those with powerful municipalities, rationing is more diverse. As we shall see, the English government is introducing a single formula to apply to the funding of all state schools. This would be considered impossible and wrong in the US, for example. Even there, the federal government has taken steps to encourage states to support the funding of schools with more poor children.

Perhaps because it is all so complicated, there are few, if any, comparative accounts of service and financial rationing internationally. One recent exception was a historical and comparative account of the way in which different countries have responded to past bouts of 'austerity' or cuts in public funding. In a devolved system such as Germany, this resulted in a complex dance, each level trying to avoid the blame, for example (Hood et al, 2014).

Overview

To conclude, publicly provided services require an open political process to allocate resources fairly. I have called this 'rationing' despite its wartime overtones. The processes adopted in the UK for each service and at national and sub-national levels have become more explicit and open over time. Periodic Comprehensive Spending Reviews by the Westminster government set overall spending targets that supposedly hold for five years in the absence of economic shocks:

- That pattern has begun to change with dissatisfaction about the priorities 'imposed' by Westminster. More taxing powers are being given to the devolved administrations from 2016.
- This will begin to devolve service rationing. Small steps towards more independent local government budgetary freedom in England are also being taken. However, local government lacks tax-raising powers that those in most other countries possess. Without that, true devolution is not possible.
- Many detailed rationing decisions are made by front-line professionals. Some have become subject to central guidance, as in the case of health care. In the present climate of austerity, the dilemmas that professionals face are harsher than for many years.

Questions for discussion

1. Who rations what kinds of social service resources in the UK?
2. Trace the development of UK Treasury control of public expenditure since 1961. What will be the implications of the Comprehensive Spending Reviews that cover the period 2015/16 to 2020/21?
3. What attempts are being made to devolve spending decisions in the UK?
4. How would you balance the need for local accountability and freedom with equal access to major services? Compare the rationing process in the UK to that of another country known to you.

Further reading

Still the best account of the kind of negotiations that take place between the Treasury and spending departments is **Heclo and Wildavsky (1974; 1981)**. For a focus on social policy, see **Deakin and Parry (2000)**.

The Treasury website (see: www.hm-treasury.gov.uk) gives the results of each latest Comprehensive Spending Review, and past public spending trends. The latter are published every July under the title ***Public expenditure statistical analyses***.

For a discussion of devolved public spending control as it is organised in Scotland, see **Heald and McLeod (2003)** and, more widely on devolution, **Lodge and Trench (2014)**.

Part Two
Paying for services

five

Cash benefits: pensions

Summary

The most expensive cash benefit paid out by the state is the state pension. Long before the state paid pensions, a declining capacity to work in older life always posed a financial problem for families. Mutual aid schemes and private pension savings have never been enough. Individuals are not good at making financial decisions about the distant future. This constrains the capacity of the insurance market to provide adequate incomes in retirement.

- State intervention can have two distinct purposes:
    - to prevent poverty in old age; and
    - to ensure that people do not suffer a major and disruptive decline in their living standards on retiring – income smoothing.
- The UK government has decided to concentrate its pension spending on the first objective. Many other countries aim to do both.
- It requires employers to *offer* their workers a pension scheme to partially achieve the second objective. Individuals can choose to opt out. That is an unusual model internationally.
- Major controversial changes to the tax treatment of private pensions are also under way.

Some history

Old age, and the frailty that eventually goes with it, brings financial problems. Thane summarises the situation that held long before the state got involved:

> the great majority in all populations in all recorded time until the very recent past worked for as long as they were physically able, though often in increasingly irregular, low skilled, and low paid work as their abilities declined. If they were lucky they might have children to support them. More probably, until into the twentieth century … their children were dead, had migrated out of easy contact in search of work or land; or were themselves too poor to assist their parents. (Thane, 2006, p 35; see also Thane, 2005)

Many would have to rely on charity or poor relief. The majority of those needing support have always been women. Working men could never amass enough savings to support their wives after their death and the husband's death usually came first. The notion of 'retirement' gained ground only very gradually. Employers began – first informally and then in more regularised forms – to give their employees a pension or some financial reward on giving up work after long service. 'Smoothing' the process of leaving work was useful for a state bureaucracy or a firm as it enabled those organisations to part with someone who was becoming less useful. Instead of making individually difficult decisions, a common rule could be applied. An age of 'retirement' could be set.

The promise of a pension also helped tie the worker to the firm. It retained the benefit of long experience and skill and fostered trust and loyalty in the workforce. Such privileges did not apply to all kinds of worker. Many were considered more dispensable. However, pensions also became something that trade unions could add to the benefits for which they were fighting. Governments began to see such developments as useful – they reduced the potential demands on the state to fund poor relief. Tax relief and other inducements to encourage occupational pension schemes began.

When state pensions were gradually introduced, they were seen as supplements to falling incomes. Workers were not required to give up work; they were expected to go on working so long as they could. However, a pension did not increase much if the employee went on working. People thus came to see the age at which you could draw a state pension as the point at which you 'retired'.

As the scale of industrialisation grew in the 20th century and as more agriculturally based economies were exposed to the risks of international trade, workers began to organise themselves to meet the risks of sickness and old age. 'Friendly Societies', the British legal entity, and 'mutual aid organisations', the American term, grew in scale and coverage. The emergence of national working-class movements in the late 19th century widened the collective logic. The focus moved from small-scale collective action to demands for some national government policy.

In an early contribution to this topic, Bentley Gilbert (1966) argued that the Friendly Societies in the UK ran into financial difficulties at the end of the 19th century because of the unexpected rapid extension of life. Macnicol (1998) challenged this story of 'impending actuarial cataclysm'; there were other factors at work, he argued. The plight of pensioners was used on the Left as a reason to press for a fundamental redistribution of wealth and a progressive income tax.

When an old-age pension was introduced in the Old Age Pensions Act 1908, it was means-tested and available only to those aged 70 or above. It was *tax*-financed. Its escalating cost and the implications for income taxation led a later Conservative government to move away from tax finance to a social insurance model (ie through National Insurance Contributions). Funding came from a flat-rate contribution paid by the employee and the employer. A flat-rate levy put a natural ceiling on what could be spent on pensions. It was adopted as the basis for Beveridge's post-war 'social security plan'.

In the 1950s, critics, notably, the trio of social policy analysts Abel-Smith, Titmuss and Townsend, convinced the Labour Party that this flat-rate principle was wrong. Over the next 20 years, successive Labour governments tried, and temporarily succeeded, in building on top of the flat-rate pension a second tier that would relate people's pension to their pre-retirement earnings. It was an attempt to move the UK nearer to the Scandinavian, German and US state pension model. This move ultimately failed. The UK has reverted to seeing the state's role as one of poverty relief – a minimum platform on which private and occupational pensions can build – the 'neoliberalising of old age', as Macnicol (2015) has put it.

Some economic theory

Pensions differ from a 'first best' free market in a whole series of ways (for a detailed elaboration, see Barr and Diamond, 2008):

- Many people have a poor sense of the financial risks they face over a lifetime, for example, how likely they are to become long-term sick or disabled, or how long they may live.
- Many are poorly informed about the nature of the financial products that are available and the interacting risks that are involved. The problem is not just one of poor information, which could, in theory, be improved; it is also a problem of processing the information – making sense of it. This makes individuals vulnerable to scams of various kinds.

- Decisions about what kind of pension you need, and of what size, have to be taken a long time in advance. People may give too high a preference to the present – spend now, forget the future. Economists call this myopia. Similarly, people are tempted to cash in a pension pot without fully realising the potential gains of investment and the risks of inflation (see Pensions Commission, 2004, ch 6).
- Even if a young person has gone to the trouble of being well informed and has grasped the risks, she may well not act – difficult decisions can be put off until tomorrow with little to lose, and to tomorrow and tomorrow.
- Even if a consumer is well informed and decisive, the provider may not be able to provide a product geared to her needs. She may have a family health history. She will want a pension that takes account of inflation. That risk is too unpredictable for a company to provide beyond a low limit. It may be able to do so only if the government offers a price-index-linked bond and hence takes the inflation risk itself. This is what economists call an 'incomplete market'.
- There is a real danger of mis-selling pension products – as happened in the UK in the late 1980s and early 1990s when the sales of half-a-million pensions were investigated for mis-selling. It may be happening today with schemes that seem to offer small employers a way to meet new government requirements.
- All schemes that rely on accumulated financial assets are at risk of volatility in the financial markets, as we saw in 2008!
- Occupational pension schemes (employer-based ones) are designed to tie individuals to the firm. That reduces labour mobility. Such schemes may also be used to rescue a firm when it gets into trouble, for example, Enron shares were held in the pension portfolios of Enron employees.
- The administrative costs of many private schemes are very high. An annual management charge of 1% of the account balance is, on one set of reasonable assumptions, equivalent to a cumulative decline of one *fifth* in the eventual value of a pension (Barr and Diamond, 2008, pp 164–8). Such an administrative charge was the average for pension plans in the UK in the early 2000s, though costs varied by type of scheme. These variations and their significance were not appreciated by pension scheme members (Pension Commission, 2004, pp 214–25).

All pensions – state and private – are a claim by those who are not producing goods and services on those who are. It might be technically feasible to hoard physical assets in the garden shed and sell them off gradually after you are 70 but that is a highly inefficient process and a risky one too. The nearest people get to doing this is to buy a house in their youth and hope to sell it later – to downsize. This has worked in a rising housing market and may finance a couple's long-term care, briefly, but it will not meet regular financial needs over a 30-year retirement, for example, housing markets may not go on rising.

'Fully funded' schemes

The mechanism that is most used to store value is to acquire financial assets, shares or government bonds, which can be cashed in when needed. Regulated private schemes are in theory 'fully funded' but there are ways around those rules. That does not make them necessarily safe or economically superior to public non-funded ones (Barr, 2001).

Those pensions will be used to buy goods and services produced by those in work. However, those in work must not be seeking to consume those resources too. They need to be saving for *their* retirement! If not, there will be inflation or a balance-of-payments problem. In either case, the value of the financial assets will fall. Asset values may crash for reasons that have nothing to do with pension scheme management.

Pay-as-you-go schemes

The other way to organise pensions is to get the younger generation to agree to be taxed to support their parents' generation. If they are paying taxes, they are not consuming. They may agree to be taxed now because they trust the next generation, and the politicians they vote for, to continue this intergenerational bargain. This political bargain is called a 'pay-as-you-go' pension scheme. It has obvious risks: will the generational compact hold? Can we rely on future governments and future voters to keep that bargain?

There was a strong incentive for governments during the baby-boom years to offer pensions that were only affordable with a large young labour force paying contributions to finance a few pensioners. Now the baby boomers are retiring. This strategy was characterised by one economist as a 'Ponzi Game' (Disney, 2000). Charles Ponzi was the originator of the use of chain letters to raise money. But, by tempering the intergenerational consequences, other countries have kept to the bargain.

Pensions as poverty relief

This is the state's minimal role. It can take various forms:

• Means- and asset-tested cash support financed by taxation. If an individual's or family's income, savings or the value of property are above a given level, they lose the right to a state pension. In many countries, including the UK, means testing begins at a low level, near the poverty line. In others, like Australia, it applies at a much higher level, excluding only the richer third of the pensioner age group. This model is called 'affluence testing'. South Africa and Chile are more recent examples.

- A flat-rate contributory pension given to those who have contributed to a state pension scheme while at work, usually with some matching contribution from their employer. Ideally this would preclude any necessity to seek additional means-tested support. This was what Beveridge claimed that his scheme would do. That is contestable and certainly never happened (Viet-Wilson, 1994). Married women who withdrew from the labour market posed a problem for this model – 'the economic risks of marriage', as Beveridge put it (Glennerster and Evans, 1994). Women were to gain rights to benefits through their husbands' contributions. This 'male breadwinner model' proved less and less acceptable as women's labour market roles and social attitudes changed (Lewis, 2001). The UK is now returning to such a flat-rate model but on an individualised basis. It is discussed later.
- A state pension scheme that gives its members a pension linked to previous earnings but with a formula that replaces a *higher percentage* of previous income for *poorer* contributors – redistribution within the pension scheme. The US Federal Social Security Scheme and the Swedish one do this. So did the UK State Earnings Related Pension Scheme (SERPS) – initiated in the 1970s but abolished in 2012.
- A flat-rate 'citizen's pension' set higher than means-tested support for the elderly. Rights to such a pension are usually based on age and length of residence, not mere 'citizenship'. Australia, Finland and New Zealand base benefits on years of residence. The Netherlands uses 'legitimate residence'.

For a simplified account of pension schemes internationally, see the Pensions Commission's First Report (2004, Volume Two, Appendix D). For current details, see the regularly updated Organisation for Economic Co-operation and Development (OECD) volume *Pensions at a glance*.

There is no decisive economic argument favouring any one of these approaches. However, a few countries have been moving towards some form of tax-funded citizenship- or residence-based pension, for the following reasons.

- Complex means and asset testing for older people are confusing for retirement planning and may deter saving or membership of a private pension scheme. A simple known state pension platform on which people can build their own pension arrangements has its attractions if the aim is to encourage individual saving. This was Beveridge's argument and it is one to which the Pensions Commission (2005) returned.
- Higher-income taxpayers will be contributing more but have a longer life expectancy. Women will draw out more than they have contributed in cash but they have been contributing more in unpaid caring roles than men.
- A rough-and-ready conclusion may be that all these factors balance out, so go for simplicity (for a full discussion, see Barr and Diamond, 2008, chs 7, 8).

The UK version – not what it seems?

Ever since the Second World War, many retired people have relied on means-tested benefits. The first post-war agency to administer such a benefit was the National Assistance Board. Now, the Pension Service administers Pension Credit:

- If you were born after December 1953, the qualifying age is 65 or over, but it is rising.
- The UK has to be your 'habitual residence'. You must have a 'right to reside'.
- A guaranteed minimum income ('guarantee credit') is set for a single person and for partners. There are additions for special needs and for housing. Income received, for example, any state pension, is subtracted to assess how much Pension Credit will be given.
- In order to retain some incentive for people to save, they are allowed to keep a *part* of their income from a private pension or savings up to a fairly low limit – 'savings credit'. This 'tax' on small additional savings income is 40%; beyond that, it is 100%.
- If a household has additional needs, such as a member having a disability, caring responsibilities or approved housing costs, income will be made up to the guaranteed level plus these additional amounts.

In essence, this approach, though more formalised and rule-based, is still recognisable from its 1948 roots. It is means-tested, tax-funded and caters for a lot of people. However, the pensions crisis during the last part of the 20th century and the consequent Pensions Commission (2004, 2005) did spark a major change in pension policy.

Since 1980, governments had increased the basic pension only in line with prices. As earnings and, at intervals, the basic 'guaranteed income' rose, so the number of pensioners becoming eligible for means-tested support grew. So long as that policy was retained, so the share of the elderly population on means-tested Pension Credit would grow. The Pensions (Turner) Commission estimated that the percentage of pensioners drawing Pension Credit would rise from 40% in 2010 to 75% in 2050. This would destroy any incentive to save for most of the population and be expensive. The Commission recommended a new *single basic pension at or above the poverty line*.

Beveridge's logic reasserted itself. If you wanted to give people an incentive to save for retirement and eliminate poverty in old age, you had to give them a basic pension that took them above the means-tested minimum income guarantee – but how was government to afford that? There were, Turner saw, two necessary changes:

- The first was to reverse successive governments' reluctance to raise the age at which the state began to give pensions. It had remained at 65 for men since 1925. Women's pension age was set at 60 during the Second World War. It was in the process of being moved to 65. In 1948, a person might expect to spend less than a fifth of their adult life in retirement. With rising life expectancy, that figure had risen to 30% of adult life in 2005 and was still rising. Instead:
    - The state pension age should rise in line with life expectancy. Special arrangements should be made for those unable to go on working. Unless the electorate was prepared to pay higher taxes or contributions, the choice was between lower pensions or improved pensions after a longer working life. It was an argument that members of the Pensions Commission thought would be very difficult to win. In fact, once put in those stark terms, it won surprising support and political agreement across the parties.
    - Turner and the Labour government proposed a long warning period before raising the pension age for both men and women. That would begin to take effect only when women's pension age reached 65.
    - The Coalition government sped up the whole process. Between April 2016 and November 2018, the state pension age will rise to 65 for women. Between December 2018 and October 2020, the age for men and women will rise to 66. Between 2026 and 2028, it will rise to 67. There will be a review of these ages every five years, the first review being completed by May 2017.
    - In the 2013 Autumn Statement, the Chancellor said that he thought future generations should expect to spend no more than up to a third of their adult life in retirement – echoing Turner. On present trends, that would imply a state pension age of 69 by the late 2040s.
- Under the Turner Commission plan, the old second state pension, an income-related supplement to the basic state pension, was to become a second flat-rate pension and then be merged into a new higher basic pension:
    - The Pensions Commission's preferred option was to introduce a citizen's pension to which every person would have a right depending on their period of legitimate residency. The Labour government rejected the idea of giving up a contribution-based system. In practice, it moved in that direction in the following ways. It reduced the number of years that people had to contribute to gain a full pension. It was to fall from 44 years for men and 39 for women to 30 for both. Building on past 'home responsibilities protection', it introduced a new Carers' Credit – the equivalent of a pension contribution for those receiving Child Benefit for a child under 12, as well as those undertaking care for the sick or severely disabled in the family and spending more than 20 hours a week doing so.

- The Coalition government sped up this whole process, saving money in the process. It legislated to begin phasing out rights to the second pension for those retiring from April 2016 onwards.

- At the same time, that government increased the size of the basic pension by applying what they called a 'triple lock'. The basic pension would rise by the highest of increases in the Consumer Price Index, average earnings or 2.5% per annum. Thus, while average earnings fell or stagnated in the recession, the basic pension rose. The present government has promised to continue with this 'triple lock' until 2020.

- From April 2016, new pensioners who lost entitlements to the varied second state pensions receive a new merged flat-rate pension. This was due to be set at a rate high enough to take people above the Pension Credit entitlement. That, at least, was the government's claim. In fact, only some people will get this level of pension. The Treasury insisted that this reform should be 'nil cost'. That could only be achieved by limiting the contribution conditions required to receive it. Those who had contracted out of the state second pension will not get the full new pension. Moreover, the number of years of contribution required to qualify will *rise to* 35 – not 30. So, less than half of new pensioners will get the new higher pension. Indeed, in the medium term, the government will save money from this change. Those who would have gained higher state second pensions will lose them.

An Institute for Fiscal Studies (IFS) study (Cribb and Emmerson, 2016) has charted the early impact of 'nudging' employers and employees into workplace pensions. The percentage of employees enrolled in workplace pensions in 2012 was 30%. By 2015, this had risen to 55%. The increase was particularly marked in the 22–29 age group. The average contribution per worker in the whole economy had risen from 7% to 8.1% (5.4% from employers; 2.7% from the employees). Since only about half of all workers are members of such schemes, that means roughly double those percentages for members of the schemes.

If we now stand back from all this complex and rapid change, we can only reflect, as another IFS study (Crawford et al, 2013) put it, that UK pension policy has travelled 'a long and circular road' since 1974 when the then Labour government introduced a previous income-related element into the UK state pension rather like the Scandinavian, German and US schemes. It was designed to smooth the transition to retirement for all citizens. The UK has now reverted to a flat-rate poverty pension with a value not that different from what it was in 1974 compared to average earnings. Its value should rise with average earnings as the basic pension did before 1974. The only major improvement on 1974 is that coverage should be more extensive. Rights to receive such a pension now include those who have had caring responsibilities.

However, the policy is not quite what is seems, or will not be for a long time. The IFS (Crawford and Tetlow, 2016) point out that the contribution rules necessary to gain the headline 'over poverty line' pension rate mean that this policy will apply to just over 60% of those reaching retirement. The rest were contracted out of the old second state pension scheme and hence do not have the full contribution record required. They should be receiving an occupational pension, which may make up for their lower state pension. The transition period will be a long one.

Pension costs

One way to measure the financial impact of all these changes is to look at the estimated cost of pension policy as it was when the Pensions Commission reported over 10 years ago and compare that with estimates of the cost of present policies. The expected ageing of the population has not changed that much since 2004. The Pensions Commission (2004, p 75) estimated that cash benefit spending by the state on pensioners would rise, assuming no change in policy, from 6% of gross domestic product (GDP) in 2003/04 to 7% by mid-century (2053/4). That assumed the size of the *basic* pension would continue to *fall* relative to earnings but means-tested pension spending would rise. The cost of the then Second State Pension would also rise. The estimates by the Office for Budget Responsibility (OBR, 2017) suggest that by 2056/7, the state will be spending 6.5% of GDP on state pensions and other cash benefits for the elderly, only a little more than now and less than the pre-Turner pension regime would have cost more despite the fact that the share of the population over 65 is predicted to rise (see later).

These figures illustrate the overall strategy. It is saving money by giving a pension only at an increasing age. It has abandoned any responsibility for cushioning family income when it moves from earning into retirement. That is a private responsibility, but the state will 'nudge' individuals to make their own arrangements, as we see later. The Coalition government and its successor promised to keep the basic state pension rising by the fastest of inflation, average earnings or 2.5% a year – the Triple Lock'. In November 2017 the Chancellor said this promise would be 'reviewed' before the next Parliament. If it is revoked pension spending would fall faster than the OBR predicts. This is difficult to justify in terms of generational equity or overall cost.

At this point, it may be useful to reflect briefly on the issue of ageing and the way it differs between parts of the country and social classes. An increasing proportion of the population is reaching age 65 for two quite different reasons:

- *Longevity*. People are living longer. This is a gradual trend over many decades (65-year-old men have seen their lives extended by five years over the past 30 years).

- *Variations in fertility.* There was a sharp increase in the number of births after the Second World War, which continued at a high level for two decades. That generation is now retiring. This is the *current* financial problem.

Table 5.1 shows that life expectancy at age 65 has been rising for both men and women in the UK and in all countries of the UK. However, it remains well over a year shorter in Scotland for men than in England. Those in higher professional occupations live roughly four more years after they reach 65 compared to those from 'routine' – working-class – occupations. This means that a higher full pension age impacts some classes and regions more than others. Over the next 25 years, the expectation of life at 65 is expected to rise by about three to four years, whether the calculations are done on a 'cohort' or 'period' basis. (Period life tables use current rates, not making estimates of future changes. Cohort estimates use age-specific rates and known or predicted changes by age group.)

Table 5.1: Life expectancy at age 65 by UK region (years)

Region	2006–08		2010–12	
	Males	Females	Males	Females
UK	17.5	20.1	18.5	20.9
England	17.6	20.3	18.5	21.1
Scotland	16.3	18.9	17.2	19.5
Wales	17.2	19.9	18.0	20.6
Northern Ireland	16.9	19.9	17.9	20.6

Source: ONS (2015b).

Consumption smoothing

If people lose their regular income from work and have to rely entirely on a state poverty-line pension, most would suffer a big fall in living standards. Their past housing, eating and leisure habits would become unaffordable. What responsibility does the state have to cushion or smooth this adjustment?

We have already seen that there is powerful experimental and practical experience which suggests that individuals are not good at planning for future financial circumstances. In the financial crisis, many organisations realised that the risks posed to their firm by their occupational pension schemes were too great to continue them. Most outside the public sector were closed to new entrants.

Given that it had given up direct state involvement in providing income-related pensions, there were three possible strategies for the government:

- The state could require people to belong to a private scheme.
- The state could introduce rules that would 'nudge' people to save for retirement. This term was popularised by two American authors (Thaler and Sunstein, 2008). Governments can adopt rules that encourage people to change their behaviour without actually requiring them to do something.
- The state could give tax inducements.

The state decided not to force individuals to take out private schemes, but to adopt a nudging approach aided by tax inducements.

Nudging

Drawing on American evidence that was just emerging (Choi et al, 2004, 2006), the Pensions Commission (2005) concluded that if the onus were placed on employees *to opt out* of a pension plan that an employer was obliged to offer, most employees would *not* opt out. The Pensions Commission recommended that if employees were not in a government-approved company or other pension plan, they should have a portion of their income paid into an approved pension scheme. Those funds would be matched by a combination of employer contributions and tax subsidy. The essence of this plan was legislated for in the Pensions Act 2008 and is being introduced in stages that will last from 2012 to 2018:

- All employees – however few an employer may have on their books – must eventually be automatically enrolled if they are earning (currently) £10,000 or more and are aged 22 or older but below state pension age. Failure to do so could involve prosecution. The scheme is being phased in gradually for small employers (fewer than 30 staff).
- The contribution rates are also being phased in:
  - Employers' minimum contribution rate started at 1% of earnings. It will rise to 2% in 2018 and 3% from April 2019.
  - Employees' contributions will rise from an initial 1% to 5%, which, under current law, will attract tax relief (see later).
  - From April 2019, the total minimum contributions from which people could opt out will amount to 8% of earnings. However, that figure only applies on a particular band of earnings. It currently omits pay up to £112 a week. Thus, the lower paid will have contributions well below an 8% figure.
  - However, the Pensions Policy Institute (2013) calculated that a lower earner will need a combined contribution of 11% to have a three in four chance of achieving what they see as their target replacement rate. A median earner would need a contribution of 13%. Thus, even if people

choose to stay in these schemes, they will get pensions below what they think of as an appropriate 'cushion'.

- Those aged under 22 are not auto-enrolled, nor are people earning below £10,000. The sum applies to each separate job. Thus, many with several jobs will not be automatically enrolled.
- More encouragingly, only about one in 10 workers in the first tranche of employers to be involved chose to opt out. This may increase as the employers in following tranches are smaller and the employees are more transient.

• Employers can choose to enrol their employees in any pension scheme that meets the Pension Regulator's rules. However, they can also choose to use a default scheme run by the National Employment Savings Trust (NEST). This guarantees that all the rules are kept to and makes things simple for small employers. The options are:

- Employees join a scheme that older generations and public employees are familiar with, called 'a defined benefit scheme'. This guarantees a pension usually related to years of service and the final salary that a person earns or one calculated from the salary earned over some period before retirement. The risks that employees may live longer than expected have to be carried by the employer. The same is true of a collapse in the stock market or poor returns on investments. The scale of these risks has led most employers to abandon such schemes.
- The majority of employers (over 70%) offering a pension are now enrolling their employees in 'defined contribution schemes'. These set a required level of contributions and the pension fund managers do their statutory duty to get the best return they can on the money that is invested. The pensioner merely gets the resulting pot when she retires. What that will mean in terms of a percentage of final salary is mostly luck, tempered by a little judgement. She can then:
  - buy a guaranteed annual pension – an annuity;
  - get flexible access to the sum; or
  - cash it all at once (limits to this option have been relaxed, as is discussed later).

• After a steady decline in the percentage of workers enrolled in a pension scheme (from 65% to 55% during 1995–2012), there has been a small increase since.

Public sector pensions

These have remained defined benefit schemes but their cost has been reduced by linking normal pension ages to the rising state pension age and moving pension linkage from a final salary to a career average salary. This covers teachers and National Health Service (NHS) staff, as well as local government employees.

Fire-fighting staff and police, as well as the armed services, have a normal pension age of 60. Contribution rates have also been raised (Public Service Pensions Act 2013). This has saved significant future public expenditure.

Tax inducements: the bad, the better and the sheer potty

As we saw earlier, governments have long used tax reliefs to encourage individuals to save for their retirement. Such tax reliefs tend to favour those with enough income to invest a lot in pension schemes. Currently, such relief costs the government about £50 billion a year – half the cost of the NHS. That is made up of reliefs to employees and their employers. The structure is sometimes called 'Exempt–Exempt–Taxed' (EET):

- **Exempt** – Pension contributions by individuals and their employers are exempt from tax.
- **Exempt** – Personal tax is not charged on investment growth in the pension fund, though it would be if this were not a pension fund – a capital gains tax and a tax on investment income would otherwise be charged.
- **Taxed** – What is taxed is the income you take out as a pension. However, individuals have been able to take out 25% of the fund as a tax-free lump sum on retirement without it being taxed.

Those able to put large amounts into their pension pot have been saved a great deal in taxation. This has not necessarily increased the amount that they have saved in total. People may have simply moved their savings into this tax-privileged means of saving.

The Labour government began to restrict the amount of tax relief available in 2006. It said that the total lifetime personal allowance should be capped at £1.5 million. The annual sum of allowances should also be limited to £250,000. The Coalition and later Conservative governments reduced these totals still further to a £1 million lifetime cap in 2016, then to be uprated in line with the Consumer Price Index. The annual allowance was reduced still further to £40,000. These are still huge sums compared to an average worker's salary.

The tax subsidy remained highly skewed towards those with higher incomes. The richest *8%* of taxpayers receive about *half* of the tax relief. Interestingly, this criticism has not been confined to those on the political Left. One of the most effective critics has been Michael Johnson (2012) of the right-leaning think tank the Centre for Policy Studies. He has proposed:

- abolishing tax relief on pensions altogether; and
- using the sum saved to increase the basic pension by 40%!

The justification for the pre–2016 arrangements was that:

- to tax income that we pay into a pension scheme and the income we draw out as a pension is wrong as it amounts to 'double taxation'; and
- the Treasury will get more tax revenue from the invested savings when it appears as a taxable pension.

Both arguments were fallacious, Johnson claimed:

1. Governments double tax all the time. If someone puts money in the bank or buys shares, it is from income on which an individual has paid tax. The government then taxes the investment income earned. Money circulates. Governments tax it as it circulates – when it is earned and when it is spent.
2. The Treasury loses money on the whole set of arrangements. Only one in seven of those who would have paid higher-rate tax on their income in working life pay tax at that rate in retirement.
3. The high charges levied on pension pots by pension companies lose the Treasury money as it is not taxable as income.

Some economists have therefore argued that tax relief on payments into a pension scheme should be taken away altogether. Pensions should merely be taxed, above an exempted floor, like any other income. Others argue that some tax relief *is* necessary to encourage long-term pension saving but only up to a low limit and at a flat rate. This could be more generous than now for the basic rate taxpayer and could be financed at the cost of reducing, or abolishing, support for higher-rate taxpayers (Tetlow, 2015).

Johnson's (2012) critique is different. He argues that encouraging people to put their money into a pension pot that they cannot access until after retirement constrains their choices – they might want to use their savings to buy a second or bigger house, or pay for their grandchildren's higher education before they retire. Moreover, the younger generation are losing faith in pensions. Traditional pensions will soon be 'finished' (Johnson, 2015). The younger generation want freedom about how to save (and some tax incentives to do so) but in flexible savings pots.

This line of argument has clearly been influential with some in the Conservative government. Mr Osborne consulted on the whole future of tax relief (HM Treasury, 2015c). However, at the time of the 2016 Budget, he decided not to do anything more. He did introduce a different way of subsidising a more flexible form of saving – a 'Lifetime ISA'. This is a 'tax-efficient' (non-taxed) savings account that can be opened by anyone aged 18–40 after April 2017. Savers can put £4,000 a year into such an account *and* receive a government bonus of up to £1,000 a year for doing so! The total sum can then be invested and the asset growth will be free of capital gains tax. Money can be taken out to buy a first home but not otherwise until the age of 60. This kind of subsidy is capped, unlike the tax relief described earlier, but is only available to those who can put aside this kind of money at a time when there are many competing financial demands. It clearly favours those with wealthy grandparents!

Freedom to spend your pension pot?

As a quid pro quo for the big pension saving tax advantages described earlier, governments put limits on how private pension pots were to be used. Since the whole point was to prevent pensioners becoming a burden on the state, they were prevented from simply cashing in their tax-subsidised pensions on retirement. If not, it was argued, the state would pay twice: once to subsidise the pension; and then to keep the individual out of poverty when they spent their pension. When people reached the age when they could access their pensions (age 55), they had to use it, mainly, to buy an annuity – a promise by an insurance company to give an annual income. However, in his 2014 Budget, the Chancellor abandoned this logic. Those with private pensions would be able to cash them in. The reasoning was:

- People can make an informed choice to spend or not. The government can make advice available.
- The state would, after 2016, be providing a pension above the means test limit. So, people who drew out their private pension savings would fall back on that but still not qualify for any means-tested state addition. As we have seen, the latter is not true in many cases for those reaching pension age.

There are, in fact, two kinds of problem with this logic: 'bounded rationality' – the problem is too complicated for most people to understand; and 'bounded will power' – most people do know what to do but they do not do it. In the case of a sudden opportunity to spend a lot of money, people rush their decision, only to regret it at leisure. They may draw down too fast, underestimating their life expectancy, or they may do it too slowly – 'I do not want to be a burden on my family', 'I should not be spending my children's inheritance'. An annuity discourages excessive self-insurance for risk-averse people.

Older people in this situation must also take account of the tax implications of what they do. The sums withdrawn in one year will count as income to be taxed. The rate will be high on high withdrawals. The Exchequer may benefit from misjudgements about this, the pensioner will not. Chancellor Osborne also proposed to remove the tax rules that deterred people from selling their annuities to gain a cash sum. His successor scrapped that idea in October 2016; the market was too small and consumers are at too great a risk of exploitation, he argued.

Handing on your unused pension

In a related move, the remnants of many private pension pots can, since 2015, be handed on to children or a spouse tax free. On the one hand, the argument runs, people should be free to do what they want with the sum they have saved. On the other hand, the size of this pot has been subsidised by other taxpayers. The post-2015 rules are as follows:

- If a person dies before age 75, the pension pot can be inherited tax free by a nominated person. (It used to be taxed at 55% of the capital sum on the grounds that the taxpayer had contributed to its value.)
- If the pensioner is 75 or over, a lump sum inherited will be taxed at 45%. An inherited annuity attracts income tax in the normal way.

This change is likely to encourage more people to leave final salary scheme pensions and opt to take drawdown pensions. (An agreed sum is withdrawn by the pensioner each year.) Individuals may get this calculation wrong, as we have seen, and hence run out of their annuity. It is a risk that they must assess (see 'Take on a private pension you inherit' at: www.gov.uk/tax-onpension-death-benefits).

Some other pension models: international perspectives

A non-contributory state pension plus private pension consumption smoothing

This model is becoming more widespread. Varied and less certain labour market involvement and a breakdown in the traditional family and the 'male breadwinner model' are driving the spread of non-contributory pension schemes. Countries with such schemes include Australia, New Zealand, Canada, the Netherlands and Chile. In the Netherlands, this pension is set at 70% of the, after tax, national minimum wage. It is financed out of an earmarked element of income tax but is not levied on those aged over 65. The Australian scheme discussed earlier means tests the basic state pension for higher earners. It is combined with *compulsory* membership of a private or occupational scheme.

The Chile non-contributory pension was introduced after an attempt to rely solely on compulsory membership of a private pension scheme failed. This did not prevent poverty in old age. Now the poorest 60% of the population receive a basic pension funded out of taxation – a 'Solidarity Pension'. Formal and informal sector workers, men and women, and the self-employed all are eligible. It is gradually withdrawn as other contributory pension income rises. Schemes compete in a bidding system to attract and hold new workers. The Chilean scheme is under review. For a simple summary of the history and debate, see Barr and Diamond (2016).

New Zealand has a basic tax-funded pension based on residence conditions with automatic enrolment in individual savings accounts. An individual can opt out. It is the model nearest to the UK's evolving scheme, though the basic pension is tax-funded.

A national pension scheme, additional required saving and a guaranteed minimum pension

Sweden is the classic example of this model (for an assessment, see Barr, 2013). A guaranteed minimum pension within the scheme is based on years of residence, so this may have to be supplemented with public assistance, especially in the case of older immigrants or those with a poor employment record. The size of the pension for each age group is linked to its life expectancy. It falls as life expectancy rises – a 'notional defined contribution'. That could squeeze levels of adequacy unless the age of retirement rises in line with life expectancy.

Individuals have to invest part of their contribution in funded schemes of their choice: 16% of their pensionable income goes into the state 'pay-as-you-go' scheme; and 2.5% more has to be invested in a personal funded pension scheme. The number of alternative schemes listed was at one point over 800. That proved complicated and costly. Most people opted for the state reserve default option. Despite these problems, the pension system has proved resilient.

Germany also has a 'pay-as-you-go' national scheme funded by contributions that are shared between the employer and employee. Together, they amount to 19.6% of earnings. The pension age is rising to 66 in 2023 and 67 in 2029. Individuals *can* supplement such contributions by paying into an occupational scheme tax free up to a set limit. As a 'third pillar' they can pay into a private pension and attract a fixed tax credit, which is higher if they have children. Thus, the scale of tax-advantaged contributions has a ceiling.

This was a clever political compromise. It combined features that appealed to the Right – private contributions and choice – and for the Left, it had a citizenship 'pay-as-you-go' element.

Varied generosity

Some overall sense of the cost and generosity of pensions internationally can be seen from *Tables 5.2* and *5.3*.

Table 5.2 compares the levels of compulsory contributions that workers have to make towards their pensions in different countries. Most comprise social security contributions paid into government pension schemes. However, there are also compulsory – mandated – payments made to private pension schemes. Most countries require combined employer and employee contributions at about

20% of workers' earnings – some significantly more. Other countries pay for their basic pensions out of general taxation.

Table 5.2: International variations in pension contributions: social insurance and mandatory public and private contributions for the average worker, 2014 (percentage of earned income)

Country	Employee	Employer	Total
Chile	11.2[a]	1.15[a]	12.3
France	6.8 + 3.0[a]	8.45 + 3.0[a]	21.25
Germany	9.5	9.5	18.9
Italy	9.19	23.81	33.0
Netherlands	4.9 + 16.0[a]		20.9
Sweden	7.0	11.4 + 4.5[a]	22.9
Spain	4.7	23.6	28.3
UK	9.05	11.9	20.96
USA	6.2	6.2	12.4

Note: [a] Mandatory private schemes.

Source: OECD (2015b).

These varied contribution levels give rise, along with the age of the population and retirement ages, to varied replacement rates. *Table 5.3* reproduces figures from the OECD, which models what pensioners should get if they have full contribution records – the best-case scenario. The figures are after tax – showing take-home pay during working life *and* pensions after tax.

The average paid worker in the UK can expect a state pension of below 40% of their previous net income, even if they have a full contribution record. This is well below that in other European countries, as well as below that in the US. A higher-paid worker can expect a state pension of only just over a quarter of previous net pay. That is the natural outcome of a flat-rate poverty-line state pension.

Table 5.3: International variations in net replacement rates: state and mandatory private schemes (pensions as a percentage of pre-retirement earnings after tax for those on 0.5 x average, average and 1.5 x average earnings)

Country	0.5	1.0	1.5
Chile	48.7	37.7	45.9
France	66.9	67.7	62.0
Germany	53.4	50.0	49.0
Italy	82.2	79.7	81.6
Netherlands	101.3	95.7	94.1
Sweden	63.9	63.6	78.2
Spain	89.1	89.5	89.3
UK	69.4	38.3	27.3
USA	54.3	44.8	38.9

Source: OECD (2015b).

Overview

In short, the UK is in the midst of a fundamental change in the way it funds pensions:

- The aim is to provide a flat-rate state pension set at a level sufficient to avoid means testing. That will not be fully achieved for many years.
- On top of this platform will be a pattern of occupational pensions into which individuals are automatically enrolled but from which they can opt out. This new strategy still has to be completed.

The tax treatment of pensions is also undergoing major change and is open to serious challenge. Nevertheless, pensioners have done well compared to benefits paid to those of working age. Pensioners have been promised rising real benefits, at least until 2020 (and continue to receive other non-means-tested payments such as Winter Fuel Payment), while working-age families face a cap in benefit spending.

Questions for discussion

1. Why are there difficulties in leaving people to look after their own pension arrangements unaided?
2. Why did the Turner Commission conclude that the UK pension system needed a fresh start?

3. Evaluate the strengths and weaknesses of the UK's current pension strategy, including the tax treatment of pensions.
4. Evaluate the merits of other international pension models.

Further reading

Barr and Diamond (2008) is the best comparative account of pension economic theory and pension reform. A simplified policy version is **Barr and Diamond (2010)** and a later version is due.

The **Pension Commission's (2004, 2005)** two reports are indispensable to any real understanding of the UK pension story and the case that underpins the latest strategy. Accessible up-to-date commentaries on pension policy, especially recent private sector pensions, can be found on the Pensions Policy Institute web site.

For a different perspective on the political economy of retirement, see **Macnicol (1998, 2015)**.

The best collection of essays on pension policy internationally (including developing nations) is to be found in **Clark, Munnell and Orszag (2006)**.

six

Cash benefits: during working age

Summary

Many people experience interrupted earnings during their 'normal' working lifetime. The state provides a range of benefits for those in that situation. It has also begun to enhance the incomes of those on low pay with in-work benefits that are withdrawn as individuals' incomes rise. In recent years, although pensions have been protected from austerity measures, except the age at which they are drawn, working-age benefits have been 'capped' and not increased in line with prices, let alone earnings. Sanctions have been imposed on those deemed not to be genuinely seeking work. Pressures to get people off benefit and back to work have been increased in most welfare systems in recent years.

Some state benefits are funded out of social insurance contributions and are only available if given contribution requirements are met and if beneficiaries meet certain conditions – they are certified as sick or have been made unemployed or have sought work but not been able to find it. Other benefits are financed from general taxation. These are often, but not always, means-tested.

- The UK government is phasing in a major reform designed to reduce the range of means-tested working-age benefits and the rate at which they are withdrawn. The devolution of some social security powers to the Scottish Parliament has begun.

- Minimum wage legislation can be seen as a complementary way of combating in-work poverty. It has its limits.
- Some advocate an entirely different approach – the state should give every citizen an adequate income whether they work or not. Others argue that this is impractical and unjust.

Some history

There are several routes by which the state became involved in giving benefits to those of working age. One may be thought of as the social insurance route. It involved creating a distinct set of payments to ex-workers excluded from paid work temporarily or more permanently. Such payments were funded from contributions paid by both employers and workers.

The initial involvement of the state in setting up such schemes came about because of legal claims that workers could make against their employers for *accidents* suffered at work. Workers lost their livelihood and blamed the employer. This led to complex legal disputes and labour unrest. The earliest solution to this set of financial and political risks came in Bismarck's Prussia. There, the government required employers' organisations to take out accident cover – a solution similar to that which we apply today when the government requires individuals to take out third-party car insurance. It was a model that spread to other continental systems.

The UK, first in 1887 and more fully in 1906, adopted a different model. Employers were held responsible for accidents at work and hence had a duty to compensate employees for their loss of earning capacity due to accident or industrial disease. That could only be avoided if it could be shown that the accident arose as a result of serious misconduct by the employee. These claims could be settled by the employer offering a lump sum to the employee – often, in retrospect, far too small a payment. This all led to interminable legal wrangles and poor labour relations. It was devastatingly criticised by Beveridge (Beveridge Report, 1942, paras 77–105). As a result, payments to those so injured became part of the UK's broader social insurance scheme in 1946. (For an account of the varied international pathways towards accident and sickness insurance, see Kangas, 2010.)

Long-term inability to work for physical or mental reasons put individuals into quite a different category. In the UK, individuals could end up in the institutionalised care of the Poor Law. In Germany, invalidity cash pensions came to be linked to some judgement about how far individuals were capable of work (Stone, 1984). That pattern became widespread.

After the Second World War in the UK, obligations were laid on employers to employ a quota of disabled people (under the Disabled Persons (Employment)

Act 1944). This was never enforced and has since been repealed. However, most other European countries do still have some disability quota system, sometimes with financial penalties if the quota is not met. There are now laws to discourage discrimination in the employment of workers in many countries.

Much later, in the 1970s in the UK, a range of benefits were introduced, funded out of taxation, not social insurance contributions, to assist people caring for those with a disability. The additional costs of meeting the mobility and other needs of such a family can also be met, in part, from state benefits. Social policy analysts, such as Peter Townsend and Alan Walker in the UK, played a major role in making the case for such provisions in the 1970s and later (Walker, 2010).

There is a remaining policy tension between seeing disability benefits as a kind of default option if you fail some required work test or seeing such benefits as a right – enabling all citizens to participate as fully as possible in the normal activities of a modern society (Walker and Townsend, 1980; Bolderson and Mabbett, 2001). European Union (EU) laws have played an important part in shaping anti-discrimination policy. Under the Lisbon Treaty and EU Directive 2000/78, discrimination at work based on disability, age or sexual orientation was made illegal. The consequences of leaving the EU have yet to be seen.

For quite distinct economic reasons, discussed later, the private insurance market does not provide cover against the risk of unemployment, except very temporarily and in exceptional circumstances. Voluntary societies and labour unions tried to fill this gap in the 19th century. They could be financially devastated by widespread unemployment in a depression. Hence, a number of continental countries' governments began to subsidise such schemes at the end of the 19th century. This tradition has continued. The UK was the first to introduce a *compulsory National Insurance* scheme for such purposes in 1911. Those with a contribution record had a right to a cash benefit if they were unemployed through no fault of their own. Other countries have followed. Some governments have seen their function as cushioning the fall in income – relating the benefit to previous earnings. In other countries, the support has been low and at a flat rate. As we shall see, the UK began with a flat-rate system, moved to introduce income-related benefits and then moved back to a flat-rate system. (For a short comparative history of unemployment benefit schemes, see Sjoberg et al, 2010.)

Many Continental European schemes evolved relatively generous unemployment benefits over long periods for those with contributory rights. This was sustainable in periods of high employment but became increasingly difficult to sustain as full employment began to falter. From the 1990s, the Netherlands and Germany, followed by others, began to reduce the length of support and made benefits conditional on individuals taking active measures to return to work. (For an account of how these approaches differ across Europe, see Hemerijck, 2013, ch 6.)

There is a quite distinct history of attempts by the state to supplement the wages of those in work because of their inadequacy. It begins with local magistrates, who administered the Poor Law in England (Daunton, 1995; King, 2000). They were charged with minimising the possibility of unrest and of sustaining community harmony. They found a variety of ways to assist those in hardship, whether in or out of work. At times of major hardship, such as the Napoleonic Wars, such intervention grew. The Victorian New Poor Law was meant to stamp out in-work relief but, reduced in scale, it continued and differed regionally. Local parishes struggled to cope with the growing problem of poverty.

With the Second World War came full employment and strong trade unions to bargain for adequate wages for most workers. However, employers could not be expected to pay higher wages to those with children, though their needs were greater. Feminists and campaigners like Eleanor Rathbone pressed this case but other pressures came into play after the Second World War (Macnicol, 1980). If the state was to administer adequate family benefits in the event of sickness and unemployment, they might be higher than the breadwinner had been earning in a low-paid job. If income was linked to family size, in both cases, that could be avoided. This argument, too, carried weight in government.

Whatever the politically deciding factor, family allowances *were* introduced immediately after the war, financed out of general taxation. However, throughout the 1950s and early 1960s, they were allowed to decline in real terms and, even more, in relation to pay. In 1975, family allowances were replaced by Child Benefit and awarded to all children, including the first.

Finally, post-war optimism that full employment would ensure a reasonable living wage for everyone dissipated. The UK government followed other countries (eg Australia in 1907) in passing minimum wage legislation in 1998. It then began supplementing low wages through tax credits.

As Hills (2015) has demonstrated, life is a chancy business. Only a half of those in the top fifth of the income distribution in 1991 stayed mostly in that relatively favourable position for the whole period up to 2008. For the next fifth down the income ranking, only a third remained in the same or a better labour market position. So, even the relatively well-off are at considerable income risk during their working lives. That is the reason this range of benefits is so important.

Some economic theory

Insurance markets do work fairly well for some purposes. It is possible to insure against the chance of being burgled, a house burning down or your car being damaged:

• Most people are risk-averse to some extent. They want to be protected from the consequences of a sudden fall in income, or large necessary expenditure that would adversely affect their accustomed lifestyle. They will be prepared to buy insurance cover so long as the value of the added security to them outweighs the cost of the premiums they have to pay.

- Some people are particularly risk-averse: they choose not to lose anything if their car or their house is damaged. So, they pay high premiums to get that cover. Others are prepared to take some risks and pay lower premiums. For the state to determine how much fire insurance everyone should take out would be inefficient. The risk-averse individual would feel underinsured; the optimist would feel over-insured.
- However, failure to insure oneself at all may bring costs to others. Failure to insure yourself as a driver against the possibility of injuring others may mean that they cannot recover damages if they are badly injured. Hence, the state requires 'third-party cover' – regulation not provision. It does not mean that the private market cannot work. Citizens may be required to use it in a regulated way.

However, there are limits to markets in the field of unemployment insurance and long-term sickness, where the market does not work at all (Barr, 2012a):

- Nowhere in the world does the private sector provide insurance cover against unemployment. Brief cover for those with mortgages is an exception. Full cover would be too risky for any private insurer because:
  - Risks of one person being unemployed are linked to others' risks. A slump would bankrupt an insurer.
  - Some individuals, such as the low-skilled, have a high risk of long-term unemployment – their premiums would be high and their capacity to pay would be low.
  - Individuals have considerable influence over whether they get a job. Knowing they would get such a benefit could encourage them not to take a job (moral hazard). Judging whether this was the case and applying sanctions would be expensive and difficult for a private company.
- No private employer will give sick pay for an unlimited period because:
  - The cost over a long period would make employers wary of employing bad risks.
  - The individual might delay returning to work – moral hazard. That would be difficult to police without complex and expensive checks that a private firm would rather avoid.

It is partly for these fundamental economic reasons that the state has come to provide benefits for unemployed, sick and disabled people.

Active labour market policy

However, economists have come to believe that lax rules governing social benefits have enabled people to stay on benefit too long. Prior to the big recession of 2008, economists argued that it was this that helped explain the persistence of long-term unemployment (Layard et al, 1991). The work ethic was being gradually eroded (Lindbeck, 1995). Certainly, where benefits were based on household income, there was an incentive for second earners, notably, married women, to work less (Blundell, 2000).

These ideas and evidence have underpinned attempts to change the rules governing in-work benefits over the past two decades in many countries. These have not only been punitive – sticks – but have also involved carrots – retraining, advice, personal support and better childcare for single parents. This mix is often given the title 'active labour market policies' and is to be found in many countries, each with a different emphasis (Bonoli, 2013). Its origins are not just economic, but political.

Paying for security

Working-age benefits are funded in two main ways: through National Insurance Contributions and through general taxation.

National Insurance Contributions

These can be thought of as a special kind of tax, not, as the name implies, some voluntary contribution. The state *requires* you and your employer to contribute to a National Insurance Fund if your pay is higher than a 'primary threshold' – £112 a week in 2015/16. Your employer is required to take a 'contribution' from your pay packet and the worker is required to make one herself. The required sum (in 2015/16) was 12% of earnings between the primary threshold and an 'upper earnings limit' – £815 a week. An individual also pays 2% of her earnings above this earnings limit. A 1% addition was introduced in 2003 to help pay for the improvements made to the National Health Service (NHS) in the Blair years. This was increased to 2% in 2011 to help the Coalition government reduce the deficit. (From 1948, a small part of National Insurance Contributions had been used to finance the NHS – a hangover from the days of the pre-Second World War National Health Insurance scheme [see Chapter Seven].) If an individual is self-employed, she must pay a flat-rate (Class 2) contribution. It is possible to pay a voluntary contribution to enhance your pension or to make it possible to qualify for a benefit where your contribution record is inadequate.

This 'tax' therefore has an odd schedule, as we saw in Chapter Four. It is nil at low incomes, then applied at a constant proportion but *falls* when incomes rise above a given level. The reason for this oddity is that these 'contributions' mostly go to finance a set of benefits that also have an upper limit. It is deemed 'unfair' for those on higher incomes to pay more to fund benefits from which they will not gain.

What makes these contributions not a normal tax, but a 'specific contribution', is that the number and scale of contributions determine whether you have enough to receive any benefit at all and, within some band, how much benefit you will receive. 'Need' is not a relevant criterion. You may have inherited a fortune but can still draw a state pension. You may be starving with no contribution record and have no right to a state pension or other contributory benefits. In this case, you must apply for means-tested help funded out of general taxation. How far this distinction makes sense is something discussed later.

An individual's contribution records can be of two kinds: 'cash' and 'credited'. The first are those described already. However, in the past few decades, they have been supplemented by National Insurance 'credits'. Under the Beveridge model, married women were mostly deemed to be dependent on their husbands, whose married man's contribution included them. However, married women could choose whether to pay National Insurance Contributions. If they did, they received benefits on their own contribution record. This was not changed until the 1970s. Women were often working and caring but gaining no contributory rights on that account. Subsequently, carers and those with childcare responsibilities were assumed to have made contributions (assigned contributions) by virtue of these responsibilities. The same applied to the unemployed on Jobs Seekers Allowance (JSA), those on statutory sick pay and those with limited capacity to work.

National Insurance benefits

There have therefore been two kinds of benefit: those where right to benefit depends on whether you have paid contributions, or been credited them, and the rest. For example:

- Contributory benefits
    - Contribution-based JSA.
    - Contributory Employment and Support Allowance (ESA).
    - Bereavement Benefits.
    - Retirement Pensions.
    - Widow's Benefit.
    - Incapacity Benefit (IB).
    - Maternity Benefit.
- Non-contributory means-tested benefits
    - Income Support.
    - Income-based JSA.

- Income-related ESA.
- Pension Credit
- Housing Benefit.
- Council Tax Credit.
- Universal Credit.
- Non-contributory non-means-tested benefits
  - Attendance Allowance.
  - Carer's Allowance.
  - Child Benefit.
  - Disability Living Allowance.
  - Personal Independence Payment.

As will be discussed later, the Conservative government is in the process of phasing out and amalgamating several of the means-tested benefits into the 'Universal Credit'.

The contributory benefits just listed are paid for, in any one year, largely out of the flow of money coming from National Insurance Contributions. This flow of income and outgoings are recorded in a separate National Insurance Fund and its accounts are published each year. In fact, there are two such funds: one for England, Scotland and Wales; and the other for Northern Ireland. A summary of the former is reproduced as *Table 6.1*.

Devolution in part

The Smith Commission (2014) on further devolution recommended that the Scottish Parliament be given new powers over some taxes and welfare payments (although Universal Credit remains reserved to the UK Parliament):

- Attendance Allowance
- Carers Allowance
- Disability Living Allowance
- Personal Independence Payment
- Industrial Injuries Disablement Benefit
- Severe Disablement Allowance
- Cold Weather Payment
- Funeral Payment
- Sure Start Maternity Grant
- Winter Fuel Payments
- Discretionary Housing Payment

Under Part III of the Scotland Act 2016, various welfare benefits can be amended as they apply in Scotland. Under the new powers, the Scottish Parliament can

Table 6.1: National Insurance Fund (UK minus Northern Ireland), 2015

Receipts	£000
National Insurance Contributions	84,112,562
Treasury grant	4,600,000
Compensation for statutory pay recoveries	2,465,000
Income from investment account	89,433
Redundancy receipts	36,392
State scheme premiums	32,622
Other receipts	23,292
Total	**91,359,851**
Payments	
Benefit payments	91,759,523
Administrative costs	806,386
Transfers to Northern Ireland National Insurance Fund	609,000
Redundancy payments	276,708
Other payments	167,370
Personal pensions	1,448
Total	**93,620,435**
Balances	
Opening balance	23,195,862
Receipts less payments	(2,260,584)
Closing balance	20,935,278

Source: Department for Work and Pensions (2015).

authorise discretionary payments that top up a range of benefits. Most significant of these are the payments made to mitigate the effects of the 'bedroom tax' (see Chapter Eleven). In addition, it will be able to create new benefits. These will all have to be paid for from Scottish funds. However, the UK government will not be able to offset any of these changes made in Scotland by reducing what that family would receive from other benefits.

The demise of the contributory principle

Over time, the number and scale of non-contributory income-tested benefits has grown (see **Table 6.2**). Between the late 1950s and the late 1970s, contributory benefit rights that had built up since the Second World War constituted about two thirds of all benefit expenditure. A further fifth were tax-funded but not means-tested – Family Allowance (Child Benefit) was followed by disability benefits and a Carers' Allowance. In the late 1950s, only 10% of all benefits depended on a means test.

Table 6.2: UK benefit expenditure 1948/49–2015/16 (contributory and non-contributory benefit spending) (%)

	1948/ 49	1958/ 59	1968/ 69	1978/ 79	1988/ 89	1998/ 99	2007/ 08	2015/ 16
Contributory	53	67	69	66	55	47	45	46
Non contributory, non-income-tested	34	23	17	17	17	20	21	14
Means-tested:								
Cash benefits	13	10	14	17	28	33	25	21
Tax credits	–	–	–	–	–	–	9	19
Total income-tested	*13*	*10*	*14*	*17*	*28*	*33*	*34*	*40*
All benefit spending	100	100	100	100	100	100	100	100

Source: Updated from Glennerster, Bradshaw, Lister and Lundberg (2009).

Then three things happened:

- Income tax came to affect most earners.
- Contributory benefits were allowed to decline as a percentage of earnings. They increased in line with prices, not earnings. As a result, means-tested additions grew in importance.
- Governments began to supplement low wages with means-tested cash benefit (as explained at the beginning of this chapter). As a result, income-tested benefits have come to form two fifths of all benefit spending.

Thus, to a larger degree than ever before, these two welfare systems – tax-funded benefits for the poor and tax relief for the rich – began to overlap with the social security system. Both were giving out benefits on a means-tested basis with different tax rates. One was the marginal rate at which income tax was levied; the other was the rate at which benefits were withdrawn. This led economists to question whether we needed these two parallel and interacting systems (Dilnot et al, 1984) – 'No', these authors concluded. We can merge them into a single system of tax credits, at least for working families. Keep the contribution system for pensions but move to a tax-based benefit system for everything else. If the starting point for income taxation begins higher up the income range, then we can further separate these two systems. That is what successive governments have sought to do and has culminated in the present government's introduction of Universal Credit. In practice, though, things are not that simple.

Universal Credit

The aim of simplifying the complex range of working-age benefits gained support from both the Left and Right (Sainsbury and Stanley, 2007; Brien, 2009) and the Mirrlees Review (2011). An important objective was to reduce the cumulative impact of overlapping means-tested withdrawal rates to which social policy writers had first drawn attention four decades before (Piachaud, 1971; Bradshaw and Wakeman, 1972). This could have serious disincentive effects for returning to work. Since then, the range of means-tested tax credit benefits has increased, as has been explained.

In 2010, out-of-work benefits were withdrawn altogether beyond a small 'earnings disregard' when someone entered work. Working Tax Credit could be paid when parents were working 16 hours a week, or more for a couple, and Child Tax Credit came on top. Both were tapered off at 41 pence in every extra pound earned. On top of that, there was the basic income tax rate and National Insurance to pay, making the overall taper, or 'tax rate', 73%. Plus, there were the tapers for housing benefit and council tax. Over half-a-million couples were facing combined marginal 'tax' rates of over 80% and 100,000 were facing 'tax' rates of between 90% and 100%. The aim was to reduce these rates. There were other objectives outlined in the Coalition government's original White Paper (DWP, 2010), notably, ease of administration and reduced complexity for the recipient.

The new Universal Credit will eventually replace:

• Working Tax Credit;
• Child Tax Credit;
• housing benefit;
• income support;
• income-based JSA; and
• income-related ESA.

New rules mean that the taper is calculated on net, that is, after tax, income. This reduces the effect of tax deductions but is less favourable to those who pay less tax and means that the benefit of raising the tax threshold for income tax is not fully passed on.

A new work allowance is designed to increase work incentives – more earnings are ignored before the taxation taper begins. Households will be subject to interviews and requirements for job search like an unemployed person if they earn less than the full-time minimum wage. This is a major extension of 'conditionality'.

A key objective is to make returning to work more financially attractive. This is to be achieved, for the first partner to enter work and for single parents, by a combination of the work allowance and a new uniform taper of 63% (originally 65% but reduced in the 2016 Autumn Statement). However, households have a *single* work allowance. Thus, once this allowance is exhausted, the second earner faces the 63% taper immediately. They thus face a higher taper than under the old system. If they are paying National Insurance or income tax, they will have less incentive to enter the labour force than before. The best analysis of the complex ways in which Universal Credit will affect different kinds of household is to be found in ongoing work by the Resolution Foundation (Finch et al, 2014 [as well as subsequent reports]; see also Hills, 2015, ch 4; IFS, 2016; Miller and Bennett, 2016).

Universal Credit will reduce the number of households that had very weak financial incentives to work. Those facing a 70% 'tax' rate should fall from 2.1 million to 0.7 million. However, it will weaken the incentives for single parents to work and reduce the incentives for a second person in the household to work. There used to be a strong incentive to work at least 16 hours a week in order to receive an in-work benefit. Now, that has gone. The overall impact is difficult to judge.

Although the original intention was to be more generous than the old system, overall, this outcome has been abandoned, with reductions in the amount that recipients earn before they lose benefit. There is also the impact of the four-year freeze to benefit rates. Two million working families will lose £1,600 a year. Rather fewer will gain a similar amount. Single parents may be £1,000 a year worse off on average.

Nor is the simplification all it seems. Council Tax Benefit, or Council Tax Support as it is now called, is excluded. For those local authorities with the highest tapers, the overall taper facing households could be 83%. Free school meals and other 'passported' benefits are also excluded and their taper rates have to be added on too. Support for housing costs is included in the scheme but local admissible rents vary a lot from one area to another. Where these are high, the common 65% taper will last over a wider band of income. Childcare costs of up to 85% will be offset – a system that will work alongside 'tax-free' childcare (see Chapter Nine).

Moreover, the need to combine and automate two streams of information – income data from people's employers and from the social security system about people's situations – has led to a longer delay between people's changing situations and receipt of benefit. A single sum of money arriving once a month, not at intervals through the month, may seem administratively simple but can cause difficulty for families living on the edge. As Spicker (2013) has commented, all benefit systems have their problems but 'Universal Credit has the lot'.

Sick pay

The UK has also evolved a compromise position on sick pay. Employers now continue to pay for short-term sickness absence but the state reimburses employers a fixed sum for up to 28 weeks – Statutory Sick Pay. A much tougher set of rules applies for long-term sickness and disability. A new benefit called the 'Employment and Support Allowance' was introduced in 2008, replacing three previous benefits. To qualify requires a 'work capacity assessment'. This can be repeated at regular intervals depending on the initial assessment. Some limited work with some benefit may be prescribed. Despite major changes over the past decade, the number of people on such benefits has changed little, at about a quarter-of-a-million people. The government announced a major overhaul to the system – yet again – in January 2016.

A cap on welfare

The Coalition government set a limit on the amount that any one household can receive in benefits and the Conservative government elected in 2015 increased the severity of this cap. The annual total of benefits that a family can receive, excluding Working Tax Credit, was set at £20,000 in 2016 (£23,000 in London). Those mostly affected were those with several children paying high rents. On average, those affected would lose £2,000 a year. Yet, this would contribute only about 1% of the total savings to the benefit bill that the government said it would make by 2020. Nor was there evidence that the measure, up to 2016, had produced a significant return to work by the families affected. Commentaries on this policy as it evolves can be found on the web sites of the Institute for Fiscal Studies, the Resolution Foundation and the Child Poverty Action Group.

A freeze in the level of most of the benefits discussed in this chapter during the period 2015 to 2020 would also reduce their real value if prices rose in that period, as it seemed they would at the time of writing in late 2016. Finally, the rules governing the new Universal Credit, as set out in 2015, will reduce the value of benefits too. They outweigh the reduced taper referred to earlier. The government planned in 2015 to reduce the value of 'in-work allowances' under the scheme. This is the sum that families can earn before their benefits are reduced as their incomes rise. Before the 2016 Autumn Statement, a single parent would eventually, on average, have been £2,480 worse off as a result of the reduced work allowance and a couple with children would have been £1,220 worse off. The reduced taper would only put back £220. The effect would be less on an after-housing-costs basis (Resolution Foundation figures). Working-age benefits have thus been squeezed and will be further up to 2020 on government plans as they stand at the end of 2016.

Current dilemmas and international experience

How generous should benefits be?

There have historically been two opposing schools of thought:

- Unemployment benefit should be high enough to make employees and their unions relaxed about temporary unemployment that may follow new technology. It would encourage new technology and productivity. This had much support in the 1960s. The Labour government's *National plan* (Cmnd 2764, 1965, p 203) said: 'To complete the structure of benefits needed to promote mobility of labour the Government have concluded that the earliest possible introduction of earnings-related unemployment benefit is essential to provide better protection during periods between jobs'.
- Out-of-work benefits should be set as low as possible to encourage people to return to work, along with other penalties. This view gained widespread international acceptance in the 1990s, as we suggested earlier (OECD, 1994).

This second view, at a time of growing long-term unemployment, persuaded many governments to impose shorter limits on the receipt of benefit and to impose stricter conditions on receiving them. The United States, Germany and Denmark led the way. The UK abolished its wage-related out-of-work benefits, cut the flat-rate benefits as a proportion of average earnings and imposed stricter conditions for the receipt of benefit. However, at the same time, it increased in-work benefits 'to make work pay'. In common with many other Organisation for Economic Co-operation and Development (OECD) countries, the UK has also put a lot of effort and money into supporting childcare and into active support for those seeking work. These are all hallmarks of the social investment perspective in social policy (Hemmerijck, 2017). The US put more emphasis on simply cutting welfare payments. Gregg and Corlett (2015) argue that UK policy has been more successful than US policy but its social investment spending levels lag behind many other countries.

The way in which different welfare systems respond to interrupted earnings varies widely. The UK stands out as relatively generous in terms of cash benefits for families, somewhere in the middle for incapacity benefits and least generous for unemployment benefits in the belief that this will incentivise work.

Table 6.3: Social expenditure on working-age benefits internationally, 2013 (percentage of gross domestic product)

	Unemployment	Incapacity	Family cash benefits
Australia	0.5	2.6	1.9
France	1.6	1.7	1.6
Germany	1.2	2.0	1.2
Italy	0.8	1.8	0.7
Netherlands	1.5	3.3	0.7
Spain	3.5	2.6	0.5
Sweden	0.4	4.3	1.5
UK	0.4	2.5	2.6
USA	0.8	1.4	0.1

Source: OECD (2016a).

A negative income tax?

The idea of a negative income tax has a long pedigree (Friedman, 1962; Lampman, 1971). The original idea was that all poor households would receive a benefit through the tax system that was reduced at a tax rate no different from the positive tax rate that most ordinary taxpayers faced– 20% in the UK currently. While that sounds attractive, it poses the key problem that faces all attempts to withdraw benefits gradually as income rises. If you keep the original benefits reasonably high to avoid poverty, and you phase them out very slowly, the cost is high. If you want to keep the cost low, you can only do so by starting with a very low benefit. This dilemma has haunted all attempts to introduce universal negative income tax ideas.

Give everyone a citizen's income?

One way to apparently avoid these problems and the complications in our current benefit system is to give everyone enough to live on simply by virtue of being a human being, or at least a citizen of a particular country. We go to great lengths not to let people starve and provide benefits of various kinds when they are unable to work. Why not just give *everyone* enough to live on whether they work or not and leave it at that? Paid work would then be a choice.

Some people have advocated this route ever since Beveridge received evidence to that effect from Lady Williams during the Second World War. It attracts those on the Right who think that the state could then get out of social service and health provision altogether once everyone had 'enough' money to live on. It attracts those on the Left interested in social justice, who see it as a way to avoid humiliating means testing.

At first sight, it is very appealing. Switzerland recently conducted a referendum on whether to introduce such a scheme. It was defeated. The central problems are those of affordability, efficiency and fairness. At the moment, we give benefits to those unable to enter paid work and we set those benefit levels above what the government see as a minimum poverty line. That would be the logical level for any income that took all citizens above the state means-test level and out of poverty. If it does not do this, a citizen's income loses its main appeal.

However, to find the money necessary would require taxing away 40% of the average person's earnings, or 50% if housing benefit were included (Hirsch, 2015). We would, as we have seen, still need a health service, schools and some defence force, to cope with climate change, and to build some roads. The resulting tax levels would tax away nearly two thirds of most people's earned incomes. It is difficult to see why many people would want to work if they already had a really adequate citizen's wage – university professors writing books about the finance of welfare perhaps, but who else? The fewer people who took the work option, the higher the tax levels needed to pay for the citizen's income and the lower the level of produced goods and services there would be to go around.

That is why, when the crunch comes, advocates retreat into suggesting a much lower citizen's income – US$1,600 a month in the case of Switzerland. This gets us the worst of both worlds – no less means testing, benefits needing to be topped up for those without work *and* an added complication to the benefit structure. The apparent simplicity is also a delusion. Different individuals have strikingly different financial needs and face different costs. That is partly why the social security system is so complicated.

Finally, there is the question of fairness. Would people consider it 'fair' to reward those who chose a life of leisure – 'those who surf all day off Malibu' to quote Rawls (1988) – by taxing those who choose to work at a rate of say 66%? There are good reasons why current working-age benefits are conditional on actively seeking work or being incapable of work for good reasons. This way of doing things has responded to some deep-seated notions of fairness that would have to change. (For contrasting views on the fairness of the whole idea, see Van Parijs, 1991; Piachaud, 2016.) The experiment underway in Finland may answer some of these questions.

Professor Tony Atkinson was a sympathetic, partial advocate of the idea for many years. His recent book, *Inequality: What can be done?*, Atkinson (2015, ch 8) presents a balanced account. Atkinson argues that for those of working age, there would have to be some requirement that individuals work or 'participate in society' in some helpful way in order to receive the income. (The original advocate of a citizen's income, Lady Rees-Williams, in the 1940s, was also clear that there would have to be a work test before such an income could be paid.)

Those who do 'participate' would then have the right to a 'participation income', as Atkinson calls it. Just how to define and impose such a condition raises serious issues. In the case of a carer, for example, or a retired person, it could be done. However, for the bulk of the population, what would constitute 'work' and/or participation and for how many hours? It would mean applying the kind of rules that we now apply to benefit recipients to the whole working-age population.

For those *not* of working age, the incentive dilemma is less central. We are already moving towards something nearer to a citizen's *pension*, as we saw in Chapter Five. An adequate child benefit would be a 'child' citizen's income, so would be a 'carer's wage'. Thus, where it is a viable policy, it turns out that we are doing it already, or could do, by increasing child benefit or introducing a decent universal pension or a carer's benefit.

Stagnant incomes and growing inequality – our future?

As we have seen, the original purpose of working-age benefits was to compensate those who had their earnings interrupted, or, in the worst case, ceased, because of personal or economic factors beyond their control. In more recent decades, governments have also come to worry about persistent low earnings, the failure of middle and lower earnings to rise much over time, and persistent long-term unemployment.

Two authors recently compiled compelling evidence of growing inequality of incomes within advanced economies, and recent stagnation in real incomes in many places. Their precise explanations for this differ (Piketty, 2014; Atkinson, 2015). Both see large structural changes in the international economy, technology and large corporations' rewards structures as contributing. Others see big demographic change as the driver – the huge growth in the manual working labour force of the Third World (Goodhart et al, 2015). This may be going into reverse as birth rates in these countries fall and flows of people from the countryside decline. 'Picketty is history' as Goodhart puts it.

Whatever the explanation, social welfare systems have had to change their emphasis as a result. Governments of different stripes and in different countries have sought to subsidise wages through means-tested in-work benefits. They have introduced and/or increased minimum wage requirements. They have tried to force workers back to work with tougher penalties. None of this has addressed the central problem of low-wage jobs, declining industries and neglected communities, nor the 'productivity puzzle'. Why is productivity not rising faster? Failure in all these respects has produced a political backlash from those most affected in Britain, America and parts of Europe. The kind of responses we see has worrying parallels with the 1930s.

Benefit policy, on its own, cannot be the answer to these fundamental issues, but it will have to be part of the response. The Scottish government has recently established new 'inclusive growth' policy frameworks aimed at helping to promote greater social justice in employment – 'a fairer Scotland' (Deeming and Smyth, 2017). It is a response that the Westminster government would be well advised to develop.

Overview

In short, support for those unable to earn or whose capacity to earn has been interrupted is a key function for any humane society to perform. The market cannot do this for reasons that are well understood in economics. However, in recent years, policy has shifted from income support to limiting the periods that people spend out of the labour market. This has been done by reducing the levels of benefit and putting sanctions on those who are out of the labour market for long periods and who are thought not to be genuinely seeking work. Although this approach is to be found in many countries, the balance between penalties, advice and practical help varies. The UK is short on practical help:

- While there has been some steady progress in rationalising UK pension provision in the past decade, cash benefits for the working-age population have become less generous, more stigmatic and no less complex.
- The gradual introduction of Universal Credit and caps to welfare payments present major difficulties for poorer families.
- Radical alternatives canvassed include introducing a citizen's income. However, there are major unsolved incentive problems with this route.

Questions for discussion

1. Why is the market unable to provide effective insurance cover for unemployment and long-term sickness? How have governments responded?
2. What benefits, if any, should be financed on a contributory basis? Does a citizen's income provide a workable alternative? What conditions should be applied to the receipt of what benefits?
3. How should benefit policy be combined with other social and economic policy to address widening inequality and low wage growth?
4. How does the UK system of in-work benefits compare with that in some other countries of your choice?

Further reading

The idea of a unified contributory scheme was best made by Beveridge. This classic exposition is worth reading **(Beveridge Report, 1942, paras 20–29, 71–105, 129–32)**.

The history of conditionality in the UK and the case for more of it was expounded in the **Gregg Report (2008)**.

A concise assessment of the move to the Universal Credit is to be found in the Resolution Foundation review **(Finch et al, 2014)**.

An assessment of the idea of a citizen's income is made by **Hirsch (2015)** and **Atkinson (2015, ch 8)**. The Citizen's Income Trust provides regular advocacy of the idea (see: www.citizensincome.org).

The growth of self-employment poses major problems for both taxation and rights to benefits. They are well discussed by Tomlinson and Corlett (2017).

seven

Health services

Summary

The UK remains unusual in providing free access to a wide range of medical services for all its residents funded predominantly from central government taxation.

- There are well-understood market failures in the private *funding* of medical care but there is more dispute about the virtues of a mixed economy of private and public *provision*.
- The costs of medical care are rising in all advanced economies, not least because of their ageing populations. Before 2000, the UK had one of the lowest levels of health-care spending among advanced economies. By 2010, it had moved near to the average for other European nations but is now likely to fall back again.
- Health funds are 'rationed' and allocated to local areas according to their varied health 'needs'. This is done somewhat differently in each part of the UK.
- Growing demands on the health budget will not be matched by the public spending envisaged by the present government up to 2021. Funding methods used in other countries are examined to see if they provide a way forward.

Some history

The National Health Service (NHS) is relatively recent and its financing is unusual by international standards (Gorsky and Sheard, 2006). In 1911, the UK introduced a limited scheme of national health insurance but only for lower-paid occupations and only to cover primary care. A 'panel' of local general practitioners (GPs) could join the scheme. Their consultation costs and the pharmaceuticals they prescribed were funded from national insurance contributions set nationally. Some additional cover might be added if the local scheme could afford it. The cover included the worker, not his family, unless the local funds ran to it. Compulsory national contributions were collected by 'approved societies', which ranged from trade unions and charities to commercial insurers, who operated the scheme as part of their business but on a 'not-for-profit' basis. These firms derived benefit from the additional insurance cover that they could sell to their users.

GPs who were part of the scheme were paid a flat sum for each individual they agreed to serve. The insurance contribution did not vary by the occupation of the member. Those societies catering for manual workers in unhealthy occupations – miners were the classic case – could barely break even, while others could offer wider cover. The upper income limit for participation in the scheme was gradually extended but only covered just over 40% of the population by 1938.

In the first half of the 20th century, local authorities began to build hospitals and take over old Poor Law hospitals as their public health powers were extended. By the beginning of the Second World War, the state was involved in funding just under half of medical care provision in the UK (see **Table 7.1**).

Table 7.1: The cost of the pre-war health services in Britain met from different sources (%)

Local authority-funded hospital services	12
Poor Law hospital services	6
Public mental and mental deficiency hospitals	10
Other local authority services	10
National health insurance-funded doctors' fees and pharmaceuticals	9
Voluntary hospitals' fees and charity income	12
Households' fees to doctors and dentists	27
Self-medication	14
Total health spending (3% of GDP)	100

Note: GDP = gross domestic product.

Source: Webster (1988).

The National Health Service Act 1946, which came into operation in July 1948, laid a duty on the minister of health:

> to promote the establishment in England and Wales of a comprehensive health service designed to secure improvement in the physical and mental health of the people of England and Wales and the prevention, diagnosis and treatment of illness, and for that purpose to provide or secure the effective provision of services in accordance with the following provisions of this Act. (Section 1)

A similar Act covered Scotland, though with a slightly different organisational structure.

The Act covered all kinds of medical care – from dentists, opticians and GPs, to hospital and specialist care. Voluntary and local hospitals were taken over by the central state and made the responsibility of the minister – he was to 'provide' them (Section 3), though with managerial and day-to-day governance in the hands of centrally appointed bodies. In a slightly modified form, this included the teaching hospitals – the professional pinnacle of the system. However, and disastrously, as described later in this chapter, closely related and overlapping services for the elderly, the long-term sick and those with disabilities remained with local authorities. They were funded in quite a different way out of local taxation, with government grants operating under separate budgets and political masters.

The NHS was not to be funded out of employer and employee contributions (except to a very small degree), as in many Continental systems, but out of general taxation. Its free availability to all residents and its tax funding were, at that time, unique internationally. This completely free service soon gave way to some measure of charging – for spectacles and dentures (in 1951) and prescriptions (in 1952).

Nevertheless, despite regular Treasury pressure at times of economic crisis – to introduce charges for hospital accommodation or payments to attend a GP surgery – the bulk of health care has remained free at the point of use and funded out of general taxation ever since. Central government had little day-to-day control over the early post-war NHS, though. Local medical politics were important in battling for budget shares. That began to change as the NHS featured in successive general election campaigns.

From 1989, Mrs Thatcher's Conservative government began to separate the funding of local health services from their provision. Central funds were allocated to local 'purchasing' or 'commissioning' bodies. Their budgets were decided on the basis of the relative size of their populations, weighted to take account of their relative health needs. It was up to these bodies to decide which health-care 'providers' to fund. Hospitals came to be paid for the work they completed – 'payment by results'.

Hospitals and other public bodies providing health care became 'trusts' – corporate bodies with boards of directors and non-executive directors like any private company. However, they were still subject to considerable central direction, targets and 'performance management'. Under Labour Secretary of State Alan Milburn, a new attempt was made to give hospitals in England greater financial independence, for example, to borrow funds for capital projects. Chancellor Gordon Brown resisted this, but hospitals were encouraged to apply for foundation trust status. This was only granted if the hospital was deemed to be financially successful and capable of running its own financial affairs effectively (under the Health and Social Care Act 2003). All hospitals were intended to reach foundation status under the Health and Social Care Act 2012. A body was set up to help them reach such status – the NHS Trust Development Authority. This process is still unfinished.

Each foundation trust is run by a council of governors – some elected, others appointed. The elected members are chosen by distinct constituencies – staff, residents and local residents or users. In this respect, these bodies resemble the way in which local school governing bodies used to be chosen. The appointed members are chosen by local councils, medical schools and voluntary organisations that have to deal with the local hospital. Each hospital has its own constitution. Some are more locally representative and nearer to 'mutual' self-governing institutions than others.

Over 30 years, the NHS has moved from being something nearer to a nationalised industry run by the Department of Health to a mixed economy. This approach came to be called a 'quasi-market' (Le Grand and Bartlett, 1993; Glennerster and Le Grand, 1995; see also Chapter Two). Private providers could take part in the competition for public funds under both Conservative and New Labour administrations. The approach was entrenched by the Health and Social Care Act 2012 in England. However, the NHS is so political that, in practice, political direction is never far away. In 2015, the secretary of state thought it appropriate to direct hospitals how to manage their parking arrangements!

After the devolution of health powers to Scotland and Wales at the turn of the century, these administrations retreated from this quasi-market model. Thus, in what follows, the reader will have to bear in mind that there is no longer, if there ever was, a *National* Health Service in the UK.

Some economic theory

There is little dispute about the existence of public goods and externalities in health care (see Chapter Two). Action to limit the spread of infectious disease, to provide instant response to a possible Ebola case, to ensure free vaccination and to make sure that public health advice is available is not contested even by neoliberals. It is when the issue of regular health provision is being debated that differences emerge. Even here, it is important to distinguish arguments about the funding of normal health care from its provision. The economic case for state intervention in the *funding* of health care is powerful and widely accepted internationally. However, the economic case for wholesale public *provision* is contested.

Market failure in funding

As we saw in Chapter Two, there are limits to the effectiveness of free-market health insurance as a way to finance health care:

- If a person has a high probability of needing care over a long period, is chronically sick, disabled, mentally ill or aged, private insurance will not cover that person or only provide cover at a prohibitive price.
- The more sophisticated and detailed the knowledge insurance companies have about us, the more they will be able to exclude potential bad risks – 'cream skim'.
- People know more about their own bodies, social habits and medical experience than insurance companies ('adverse selection'). Insurance companies take account of this by being reluctant to offer insurance to those they think may be high risks or charging a higher price.
- There is a separation between the individual who is claiming medical insurance, her doctor and the eventual provider. At each stage, 'moral hazard' (see Chapter Two) problems arise. The doctor has little reason not to refer if in doubt or the hospital not to treat. The patient has less reason to be careful about her health. To counter this, insurance companies take measures to restrict or ration health care.
- Companies go to great lengths to ask for justifying information. This makes the whole process of seeking care and paying for it time consuming ('transaction costs'). Administration and billing costs for the insurance companies and care providers are very high. A quarter of all health expenditure in the US goes on administration, twice that of Scotland (Himmelstein et al, 2014). (For a fuller, more technical, account of these issues, see Zweifel, 2011; Barr, 2012a, ch 10.)

As a consequence, the state has become heavily involved in funding health care in all advanced economies. Even in the US, where private insurance is widespread, the government has stepped in to fund health services for the old and the poor (Medicare and Medicaid). More recently, the federal government has required people at work to take out health cover and subsidises them to do so. It has also required health insurers not to exclude individuals because they have a 'pre-existing condition'. All this will change under President Trump but much will be difficult to undo entirely precisely because of the market failures that gave rise to such legislation.

A provider market

Here, the arguments for and against 'markets' become less clear-cut:

- Individuals have poor information about their medical situation – they are not able to readily diagnose their own condition or legally prescribe their own medication, except for minor ailments. Full information is expensive to gather, though less so now with the Internet, but needs expert judgement. Power and information in the market are unequally spread between the service provider and patient. Nevertheless, the UK system is fortunate in having a well-established pattern of GPs, who act as gatekeepers and professional guides through the secondary care system. This, and the new grading system for hospital quality with much more information available to users, enables the patient to exercise a degree of informed choice.
- Profit-making institutions have an incentive to oversupply – persuading patients to accept unnecessary treatment. However, NHS commissioning authorities have a set budget and an incentive to minimise this tendency. They have independent advice on the clinical efficacy and cost effectiveness of different treatments prepared by the National Institute for Health and Care Excellence (NICE).
- There are barriers to entry and exit in the health market, especially one so much engrained with politics. Providing a new district general hospital or a new cancer treatment centre would entail a very large investment. It would also be a politically uncertain investment. A new government could come to power and reverse the plan. Where private providers have been successful, they have tended to be small-scale and specialist organisations that supplement what the NHS already does. Exit is also difficult. Traditional markets work because firms that are doing badly go bankrupt and close. This seems to work to some extent in the US. In the UK, the closure of a local hospital is a politically painful rarity. It is not like the closure of some high street bank branch or the local Tesco.
- The NHS is also currently not very attractive to most profit-making providers. The current budget is nearly static in real terms and prices paid per treatment are low. The NHS culture is suspicious of private profit-making providers. The wider political climate is unfriendly and commercial failure could be damaging to a company's reputation. There have been some high-profile private failures in recent years. Private providers gained 7.6% of the NHS budget in the audited accounts for 2015/16 (Department of Health, 2016). This was a

share up from 4.4% in 2009/10 (Glennerster, 2015b). This is still far from a privatised health service.

- There is some evidence that the introduction of greater patient choice prompted hospitals to improve their management and sharpen their organisational practice. Competition may have even improved patients' chances of survival (Cooper et al, 2011; Gaynor et al, 2013; Bloom et al, 2015). Such findings have been challenged and robustly defended (Bloom et al, 2011; Pollock et al 2011). Competition also seems to have prompted shorter waiting times (Cooper et al, 2012).
- An alternative view is that this whole debate has been driven by pure irrationality and neoliberal ideology, not evidence (Paton, 2014).

The sum total of economic evidence so far can hardly be said to be conclusive, but it does not reject economists' view that competition can spur efficiency in health delivery. The most powerful case, however, is probably political. In a world where consumer choice is pervasive, telling people that they have no choice when it comes to public services may destroy taxpayer support. That is especially true when those services are central to voters' interests – access to hospital, an old people's home for their parents or their children's school. Most people do not accept the idea that local officials should tell them what to do or where to send their children.

Yet, it has to be said that despite the divergent approaches taken since devolution in the different parts of the UK, a Nuffield Foundation study concluded that there had been very few major differences in health *outcome trends* in the four parts of the UK (Bevan et al, 2014). Less dogma and more evidence would help.

The cost of health care

For much of its post-war history, the UK has been a relatively low health spender. In the period from 1948 to 2000, the UK was near the bottom of the health spending league, both as a share of gross domestic product (GDP) and in absolute terms per head of population. There are some good and less good reasons for this (Propper, 2001):

- One good reason dates back long before the NHS was founded. It is called the 'gatekeeper' principle. Except in cases of emergency, someone in the UK will only be seen by a specialist hospital doctor if they have a referral letter from their GP. The GP undertakes a preliminary diagnosis and decides whether you need to be seen by a specialist; 90% of all contacts with the NHS get no further than the GP. That is despite the fact that primary care has regularly taken only 10% of the NHS budget, much too low given its importance.

- A second reason is that GPs are paid on a 'capitation' basis. They are paid for each patient they have on their books, not for every time someone comes into the surgery. However, they are paid to monitor patients at risk of hospitalisation or deterioration – part of a new contract with GPs in 2004.
- Another *partially* good reason is that in most tax-funded health-care systems, ministries of finance are better able to control spending than in systems where numerous agencies reimburse medical fees charged by diverse providers.

However, a ministry of finance can be too powerful. Worried that the NHS was not performing as he promised it would, Tony Blair asked an outsider, Adair Turner, to look at the NHS's inability to improve waiting times and treatment volumes significantly. His response was, essentially, 'if you give the NHS much less money than other European systems you can't expect anything else'.

Knowing that the Treasury would oppose any major change, Blair decided to announce, in a television interview, that his government would increase the NHS budget until it matched average European spending – what average and how it was calculated was left unclear. An outraged Chancellor was left to find ways to pay for it. This was not the most rational or politic way to do things, but it worked. In 2000, the UK devoted a little over 6% of its GDP to health care (see *Table 7.2*). By the time the Labour government left office in 2010, total health spending had reached 8.6%, the increase being the result of a rise in public spending. The total of over-the-counter drug spending, private health insurance and fee payments amounted to only 1.5% within that total and had not changed significantly.

More recently, two things have changed. GDP fell and then increased slowly. Funding for the NHS, however, was increased, nothing like enough to meet the demands of an ageing population, as will be seen, but it grew. Then, the way private spending was calculated in international statistics changed. It either grew or was deemed to be larger following a new form of estimation. In 2015, the Organisation for Economic Co-operation and Development (OECD) put it at 2% of GDP. Thus, public *and* private spending on health care reached nearly 10%. That will change again by 2020 for other reasons. The NHS budget is to rise very slowly from 2017 but GDP should grow faster.

A group of leading health think tanks (Nuffield Trust et al, 2015) suggest that the share of GDP taken by the NHS will fall to 6.7% by 2021. Another way to view the UK's comparative position is to look at what is actually spent per head of population, taking account of general price levels internationally (see *Table 7.3*). The UK spends considerably less than half what the US does on each member of its population and about a fifth less than Germany. We spend more than Spain and Italy – other tax-funded systems – but less than Sweden, which is also largely tax-funded. As we shall see, some other European countries have increased the scale of their charging or 'co-payments' in recent years. The UK has not done so. Indeed, in Scotland and Wales, these charges have been reduced or abolished.

Table 7.2: *Health-care spending as a share of GDP internationally (percentage of GDP)*

	Total				Public (2015)	Private (2015)
	2000	2010	2013	2015		
Australia	7.6	8.5	8.8	9.3	6.2	3.1
Canada	7.9	9.9	10.4	10.4	7.2	3.0
France	9.5	10.8	10.9	11.0	8.6	2.4
Germany	9.8	11.0	11.0	11.0	9.3	1.7
Italy	7.6	8.9	8.8	9.1	6.8	2.2
Netherlands	7.0	10.4	11.1	10.8	8.7	2.1
Spain	6.8	9.0	8.8	9.0	6.3	2.7
Sweden	7.4	8.5	11.0	11.1	9.3	1.8
UK	**6.3**	**8.6**	**8.5**	**9.8**	**7.7**	**2.0**
USA	12.5	16.9	16.4	16.9	8.4	8.6

Note: The public–private split does not always quite add to the total because of rounding.

Source: OECD (2016c).

Table 7.3: *Health-care spending in dollars per head per annum, 2015 (US dollar purchasing power parity)*

	$
Australia	4,420
Canada	4,608
France	4,407
Germany	5,267
Italy	3,227
Netherlands	5,343
Spain	3,153
Sweden	5,228
UK	4,003
USA	9,451

Source: OECD (2016b).

Ageing and cost

Spending on health care is strikingly different at different stages of life. ***Table 7.4*** shows the additional demands that older people make on their GPs, in their use of medicines, and in the demands that they make on hospital and community services. ***Table 7.4*** shows the results of research undertaken by the Advisory Committee on Resource Allocation (ACRA). If we take spending on male 5–14 year olds as our base equal to 1, then a boy aged 15 to 44 will cost nearly the same. However, a man aged 85 or more will cost just over seven times as much. One aged between 75 and 84 will cost six times as much, calculated from the workload put on a GP. A male child under 4 will consume pills or medicine with a baseline of 1. A man aged 75 or more will cost 21 times as much! The baseline for hospital and community services consumed by a child under 4 is taken as 1. The cost for over 85s is 8.5, and for 75 to 84 year olds, nearly five. This is the multiplier scale that we are talking about when we refer to the effects of 'an ageing population'. It may seem offensive to talk about old people in this way but it is reality, whatever other great things old people do – like writing textbooks.

Table 7.4: Relative costs by age, England, 2011/12

		0–4	5–14	15–44	45–64	65–74	75–84	85+
Primary care (GPs)	Men	3.97	1.00	1.02	2.16	4.23	6.01	7.22
	Women	3.64	1.04	2.20	3.37	4.95	6.95	8.85
Pharmaceuticals	Men	1.0	1.1	2.0	7.0	15.9	21.1	
	Women	0.8	1.0	3.0	7.9	14.5	18.5	
Hospital and community services[a]	Men and women	1.0	1.2	1.3	6.3	5.0	4.8	8.5

Note: [a] An age constant that interacts with other factors.

Source: Department of Health (2011).

The figures in ***Table 7.4*** date back to 2011/12, when this author was working on them, but since then, an additional factor has been at work. Social services departments have had their funds cut significantly in relation to the age of the populations they serve (for more on this, see Chapter Eight). This has increased the demand that older people have been putting on the NHS. Moreover, the NHS is also grossly deficient in a number of other respects (Chief Medical Officer, 2014). Mental health absorbs 13% of the NHS budget but accounts for a quarter of the burden of disease.

In the 2015 Spending Review and Autumn Statement (HM Treasury, 2015b), the Chancellor increased the planned spending for the NHS in England to £133 billion – a *real* increase of £4.5 billion. Half of that was to come in 2016/17.

Over the whole period from 2009/10 to 2020/21, the average real increase per annum in NHS spending will be 0.9%. According to the Institute for Fiscal Studies (IFS), a rise of 1.2% a year is necessary merely to maintain spending per head weighted by age (Emmerson et al, 2014, p 45, Table 2.6). NHS England's original figures on demographic cost pressures were nearer 1%, not that different (NHS England, 2013, 2014). Then, the government committed itself to a health service open for business seven days a week.

The conclusion must be that the Spending Review of 2015 gave the NHS less than was needed to accommodate the costs of an ageing population, let alone the other deficiencies and demands it faces. Growing deficits by foundation trust hospitals and other strains, like growing waiting times, are the outcome. The revised spending plans announced in November 2016 (see Chapter Four) produced no material change in the planned NHS budget.

Moreover, through 2016 the Office for Budget Responsibility (OBR) conducted a major review of the pressures that were causing an increase in health care costs not just in the UK but internationally (OBR, 2016). They then increased their assessment of the likely future costs of health care over and above the impact of demographic change. The OBR's central projection 'on present policies' suggested a likely rise in NHS spending from 6.9% of GDP in 2021/22 to 9% in 2036/37 and 12.6% in 2066/67. However, its *upper bound* estimate was *15%* for 2066/67! That, it should be noted, made no allowance for the cost of meeting the deficiencies in care discussed elsewhere in this chapter.

Who pays?

The NHS is usually described as being financed out of general taxation. That is not strictly accurate – about 80% of NHS spending is financed in this way; 18% comes from transfers from the National Insurance Fund – contributions from employees and employers.

Beveridge recommended this small link with social insurance funding and it has remained ever since. After Blair's raid on Gordon Brown's Budget, described earlier, the Chancellor raised National Insurance Contributions from April 2003, adding 1% to all employees' contributions above the National Insurance starting point. That increased the rate from 10% to 11%. He raised the employers' contributions by 1% too (from 11.8% to 12.8%). This applied to the whole of the earnings range above the lower earnings limit. The promise was that this revenue would be spent on the NHS. Patient charges contribute just over 1% of the NHS budget. Prescription charges have now been abolished in Wales (in 2007), Northern Ireland (in 2010) and Scotland (in 2011).

How National Health Service funds are allocated

The government makes no distinction between these forms of revenue and allocates the NHS budget to various specialist purposes like public health and to local health agencies as if it were a single pot of money. Each devolved parliament or assembly decides what to spend on health and where to allocate it. Different formulas are used in each country to decide how much each local area should get. There are also different allocation processes for each service – GPs and primary care, dentists and opticians, hospitals and community services, and public health (see *Figure 7.1*). In England, in 2016, Parliament voted for a budget of £120 billion for the Department of Health for the coming financial year; £5 billion was siphoned off to fund the regulators that inspect and oversee hospital trusts and other services. Under new arrangements, another £3.4 billion goes to fund public health services that are now run by local authorities. The Department of Health then passes over to the arm's-length body NHS England nearly £107 billion. Of that, nearly £80 billion goes to the clinical commissioning groups who actually decide which hospitals and community services will be paid to provide services locally. By 2017/18, these bodies will commission and pay all primary care providers – mostly GPs. A small part of this budget is also taken to fund the Better Care Fund, which is designed to support services in the community often run by local authorities that assist patients to leave hospital sooner.

Funding general practitioners

After 1948, each GP was paid a set sum for each person who signed on at their surgeries as an NHS patient. In addition, GPs were paid for the staff they employed to run their practices and any additional staff – nurses, for example, or for extra functions. In 2003, a major revision of the GP contract was negotiated, and revised in 2006. Under it, each practice received a single payment. The partners could use their income to fund any mix of doctors, nurses and extra staff they wished. However, they had to deliver a much more rigorously defined set of services. They could employ outside staff to cover during the night and at weekends. Payments come under three headings:

- A *global sum* to cover defined essential services. The practice receives a sum for each patient registered at the practice weighted to take into account the demand that different kinds of patient are likely to make. This formula derives from a study of GP patient visits undertaken with a national sample of GPs over several years. From this, it is possible to measure the 'workload' generated according to the age and sex of the patient, their long-standing illness rates, the practice's average mortality rates, and a count of patients in residential care.

Figure 7.1: Flows of NHS money in England 2016/17

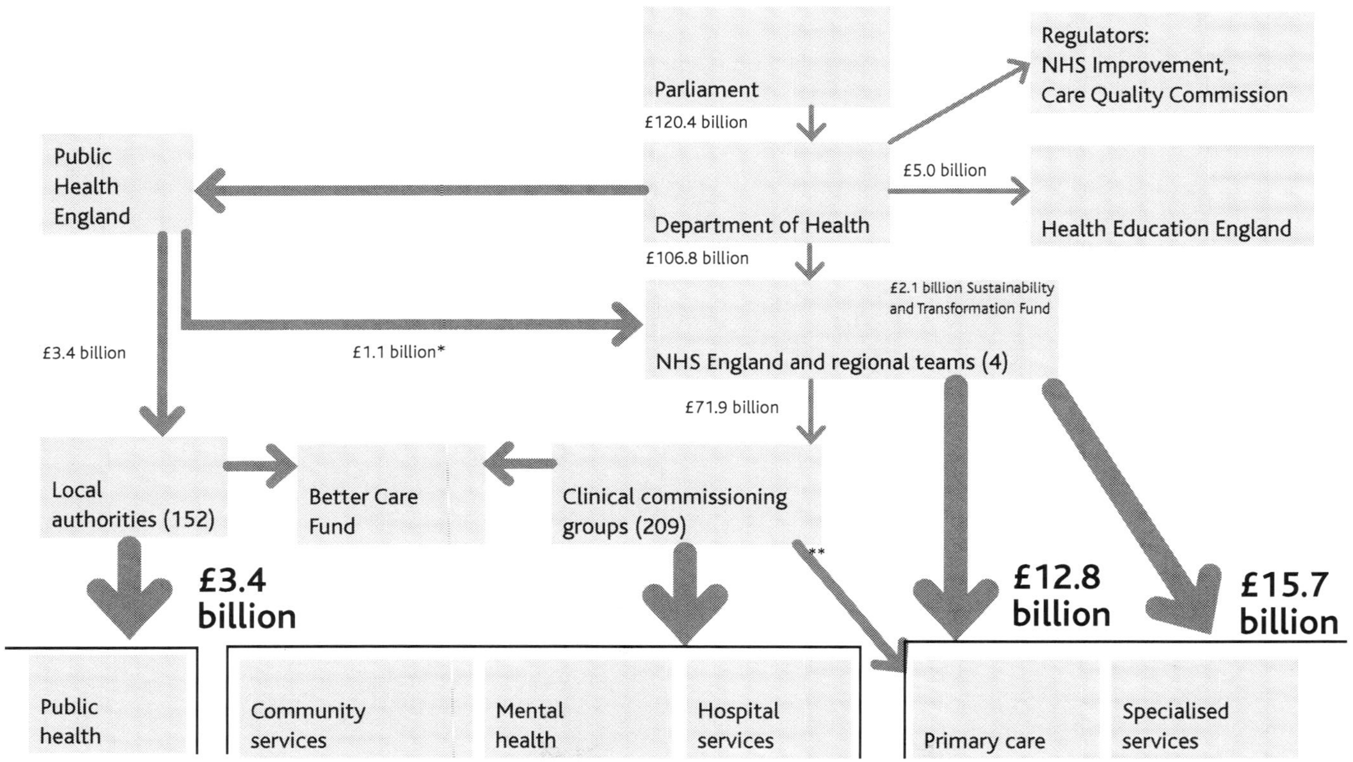

Parliament
£120.4 billion

Department of Health
£106.8 billion

NHS England and regional teams (4)

Regulators:
NHS Improvement,
Care Quality Commission

£5.0 billion

Health Education England

£2.1 billion Sustainability and Transformation Fund

Public Health England

£3.4 billion

£1.1 billion*

Local authorities (152)

Better Care Fund

Clinical commissioning groups (209)

£71.9 billion

£15.7 billion

£12.8 billion

£3.4 billion

Specialised services

Primary care

Hospital services

Mental health

Community services

Public health

**

* Screening/immunisation programmes run by NHS England.
** In 2016/17 a total of 114 CCGs will have assumed full responsibility for the commissioning of primary medical care services under delegated commissioning arrangements. Nearly all CCGs are expected to have taken on delegated arrangements by 2017/18.
Source: Adapted from King's Fund website (accessed 11 April 2016)

- Payments are made for additional services that most GPs provide, like child vaccinations, screening and check-ups for those at particular risk.
- Payments for enhanced services that fewer GPs provide.

Although expensive, this was a major improvement on the contract that preceded it. However, it did not require out-of-hours visits by GPs at weekends or at night. It encouraged the more widespread use of 'out-of-hours' services provided by a separate agency. Negotiations on a new contract are underway that will involve some kind of 24-hour access to primary care, including weekends.

Dentists and opticians

Central funds are devolved to local areas on an age-weighted basis. Local private providers receive sums from these local commissioning bodies that enable them to provide free diagnosis and care for certain categories of people who can access NHS treatment. These include those under 18 or 19 if in full-time education, pregnant women and those with recent births, those on various social security benefits, and, for opticians, those aged 60 or more. There is also partial help for low earners. Otherwise, individuals pay for these services.

Public health

At the centre is a devolved agency, Public Health England, which monitors public health nationally and puts in place measures to prevent and combat epidemics and potential risks like Ebola. More generally, its statutory duty is to 'protect and improve the nation's health and well-being and reduce health inequalities'.

Local public health functions in England were devolved to local authorities under the Health and Social Care Act 2012. A new formula was devised to allocate central funds to local authorities to cover this function. Areas with the greatest challenge of reducing health inequalities will get more money. However, there are also incentives to reward and punish local authorities that do or do not make progress in reducing health inequality. Since there is uncertainty about how far local authorities can reduce many of these indicators, this is going to be a fraught process.

Scotland has moved in the opposite direction. The Public Health (Scotland) Act 2008 transferred the major public health powers from local authorities to the Scottish regional health boards financed by the Scottish Government. There is a national public health and intelligence function provided by NHS National Services Scotland that supports the local health boards and social care authorities. However, the key bodies that deliver local services are the regional health boards. They work with local authorities in health and social care partnerships. Separate and run at the Scotland-wide level are special health boards responsible for the ambulance services, education and training, secure facilities, and other specialist functions. Public Health Wales was created in 2009 as part of their devolved powers with a Wales-wide set of functions.

Hospitals and community health – rationing by formulae

Before 1976, money was allocated to individual hospitals and other facilities on the basis of last year's budget plus a little extra – 'incremental budgeting'. If a new facility was built, more money was given to staff it (the 'Revenue Consequences of Capital Schemes'). The main beneficiaries of this 'historical approach' were the richer areas of the country where charitable support had founded voluntary hospitals before the NHS was formed – mainly in the big cities and, above all, in London.

Research in the 1970s revealed just how badly matched resources were to health needs (for a discussion of the analytical issues, see Holland, 2013, pp 160–71). By the end of the 1960s, this had become a political issue. Labour Secretary of State Richard Crossman set in train an attempt to allocate money more fairly. It was continued by his Conservative successor but was, everyone agreed, crude.

When Labour returned to power in 1974, new Secretary of State Barbara Castle and Health Minister David Owen agreed to set up an expert committee to produce an empirically robust formula that would carry the medical profession with it. That committee, the Resource Allocation Working Party (RAWP, as it came to be called), proposed a new approach to distributing health service resources. It has set the pattern for what has happened ever since (Department of Health and Social Security, 1976).

Allocations should be made, RAWP argued, on the basis of the size of each region's 'weighted' population. The weights took account of the population's age and relative ill health, measured by each region's standardised mortality ratio (SMR), that is, its death rate relative to the nation as a whole. The formula was applied first in England. Similar, though differently calculated formulae, were developed in each of the constituent parts of the UK. The original allocations were to the rather large regions of England. Various methods were then used to allocate funds to smaller areas.

When the Conservative government reorganised the NHS in England in the early 1990s, it needed to allocate funds down to much smaller entities – district health authorities. They were to purchase services from a variety of public, and, in theory, sometimes private, providers, as explained earlier. A major rethink of the formula was then undertaken. Instead of relying on SMRs as an indicator of need, economists at York University turned instead to measure the *demand* that different kinds of population put on services, independent of the effect that a more generous *supply* of services in any one area might have on demand.

The results showed how much more demand older people, pregnant mothers or those living in deprived areas, for example, put on local services. GPs only send patients to hospital if they suspect them to be in need and hospitals only treat if they agree. Thus, the *relative use* of local services, free from contamination by supply factors, *was* 'revealed need' – or so went the argument. There was, certainly, need that never got expressed – 'unmet need' – but that, it was felt, was too difficult to measure.

In the past, no account – apart from London weighting – had been taken of the differential costs that local hospitals faced. In areas where labour was scarce, staff wages tended to be higher. In the new calculations, this was taken into account. A 'market forces factor' was used to estimate the differential labour costs that faced a local provider. That affected the price such hospitals were allowed to charge for the work they did; hence, that had to be taken into account in setting the level of funds that they got from central government. This combined demand-and-supply approach underpinned the statistical formulae that allocated funds to district health authorities and then the local primary care trusts that succeeded them.

The body charged with advising the secretary of state in England on the precise formulae used was ACRA. The author was a member from 1997 to 2010 (for a history of the arguments that lay behind the changing formulae, see Glennerster et al, 2000, ch 4). The committee was made up of medical statisticians, social policy and public health experts, a representative of the British Medical Association (BMA), and local managers. It made recommendations on the formula, drawing on research it commissioned. Every year or two, the formulae was reassessed in the light of more research and external criticism. All the research was published, as well as the recommendations that went to ministers. Its work was commended by the Public Accounts Committee as an exemplar of openness and rigour.

If the old RAWP formula were still in operation, it would have given 24% more money per head of population to the 10% most socially deprived areas. The York formula of the 1990s gave them 27% more. The formula adopted after 2000 (the AREA formula) gave them nearly 40% more.

Labour ministers in the Blair/Brown government wanted more to be done to address inequality in health outcomes and to tackle the unresolved issue of 'unmet need'. In 2008, ACRA finally concluded that it was not possible to combine the goals of ensuring equal access to health care for those who presented themselves for treatment *and* unmet needs or unequal health outcomes. The latter two objectives needed a separate formula. It concluded that the main basis for such allocations should be inequalities in 'disability-free life expectancy'. Those areas with very poor healthy life expectancy should get more money on a sliding scale. Ministers were asked to use their own judgement to decide how much of the budget should be allocated for this purpose, with examples of the outcomes. They chose to allocate 15% of the hospital and community care budget on this basis in 2009/10 and 2010/11.

The Coalition government abolished the old primary care trusts and replaced them with clinical commissioning groups, whose populations were combinations of people registered with their local GPs, not an administrative area. This required more changes to the way in which the formula was calculated. ACRA now reported not directly to the secretary of state, but to the new NHS England – an 'arm's-length' agency.

The populations used in the calculations were those registered with GPs. Estimates of need were based on individual patient data weighted for age and additional need. These were based in large part on the previous recorded conditions of the registered patients. This approach was developed from work done by the Nuffield Trust. There is one formula for general and acute hospital services and separate ones for mental health and maternity services.

In their original recommendation, ACRA reverted to its old position – that it was impossible to measure 'unmet need' or cope with health inequality within this new methodology. NHS England pointed out that this would leave the least healthy in the most deprived areas with disproportionately fewer resources. ACRA was asked to think again.

After a lot of discussion and more work, an 'adjustment for unmet need' was retained but measured in a different way. It now rests on the SMR (under 75) for the areas covered by the new clinical commissioning groups – a reversion to RAWP for this particular element. It reflects a view taken on the whole area's health status. It is weighted so that small areas with the worst health carry five times the weight of those with the best health. This whole approach is under review. The central point is that the NHS still makes a major attempt to allocate resources according to *need* and *health inequality*.

Scottish and Welsh equivalents

The account outlined earlier relates to England. Other parts of the UK have similar allocation mechanisms based on attempts to measure relative health needs. The Scottish government allocates the largest part (70%) of its health budget to local health boards. This budget covers hospital and community health funding and GP prescribing.

The 'Arbuthnott' Review in Scotland decided on four indicators that research had shown were strongly related to health-care costs and used an unweighted average of those indicators (Scottish Government, 2000). This was a simpler measure than the English one. It did not seek to take into account as many indicators, but it did try to include potential unmet need rather than differential demand generated by different population types. The later English review built on some of this work.

In 2005, the NHS Scotland Resource Allocation Committee (NRAC) was set up to review the Arbuthnott formula and keep it under review. There are now three elements to the formula: age and sex differences; morbidity and life circumstances of those in each area; and unavoidable cost differences – including rurality and the remoteness of areas.

The comparable Welsh Review (National Assembly for Wales, Health and Social Services Committee, 2001) was chaired by Peter Townsend. It recommended using a range of epidemiological indicators, including self-reported illness by respondents to the Welsh Health Survey. This 'direct needs model' was felt to be preferable to one that relied primarily on differential demand for health services. Experience in using it was reviewed by the Welsh Assembly government in 2005. Here, too, health inequalities and what to do about them have been a concern. In short, each devolved administration and England has given more money to poorer, less healthy and older communities.

Paying providers

Once local commissioning agencies in England receive funds, they make contracts with local hospitals and other organisations to provide particular kinds of service of a particular scale. The more procedures they undertake, the more they receive up to a given level ('payment by results'). This is a problematic method in many ways. It rewards things done ('inputs'), not quality or outcomes. It also rewards individual treatments rather than collaborative integrated care. There are now underway a series experiments testing different kinds of contract that attempt to reward close and effective collaboration and better 'outcomes'. None of this is easy to do well without producing perverse effects. However, simply increasing the funds that existing providers gain with no relation to outcomes or quality is even worse.

Where now? Too little informed debate about alternatives

Little serious attention has been paid to the grave situation that the NHS is facing in the absence of a proper funding settlement (NAO, 2016). Health authorities in each region in England have been told to make savings totalling £22 billion by 2020. They have drawn up 'Sustainability and Transformation Plans' (STPs) to do this. Readers should inform themselves about these. The government claims that there is no funding problem – that they have given the NHS enough and that it can make efficiency gains to meet any shortfall as a result of these plans. We have seen that this is a highly dubious claim. The Labour Party simply says that more money should be found. Local NHS authorities are having to produce major reorganisations and closures to meet this inadequate budget limit.

However, the problem goes far beyond funding the NHS. As explained at the beginning of the chapter, the post-war funding structure separated the finance of health care from the closely interrelated social care services – looking after elderly people in their own homes or in residential care and rehabilitating and supporting those coming out of hospital. Unless these services are closely integrated, the NHS can spend large sums keeping people in hospital or having to accept people who need not be there. NHS England's plan for the last half of the present decade includes a series of 'vanguard' sites, where local services experiment with different ways of organising their services together with their local authority partners. Some of these experiments keep their budgets separate but agree working relationships. They may have joint commissioning budgets for some non-GP services, or they may aim for a fully integrated budget for a whole population and long-term joint contracts for particular groups of patients (King's Fund, 2016).

However, the separate funding of the two services and the cuts to local authority services have made any of these very difficult to undertake. A new way to jointly fund such services is crucial to any lasting and effective integration of services – at least in this author's view. It is a view that he has held since he first studied the supposed joint working of these two kinds of service at close quarters over 30 years ago (Glennerster, 1983). Many of the new arrangements studied by the King's Fund involve linking acute hospital and community health services and GPs. This is all potentially helpful but does not fully address the social care–health care divide. Some experiments do try to do that but are made very difficult by the funding split. The National Audit Office (2017) concluded that their overall contribution so far was modest.

One major contribution to a proper debate on these issues was made by a commission appointed by the King's Fund (2014), chaired by Kate Barker, a distinguished economist. It was rightly charged with considering the funding of both health *and* long-term care. The separate funding of these services – one national, one local, one means-tested, the other free – creates perverse incentives that can only be partially remedied by local organisational ingenuity. The Barker Commission recommended:

- Increasing the share of GDP devoted to state health *and* social care spending to between 11% and 12% by 2025. This compared to just over 9% when they reported, but by 2020, it could be nearer 8% on current plans.
- This funding should be combined into a single stream with a single local commissioner for these combined services, including the allocation of attendance allowance funds.
- There was no clear case for significantly increasing charges for treatment or attending a GP unless the intention was to reduce the demand for services – 'unnecessary visits' (see King's Fund, 2014, pp 25–30).
- Some adjustments might be made to the prescription charging regime – exemptions apply from 60 – below retirement age. Exemptions could be removed, the charge lowered and the cap on payments retained.

- More radically, the Commission discussed an income-related 'health and social care tax' (King's Fund, 2014, pp 31–3). It could be set by an independent Office of Health and Social Care after reviewing all the evidence on demographic and medical care technology trends. The Commission finally proposed:
  - An increase of 1% in National Insurance Contributions for those aged 40 and over, the age at which people may begin to think more about later life and when their family responsibilities are on the decline. People might be more prepared to accept such a contribution so long as it was explicitly linked to improvements in combined health and social care for the elderly.
  - At the moment, National Insurance Contributions cease at the state retirement age. Contributions should continue for individuals, not employers, after retirement but at a reduced rate – half the existing rate of 12%. It should be a flat percentage right up the income range.
  - Benefits to all elderly people regardless of income should go – free TV licences and winter fuel allowances were examples.
  - Wealth and inheritance should be more effectively taxed. The elderly have acquired significant increases in wealth, especially from rising house prices.

Objections can be levelled at some of these proposals but they do provide a basis for discussion. Above all, what is needed is a properly supported inquiry of the calibre of the Turner Commission to deeply consider how we fund health and social care in the next 20 years of massive demographic change. Cross-party agreement on this is crucial.

Funding health care: international perspectives

Despite being a 'protected' budget, the planned funding for health that we have described is incompatible with meeting the major existing deficiencies in the NHS and a more costly older age group. Most advanced economies face the same problems. However, most finance their health systems in a different way. What are these other funding models?

Social insurance-based funding

The essence of this model is that employers carry more of the cost. Both employers and employees contribute to a central fund during working lives, just as they do for pensions. This has the apparent advantage that the employer pays, not the ordinary voter. However, this is an illusion. Unless employers somehow absorb those costs in higher productivity, they will get passed on in higher prices or it may lead to employers hiring fewer staff.

Most health costs do not stem from people of working age. Costs arise, above all, from those who are long-term sick or retired. They are precisely the people not paying social insurance. As with the UK National Insurance scheme, there is usually a cap on contributions at a given income. This means that the funding is proportional up to this point and regressive beyond it. Such schemes also tend to have several layers – the basic all-encompassing scheme, a voluntary add-on one and a private opt-out one.

These problems have been played out in the recent history of various schemes. (For an overview, see European Observatory on Health Care Systems, 2002; to bring this up to date, see individual country descriptions at: www.euro.who.int.) Germany and France are good examples. Both spend more in total than the UK but put more of the cost directly on the employer. Both have moved towards something more akin to tax funding over recent years, for the reasons outlined earlier, and have separate tiers of funding.

The *German* scheme is worth looking at briefly as it is more costly and complex than the UK's. It is a good example of a purchaser–provider split with significant private provision. The Social Health Insurance (SHI) scheme only funds about 57% of all health expenditure. Membership is required for all people earning up to a ceiling. Just over 10% of German people opt out. This includes some civil servants who have separate cover and can top it up in private schemes. There are a range of other state insurance schemes that cover medical rehabilitation, industrial accidents and long-term care insurance. Such insurance does not cover all health costs. In the past decade, there has been a growing number of co-payments or charges to contain costs.

The contributions collected are then assigned to the sickness fund to which the individual belongs. Prior to the 1990s, only white-collar employees could choose which scheme they would be assigned to. After 1993, people had the right to choose their scheme. This led to a new risk-adjusted flow of money to ensure that a scheme did not become bankrupted by too many high-risk members joining. After 2009, everyone has to be a member of some health insurance scheme – the SHI or a private one. The sick funds then make arrangements with public or private providers to take care of their members.

The costs of approved hospital building have come to be shared between the federal government and the 'Lander' – provincial governments. The hospital-owners may be private or public but the need for a new hospital has to be agreed by the various government agencies. Anyone who finds UK health funding complex should read Buss and Blumel (2014) on the German model!

Patients pay – in part

It is common practice in both social insurance and some tax-funded health schemes for patients to make 'co-payments' towards the cost of their treatment on a sliding scale of income. In some social insurance systems, co-payments fund about a fifth of their health expenditure and a similar scale of co-funding is found in tax-based systems like Spain and Italy. England has prescription charges, as we have seen, but they only produce about 0.5% of NHS income in England. In the rest of the UK, they have been abolished.

UK families, of course, buy some health products at 'the chemist' and others have private health cover. Currently, about 15% of UK health care is paid for by 'out-of-pocket' expenditure – across-the-counter spending at pharmacists, private health insurance premiums or the direct payment of medical, dental and optical service fees and charges. This compares with about 20% in high-income countries in general (OECD, 2016b). Is there a case for more charging within the NHS? International research on the impact and consequences of co-funding is instructive.

Experiments in developing countries on the impact of charging for preventive health care and primary care show very steep declines in take-up and access for small increases in price (Kremer and Glennerster, 2011). Charging does not improve targeting; most of all, it tends to deter those in most need. The abolition of user fees in South Africa and Uganda produced a big increase in access (Gilson and McIntire, 2005). Evidence from richer countries shows less dramatic results but charging is still a deterrent to access. An old, but much analysed, experiment supported by the Rand Corporation in Puget Sound, Seattle, showed significant, if moderate, reductions in service use. Co-payments did not result in reduced overall health. However, the sickest and the poorest suffered most from higher charges (Newhouse, 1993; Rand Corporation, 2016) – a finding in line with evidence from the developing world. Work of a non-experimental kind has produced similar results. The international evidence was usefully reviewed by Schokkaert and Voorde (2011). Thus, there are real risks in the extensive use of co-payments, especially of damage to the least healthy and most vulnerable. That has to be the conclusion from this evidence.

Introducing charging across the board also brings administrative problems and costs. It has been relatively easy for social insurance systems that charge and then reimburse the user to simply increase those charges and reduce the repayment percentage. It merely involves a change to the computer billing instructions. In the UK, it would mean introducing a wholly new patient charging administration in each hospital and GP practice. The US devotes about a quarter of its health budget to administration and much of that concerns payments systems.

Finally, there is the politics. When prescription charges were introduced in the UK and then increased at each economic crisis from 1951 onwards, political objections were made to charging older people, the poor, the long-term sick, pregnant mothers, mentally ill people and the unemployed. Hence, nearly nine out of every 10 people do not pay such charges. None do outside England. The largest part of the NHS budget is devoted to precisely these groups. Trying to raise 2–3% more of GDP for health and long-term care, as the King's Fund, see later, argued is necessary, by raising charges from a minority of the population looks politically infeasible. It would involve very high charges indeed. It may be that it becomes necessary to charge some token amounts to convince those on the Right of politics to agree to more taxation, essentially the story of prescription charges, but that is a political game, not good economics.

Required private insurance

Another way to finance health care is to require citizens to insure themselves privately. The Netherlands and the US provide different routes. Each has tried to counter the market failures discussed earlier, though in different ways.

The Netherlands now has a tightly regulated market at work on both the funding and the providing side. It has the unusual advantage that it has a strong system of GPs, as in the UK, who act as gatekeepers to expensive secondary – hospital – care. It also has a separately funded system of long-term care insurance, with income-related contributions. This removes the most costly bad risks from the main scheme. We discuss that scheme more in Chapter Eight.

Since 2006, after two decades of planning, every citizen in the Netherlands must now take out a policy with a private insurer – unless they have religious or philosophical objections! Special arrangements cover these objectors; they do not escape payment. Children under 18 are exempt but they have to be in their parents' policy.

All insurers in the scheme have to offer a standard package. It is comprehensive in cover, though some elements have limits – the number of visits to a physiotherapist, for example. Most of the costs are met through a compulsory income-related levy on employers (7.75% of salary up to a ceiling). There is also a small additional premium paid by the insured to the insurer. The state pays a standard flat sum to those with lower incomes to offset this payment whatever the actual private insurance premium. People thus have some incentive to shop around for a low premium. People can add to the state's basic package with additional premiums.

The levy is paid into a national Health Insurance Fund and then paid on to the private insurers for each member on a risk-adjusted basis – those who have a poor health record or are older bring more central funds with them. This is designed to prevent cream skimming. (For a history of this long process of reform and its logic, see Van de Ven and Schut, 2008.) Providers recover the costs of care from the insurer but there are 'co-payments' charged to the user for all care other than for GPs, obstetrics and maternity services.

141

About two thirds of health costs in the Netherlands are paid out of compulsory contributions, 14% comes from the government and the rest from charges and additional voluntary insurance. In all, about 70% of the funding comes from 'taxation' in all but name. The Netherlands had the highest share of GDP spent on health care in the European Union (EU) in 2015, at just short of 12%.

Citizens can shift insurer each year. They can choose one that determines which hospital they can use, or they can be paid a cash sum and decide which hospital to attend and pay. They can do a mix of both. There is thus competition between providers to gain this custom. Most are private but 'not-for-profit' organisations. Is too early to be sure how far this has increased the efficiency of the system or what other consequences it has had.

The US, for a time, chose to follow a somewhat similar course with 'Obamacare' – the title given to the Act passed under President Obama and strongly fought for by him. The title of the legislation introduced in the House of Representatives was the Affordable Care Act and that has stuck in popular language, though after compromise with the US Senate in 2010, a longer title appears on the statute book!

In the 1960s, the US introduced a federal scheme to finance health-care services for the elderly – those who receive social security retirement pensions (Medicare). It also began joint federal- and state-funded care for the poor (Medicaid). The former was financed out of additional social security contributions. It has continued in being, albeit with increased user charges. (For a concise history of Medicare, see Oberlander, 2015.) Medicaid has also survived with additional federal tax support so that states can provide for potentially excluded groups like pregnant women and children in two-parent households.

It is important to note that while both Medicare and Medicaid are publicly funded, the funds are used to buy *private* services from many approved providers. (For a concise history of Medicaid, see Grogan and Andrews, 2015; for a comparative history of US/UK health policy and unlikely interactions see Glennerster and Lieberman, 2011).

Extensive private occupational insurance schemes had developed during and since the Second World War, covering half the working-age population. In 2008, there were gaps in Medicare coverage – prescription cost coverage and preventive care, for example – but, above all, there was a gaping hole for those who were not covered by any health cover – those just above the means-tested Medicaid system but not in an employer-based scheme. What the Affordable Care Act did was to fill in the gaps – above all, seeking to cover the non-insured and the underinsured and to fill in the gaps in Medicare coverage. This proved extraordinarily controversial.

At its heart, Obamacare was an attempt to regulate the private health insurance market to remove or mitigate market failures, to require membership of a private scheme, and to give financial aid to poorer citizens to enable them to pay for it. For reasons already discussed, private insurers seek to exclude 'bad risks'. To limit this, the Affordable Care Act 2010:

- prohibited companies from putting a cap on their annual spending on any individual;
- prohibited discrimination or exclusion on the basis of health status – excluding those with 'pre-existing conditions' – a hugely important component;
- guaranteed renewal – no exclusion if you cost a lot last year;
- limited the waiting period before insurance cover takes effect; and
- required coverage for families, including children up to 26 – crucial for students.

States were meant to create a regulated marketplace for genuinely competing insurance offerings. Many states refused to do so and the federal government had to take over the responsibility. If an individual bought coverage on these exchanges – a federal-approved scheme essentially – they received a federal tax subsidy. How many, if any, of these provisions will survive the Trump presidency remains to be seen.

In short, we can see that there are no easy alternative routes to health-care funding provided by other countries. The aforementioned 'solutions' turn out to involve requiring employers to pay, or requiring individuals to pay for their own private insurance but with large state subsidies. The other 'solution' increasingly adopted, as economic times have worsened abroad, is to require people to pay something towards their treatment or medical consultation – co-payments. However, that has its political and administrative difficulties, has not provided major new income, could delay access, and could end up being more costly. Even so, we need to be open to alternatives.

Overview

To conclude, the means by which medical care came to be funded from 1948 onwards in the UK is popular, fair and largely cost-effective. However:

- Future planned spending is completely inadequate to meet expected demographic demand and the need to fill known gaps, such as mental health provision.
- The current separate funding of health and social care is damaging.
- The allocation of resources between areas on the basis of need differs somewhat between the nations of the UK, but is open and evidence-based.
- Other countries' funding mechanisms do not provide easy solutions to the dilemmas facing the NHS.
- The Barker Commission appointed by the King's Fund produced a report that provides a good basis for discussion but a full-scale independent enquiry is needed to forge a

cross-party settlement for the combined funding of health and social care that would meet the challenges of the demographic tidal wave that is now hitting these services.

Questions for discussion

1. What advantages and disadvantages are there in the way in which the UK funds health care compared to other countries?
2. What is the scope for, and problems that attach to, a 'quasi-market' and choice in health care? Draw on local experience.
3. How does the NHS allocate funds to local health agencies? What advantages and limits does it have? How does it differ between parts of the UK?
4. How should the UK set about increasing the funding for health care and integrating it with long-term care?

Further reading

For a review of the economics of health care and international examples that illustrate attempts to counter market failure, see **Barr (2012a)**.

For an account of the comparative advantages and difficulties to be found in various European countries' funding arrangements, see **European Observatory on Health Care Systems (2002)**. Although a little out of date, it is well organised and succinct. It can be updated by using the WHO European Observatory on Health Care Systems website, available at: www.euro.who.int.

For a good, balanced summary of the impact of competition in the English NHS but with comparative material, see **Propper (2012)**.

For a discussion of ways to fund increased spending on the NHS, see the Barker Commission Report **(King's Fund, 2014)**. This issue has become so pressing that much more will be written for students to follow and discuss.

The National Audit Office has provided a useful review of past and present attempts to integrate health and social care services and a sobering view of their effectiveness. See **National Audit Office (2017)**.

eight

Paying for care

Summary

It is difficult to draw a clear distinction between medical care and social care, between housing and residential care, and between formal care and informal family support. Indeed, the best care is a sensitive mixture of all these. It is one of the UK's major failings that it has not devised a pattern of funding that facilitates such a flexible mixture. Each of these forms of care is financed in different ways by different statutory agencies.

- Social care is funded partly from national taxation and partly from local taxation. It is not provided free, but only after a test of income and financial assets. The reasons lie in post-war history.
- Responsibility for specialist housing is held by local housing departments.
- The result is a complex maze to be negotiated by vulnerable people and their families.
- Informal family care forms a growing element. Formal state support has been increasingly limited to cases of extreme need, putting greater strain on carers.
- Market failure in private long-term care insurance is even greater than with health. It barely exists. However, private insurance and wider market provision might be fostered by the state promising to cover the most costly cases.

Some history

Paying for and providing personal care, with all its intimacies and feelings of family obligation and resentment, has always been a complicated affair (Lewis and Meredith, 1988). Partners and family, not least daughters, have always been the first call for support. Only when they could no longer cope did charity or the state step in, often in the form of institutional care. This became *The last refuge*, as Peter Townsend (1962) put it in his classic study (for Townsend's view of the history, see chapter 2 in that book).

Nearly half of all those in Poor Law workhouses were aged 60 or over at the beginning of the 20th century. Specialist homes for the elderly were gradually developed under the Poor Law but many older people were deemed 'too unruly' to be accommodated within them, even by a 'reformer' like Beatrice Webb (Townsend, 1962, p 24, fn). Responsibility for such institutions passed to local authorities in 1929.

It was the coming of the National Health Service (NHS) in 1948 that produced the sharply divided system of funding that we still have today. A distinction was made between those who were 'sick' and those who were in need of 'care and attention'. Local authorities took over responsibility for the latter and the NHS for the former, each funded in different ways.

Residential care for elderly people was to be provided in 'small comfortable homes'. The old workhouse accommodation was to end. However, given the acute housing shortage after the Second World War and the need to build schools for a growing child population, these 'small homely' residential care units were given low priority. Old Poor Law accommodation remained, sometimes in the joint ownership of regional hospital boards and local authorities.

At the time of Townsend's study, there were 300 such institutions and he painted a shaming picture of them, as he did of the then unregulated private homes. Not least because of this study, the government urged local authorities to replace all old Poor Law institutions within a decade (Ministry of Health, 1963). With more central government funding, local authorities did replace the Poor Law *physical* legacy (for a comparative account of services then and now, see Johnson et al, 2010).

The source of state funding for social care was divided roughly equally between central government grants and the local property tax – then called the 'rates'. However, while health care was free, social care carried a charge on users. Bevan's justification for this on the second reading of the National Assistance Bill in 1947 is fascinating. Charging, he argued, would remove the stigma of being looked after by the state:

> There is no reason at all why the public character of these places should not be very much in the background, because the whole idea is that

the welfare authorities should provide them and charge an economic rent for them, so that any old persons who wish to go may go there in exactly the same way as many well-to-do people have been accustomed to go into residential hotels. (HC Debates, 1947, col 1609, quoted in Judge and Matthews, 1980, p 32)

Local authorities still charge the full economic cost for residential accommodation *and* the home care they provide on an income and asset test, as we shall see.

An important change came in the 1980s. The income support system could make exceptional payments to help people who got into financial difficulty while staying in private residential homes. This practice became more widespread – strikingly so. It was in the financial interest of a family that their elderly parent not use their savings to pay for care. There was also an incentive for local authorities to privatise *their* homes or transfer older people to private ones and let the social security system pay.

These 'exceptional' social security payments made to private residential home-owners rose from £10 million in 1979 to £2,500 million in 1992. A report by Sir Roy Griffiths (Department of Health, 1988) recommended that the sums then being spent by the social security system be transferred to local authorities. A transitional payment was made to local authorities between 1993 and 1996 on condition that the 'new' money was spent on private sector accommodation. From 1996/97, this funding was absorbed into the normal central government grant to local authorities. The Labour government removed the 'independent sector' requirement (for an account of these developments, see Lewis and Glennerster, 1996).

The practice of local authorities paying private sector providers to take residents continued on a large scale during the New Labour period after 1997. Local authorities could use their buying power to hold down the fees that they were prepared to pay. Many new firms entered this market, bringing with them new capital investment that had largely ceased to be invested by local authorities after the economic crisis of the mid-1970s. Over four decades since then, private firms have invested £30 billion in residential care and provided 350,000 new beds (Laing, 2014).

Figure 8.1 illustrates the huge shift in the public–private pattern of residential care that has taken place in a relatively short period. Whereas local authority-run homes provided two thirds of residential places for older people in 1980, that share fell to just over 2% by 2015 in England. Less well known is the privatisation of care and support in people's own homes. It, too, is considerable (Laing, 2014, Figure 2.2). After a series of sudden closures, the Care Act 2014 tightened controls over the private sector.

Figure 8.1: Privatisation of the supply of care in residential settings for older people in the UK, 1970–2013

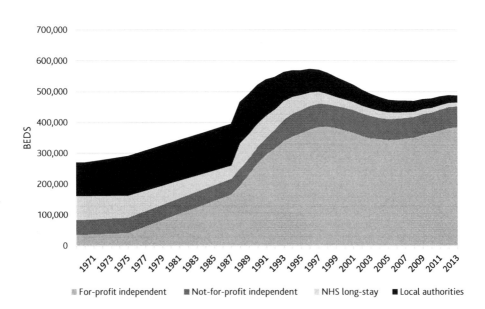

Source: Laing (2014), © Laing and Buisson

A third financial issue has unhelpfully dominated political debate. The fact that individuals might end up having to sell their own home to pay for local authority care proved a growing political irritant. Blair appointed a Royal Commission on Long Term Care (1999). It recommended that the state finance free social *and* personal care, but not meet housing costs except on a means–tested basis. The Royal Commission defined 'personal care' as 'care needs, often intimate, which give rise to the major additional costs of frailty' (p xxiv).

This recommendation was rejected by the Blair government for England and Wales but was adopted in Scotland when social care powers were devolved. The Royal Commission's reasoning is worth recalling. Since there is no clear differentiation between nursing, social and personal care, its funding should come from a common source. Funding on the same basis as the NHS seemed to be the most obvious route.

That conclusion was resisted by David Lipsey, now Lord Lipsey, in a minority report. Such a policy would, he claimed, result in a 'Croesian flood of expenditure' (Royal Commission on Long Term Care, 1999, p 119). Families and partners would claim state cash for all the informal care that they were undertaking already. The state *should* fund nursing care wherever it was provided, but no more. That became government policy in England and Wales. However, it failed to satisfy. When the Coalition came to office in 2010, the Conservative and Liberal Democrat partners agreed to try for another compromise and gave the task of constructing one to the economist Andrew Dilnot. His report (Dilnot Commission, 2011) is discussed later.

Some economic theory

As in the case of health care, it is important to distinguish arguments about *funding* long-term care from those that concern public versus private *provision*.

Market failures in the funding of long-term care

Demand-side issues include:

- Although people know that there is a good chance of needing some kind of expensive support when they are over 80, they put off doing anything to pay for it.
- Many individuals needing social care do not have the capacity to use information and make choices effectively. Their parents or partners may act on their behalf but they are not necessarily best placed to do so. They have an interest in inheriting what resources are left. Some independent safeguards are necessary.

Supply-side issues include:

- Long-term care is open to 'adverse selection' (see Chapter Two). People know their own family history and their past medical and social behaviour. They may know better than any insurer about their likely risks of needing care. This may make insurers cautious and raise premiums.
- Uncertainty about the future nature of care and survival rates makes future costs difficult to predict.
- Moral hazard problems are particularly severe. Since families do most of the caring, adequate private insurance cover might encourage families to rely on it, abandoning, or at least minimising, family roles.
- Providers, whether public or private, may be in a position to exploit vulnerable people who have no advocates or involved family.
- Local markets are polarised and some are potentially unstable (Laing, 2014). In some, labour costs are high but local authorities have very limited resources. In others, affluence has permitted high fees and encouraged the cross-subsidisation of local authority-supported residents. This may not last. Some homes have closed suddenly.

Partly to address these problems, the state has increasingly stepped in to regulate this sector. It first began to inspect private residential care in the 1960s after the Townsend study we have already cited. Public and private homes (now the majority) are inspected to see if they are providing the standards of care required by the regulations. Inspections take place regularly, and more frequently where past inspections have thrown up problems. The reports are publically available. In England, homes are rated on a scale. This is not done in other parts of the UK. The regulatory bodies responsible are:

- the Care Quality Commission in England;
- the Care Inspectorate in Scotland;
- the Care and Social Services Inspectorate in Wales; and
- the Regulation and Quality Improvement Authority in Northern Ireland.

The Care Act 2014 extended the powers of the Care Quality Commission in England to improve the inspection and oversight of market-dominant providers. Local authorities have a duty to make sure that older people's care continues if a provider is forced to stop providing care through bankruptcy or otherwise.

Regulation cannot succeed in ensuring high standards on its own. Declining public resources available for each at-risk person (see later) are incompatible with the high standards required by regulators. This is driving some providers out of business. In theory, a free market in care for older people and others should produce a flexible range of integrated services. Where most people cannot afford, or design, their own care package and where the state agencies buying the care are funded in perverse and separate ways, this is not going to happen. (For an examination of such economic issues internationally, see Comas-Herera et al, 2012.)

The cost of care

Informal care

The largest share of the costs of caring falls upon family members. Disproportionately, these costs fall on women. The care of older sick or incapacitated people is now more evenly spread across the genders but women still do more of the intimate personal care (Maher and Green, 2002; ONS, 2013). These caring activities give rise to 'opportunity costs' – time that could have been spent earning – as well as the more tangible direct costs of extra accommodation, food and heating where the person is in the same dwelling as the carer. As a result of the 'bedroom tax', extra accommodation may also *reduce* state benefit support (see Chapter Eleven).

Academic estimates of these 'informal costs' (Parker, 1990; Parker and Lawton, 1994) were followed by official ones. One approach is to calculate the cost of waged and unwaged time, accommodation, and food. Richards et al (1996) put the cost of all informal care of older people at about 2.5% of gross domestic product (GDP) – twice the cost of publicly funded care in 1995. Holloway and Tamplin (2001) (of the Office of National Statistics [ONS]) took a different line – they calculated the *cost of buying* in the formal market what we do informally.

More recently, official statisticians have looked at the scale of informal care for adults in more detail (Foster and Fender, 2013). They conclude that the value of such care has tripled over 15 years, from £21.5 billion in 1995 to £61.7 billion in 2010 – 4.2% of GDP. Given the growing elderly population, the need for informal care will grow. One official estimate suggested that it will double in the next 20 years (House of Lords, 2013, paras 256–61). (For an international comparison, see Wiener, 2003.)

Privately funded care

The next largest source for funding care is individuals' own spending. According to the magazine *Which* (see: www.which.co.uk./elderly care), the average cost of care in a nursing home in 2015 was £600 a week in the North East of England and £900 in London, with a national average of £700. Residential care prices varied from £660 a week in London to £505 in the North East of England, £589 in Scotland and £540 in Wales. With an average stay of just over two-and-a-half years, the total cost would amount to £116,000.

As we have explained, local authorities will only help with these fees if the individual's assets are below a given level. In 2016, all state help ceased when a person's assets rose above £23,250 in England. Help was given on a sliding scale for someone with assets between £14,250 and that cap. This asset limit has not risen in line with house prices since 1948 (Hills and Glennerster, 2013). The average price of a house in England and Wales topped £300,000 in 2016. Housing assets are ignored if the spouse is still living in the house but not if the person is single. Thus, virtually all single people owning a house will be above the limit for receiving state help. Moreover, the scale of owner occupation grew rapidly in the generation that is now retiring. Wittenberg and Hu (2015) estimate that the number of those fully funding themselves in care homes will more than double between 2015 and 2035 (see *Tables 8.1* and *8.2*). Public spending grows by 150% between 2015 and 2035 but private spending nearly trebles. Individuals' attitudes to selling their house – equity release – as a means of funding care are usefully explored by Overton and O'Mahony (2017).

These estimates assume that there will be no major policy change. There will, indeed, be none before 2020, though there was meant to be. The Dilnot Commission (2011) suggested raising the asset limit beyond which people would have to pay for their own care to £123,000 – a large apparent rise but still well short of the average price of a house. He also proposed that there should be a cap on what individuals should have to pay for their care. The local authority's standard fee for the care that the individual is deemed to need is taken as the assumed cost of care paid for privately. The Coalition finally accepted the proposals setting the cap on private spending at £72,000 – a higher figure than Dilnot's. Beyond that, the local authority would pay.

Table 8.1: Projected expenditure on social care for older people, 2015–35, England, in £billion at constant 2015 prices and percentages of GDP

	2015	2020	2035	% growth 2015–35
Social services public net expenditure	6.9	8.4	17.5	155
User charges	2.5	3.0	5.0	100
Private expenditure	6.8	8.7	19.9	191
Total expenditure	16.2	20.1	42.4	162
Total spend as % of GDP	*1.02*	*1.13*	*1.68*	*64*

Table 8.2: Projected public expenditure on social care for younger adults required by population need factors, England, £billion at constant 2015 prices with wage costs rising at 2.2% a year

	2015	2020	2035	% growth 2015–35
Community care	3.0	3.8	6.6	122
Care homes	3.9	4.9	8.8	125
Assessment and other services	1.6	1.9	3.0	95
Net social services expenditure	8.4	10.6	18.4	118
Net expenditure as a % of GDP	*0.53*	*0.59*	*0.73*	*37*

Source: Wittenberg and Hu (2015).

This set of proposals was legislated for in the Care Act 2014. However, in July 2015, the new Conservative government decided to put off implementing the changes until 2020. At the time, it was officially forecast that Dilnot would cost £1 billion by 2020 (House of Lords, 2013, p 62, fn 20). The prime beneficiaries would have been modestly well-off property-owners (Dilnot Commission, 2011, Figure 11).

So far, the discussion has centred on the English debate and with minor differences in Wales. However, after devolution, Scotland decided to take a different route and implement the 1999 Royal Commission's recommendations. In England, those institutions providing residential care are paid a flat sum towards nursing care costs. The Scottish Parliament added a sum to cover personal care costs – up to a maximum of £171 a week in 2015/16.

It cost the Scottish government more than it might have done. The Scottish Executive could not persuade the Department of Work and Pensions in London to change the rules for those receiving Attendance Allowance or the care component of the Disability Living Allowance. Those receiving the personal care payment lost their rights to claim these benefits (Bell and Bowes, 2006; Bell et al, 2007). Fees in Scotland still have to cover accommodation, food and other facilities.

Not-for-profit providers

Not-for-profit, non-state providers play a more important role in this field than in the other services covered in this book, though less than in other parts of Europe. Why is it that the not-for-profit sector is so well represented in the social care field compared with other human services? In the European Union (EU), for example, just over half total employment in the social care sector is in such organisations. The comparable figure for health and education is about half that. Kendall (2003) suggests that governing elites have been less engaged with social care compared to, for example, education. There has been no high-status profession to press its claims as with health. Only the Church, in its various denominational forms, has been heavily involved in pressing this case.

Economics has played a part too. Social care is less capital-intensive, and small firms can enter the market relatively easily. The varied needs of relatively small groups and links with informal carers may be most effectively achieved by small, relatively adaptable organisations (Billis and Glennerster, 1998). For whatever reason, the sector is important in social care. Its total expenditure, not just in social care, amounts to about £40 billion a year. Of that, individual donations fund just under half the activity and government about a third. Earned revenue from other sources makes up the rest (NCVO, 2015).

Local authority services

The final statutory responsibility, however, lies with local authorities throughout the UK. For many years, responsibility for child and adult care lay with the same department. Then, in England from 2006 under the Children Act 2004, responsibility for 'safeguarding and promoting the welfare of children' was combined with schooling, pre-school, day care and further education. Directors of Children's Services became the chief officers with a duty to ensure that vulnerable children did not slip between various agencies (Department of Health, 2003).

Adult care services became the responsibility of a Director of Adult Services, though, in some places, the posts were combined. Their responsibilities include those with disabilities, those with learning difficulties and people with mental ill health living in the community. Local authorities both provide services directly and pay other agencies to do so under contract. They can also pay individuals like foster parents to look after children on their behalf.

In Scotland, social work departments have wider responsibilities for children at risk, people with learning difficulties, those suffering from mental ill health in the community and probation services. This difference derives from what is still the key founding legislation – the Social Work (Scotland) Act 1968, which also began children's hearings to separate them from normal court proceedings. Criminal justice social work is largely funded by central government grant aid. From 2016, local authorities and the health boards must collaborate more directly in delivering adult social care services. They can choose one of two routes:

- create an integration joint board to plan, resource and deliver integrated adult health and social care services; or
- decide which authority is going to take the lead in doing so in each area.

This will require some kind of joint budget and planning between these two agencies. In Northern Ireland, social service and health functions have been merged, at least in theory, for a long time.

Total spending

In England, older people absorb half of all gross spending on adult social care services. ('Gross spending' includes the fees paid by users.) Those with learning disabilities take a third (see **Figure 8.2**).

Figure 8.2: *Proportion of gross current social care expenditure 2013/14 by service and client type, England*

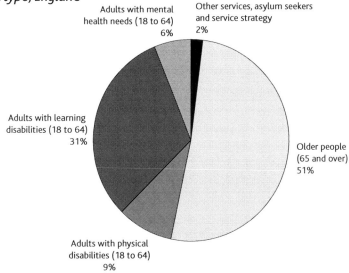

Source: Health and Social Care Information Centre, 2015.

Only about a quarter of this expenditure is used for services provided by local authorities; 15% of their income comes from clients in charges and about 7% from the NHS in transfers from the Better Care Fund designed to help patients come out of hospital earlier. In 2015, net public expenditure (excluding payments by users) on adult social care amounted to 0.7% of GDP (see ***Table 8.1***). Net public spending on services for children and families at risk, which now falls within the Department of Education's budget, amounted to £8.4 billion in 2015, or 0.53% of GDP. That brings the total spending on what used to be called 'personal social services' to about 1.2% of GDP. That is less than in 2005/06, before the services were split, when it was 1.8%. That is the lowest share of any of the services we discuss in this book.

Projections by the Office of Budget Responsibility (OBR, 2017) suggest that under current policy public spending will remain low. Even assuming that the Dilnot changes are eventually implemented, public spending in the UK on long-term care is only expected to rise from 1.1% of GDP in 2021/22 to 1.6% in 2036/37 and to 2.0% in 2066/67. New population projections reduced the cost in the long run by a little because they assume higher mortality than before in the older population. But these projections do not take fully into account the rising labour costs that will arise because of the 'living wage' increases that are expected.

Government grants

In all parts of the UK, local authorities receive grants from the appropriate 'central' government to cover the bulk of their spending – 80% or more depending on the devolved government. In Scotland, social work and social care services are 85% funded from the Scottish Executive through its Revenue Support Grant. This takes account of any income a council may receive from non-domestic – business – rates or other specific grants. These allocations are made on the basis of a 'needs' formula.

In Wales, support is based on the age of the population, various deprivation factors and the geographical dispersion of the population (Welsh Government, 2016, Annex 2, Table 1). Local authorities receive about 80% of their funding from the devolved Welsh government.

In England, there is again a formula to allocate funds. This changed during the period of the Coalition government and so did the scale of funding. A study by the Institute for Fiscal Studies (IFS) (Innes and Telow, 2015) calculated that total local government spending per person in England had been cut by 23% in real terms between 2009/10 and 2014/15. Those cuts were planned to continue on the same scale. Deprived areas and those with the fastest-growing population suffered most. General grants from the central government, excluding education and police but including social care, had been cut by 36% (39% per head) in that period. Much the same is planned for the period 2016–2020. This will be a completely unprecedented scale of cuts.

From 2016, local councils in England will be able to increase their council tax by an additional 2% a year (over the previously set ceiling of 1.99%) if they use the proceeds to fund adult social care. Councils can call a referendum to raise the tax by even more. The government has promised more money from the NHS to help hospitals discharge more quickly – the 'Better Care Fund' – and in the 2017 Budget, but this will not be anything like enough to bridge the gap.

Direct payments

As part of the more general move to giving individuals more choice and control over the services they receive, direct payments began from 1997, though initially only to those under 65 with disabilities. Their scope has been steadily expanded. To receive such payments, someone over 16 has to be assessed by the local authority as needing care and support services. This principle applies throughout the UK. Those eligible are:

- disabled people over 16;
- disabled parents with children needing services;
- carers over 16, including parents with disabled children; and
- elderly people.

People can use the money to buy services from an agency or employ someone themselves. They can, in some cases, employ someone in the family. In each case, the person receiving the payment must keep track of the payments made and be able to produce receipts or bills. If they pay someone directly, they become an employer. This complexity and worry may be something that people want to avoid but the practice is growing in scale.

A mixed market?

Personal social services have travelled further down the road to private provision than health care. The reasons have much to do with the different nature of these 'service economies' (Knapp, 2007):

- The balance of information and power between the user and provider is very different from that in medical care. Most people at least think they can judge the merits of an older person's care home but not a hospital.
- The costs of entry for any company wishing to enter the health–care market are considerable. To set up or even take over the running of a large district

hospital is very different from a couple deciding to convert a house and run an old persons' home.
- The reputational costs of failure for a company in health care are probably greater.
- Not-for-profit organisations knowing the needs of a particular client group are in a good position to give a specialist service.
- Much of the motivation for this move has been cost saving – this is more difficult to achieve in a high-profile NHS.

What difference has this made? Knapp (2007) and Hatton (2004) concluded that for clients, not much may have changed as local authorities and care managers still had a large say in what could be provided. However, since then, local authorities have had their funds cut massively and have forced providers to cut their costs and their quality. Local authorities have also sharply raised the level of need that is required before any service at all is provided (Burchardt et al, 2016).

Where now?

Given the scale of the problems that local authorities and the NHS face, there has been remarkably little government response or full debate until recently. The one concern that the government and other political parties have shown is to *reduce* the call on individuals' contribution to the costs of care. The Dilnot Commission (2011) was only asked to address the concern that someone's house might have to be sold to pay for long-term care. Its recommendations were discussed earlier and the implementation of the resulting legislation was put off until 2020.

The costs of implementing Dilnot were examined by colleagues Hancock, Wittenberg, Hu, Morciano and Comas- Herrera (2013). They concluded that they would add £2 billion to the cost of long-term care by 2030. Expressed as a percentage of GDP, that raised the public sector cost of long-term care in 2030 from 1.3% to about 1.4%.

There is now a general recognition that the divided administration and funding of health and social care is inefficient and destructive of a fully integrated system of care. There is no agreement on a new model. One option is to adopt the German or Japanese model of a merged tax-funded scheme, discussed later. The opposite route is to use such a merger to justify charging users of long-term *health* care just as we do such users of social care, perhaps with a 'catastrophic' limit to such charges, as Dilnot suggested, and perhaps compulsory private health and long-term care insurance cover. There are big political as well as practical issues to argue through. However, there has to be such an argument.

Funding long-term care internationally

Social care systems worldwide reflect the market failures with which the chapter began. Most are in a process of adaptation designed to cope with ageing populations. Everywhere, informal and family care is important. Attempts to assist carers are growing and technology is helping to keep people independent. (For a comparison of the funding of long-term care internationally, see Forder and Fernandez, 2011; OECD, 2011; Costa-Font and Zigante, 2014; Robertson et al, 2014.)

Private insurance

Nowhere is this the dominant model. Even in the US, where private health insurance is important, it is not true of long-term care. The reason lies not just in the market failures discussed earlier, but in the fact that people know if their assets fall below a given level, they will become eligible for Medicaid. In response to the recession, federal matching funds for Medicaid were increased substantially. Medicare only funds short-term care. Even so, two thirds of nursing home care is publicly funded and so is a great deal of home care.

Many countries *are* trying to encourage individuals to take out private cover. In Germany, everyone of working age has to take out long-term care insurance either with the state or privately. About 9 million people do the latter. Such schemes are highly regulated. People with pre-existing conditions must be included and such schemes cannot undercut the statutory scheme with lower premiums.

The Netherlands has gone the furthest, requiring all citizens to pay an income-related premium and employers to pay a levy for each worker. This revenue is then passed to and administered by private insurers. Even so, there are co-payments to be paid that are remitted on a means-test basis. As in the case of health care, low-income workers are assisted with their contributions. About a quarter of the cost thus comes from general taxation. Services for current older people are still heavily supported from public funds.

Private insurance is also significant in *France*, where 3 million people are privately insured. The state does have a universal social insurance scheme for long-term care that people can join. In its latest form, this has proved popular, but the amount of care it will cover is low. Individuals must have relatively high levels of need to qualify and co-payments are substantial. Someone on an income of about £26,000 would face charges equivalent to about 90% of the cost (Forder and Fernandez, 2011).

Means- and asset-tested provision

Classic examples of this residual means-testing model are US Medicaid and the Australian federal government scheme. Medicaid meets the long-term care bills (residential and home care) of those with low incomes and no or few assets. The Australian federal government funds residential and nursing home care on a means-tested basis, with most *provision* in the hands of profit and not-for-profit agencies. Residential care users can pay about half the cost of care but care in people's own homes has more state support – recipients pay nearer 10% of the cost.

Since 2012, people who do qualify for help have the option of receiving a cash budget to buy their own care, much as in the UK. The Productivity Commission (2011) – a highly respected independent advisory body to the Australian government – recently reported on the future funding of long-term care. It examined three options:

- Require people to save in schemes designed for the purpose. The problem is that the potential costs of care vary hugely. Some required 'average' savings target would be more than most people would need. However, for some, the savings would be nowhere near enough. Hence, such a requirement would be set at a level enough to cover moderate needs, with the state meeting catastrophic costs – a Dilnot Commission (2011) type of solution but with compulsion.
- Encourage the use of capital tied up in people's homes to pay for their care if needed – 'equity release schemes'. In Australia, even more people own their houses than in England – 80% or more of the retired population. These capital assets would pay for most of people's care, even at the high end. However, as in England, it is rarely used, partly because of past scandals. The Commission recommended a state equity release scheme to build confidence.
- A state long-term care insurance scheme. They concluded that it was too late to do this – the population was ageing too fast for the additional taxes to be politically acceptable.

This menu has particular relevance for the UK.

Social insurance- or tax-funded entitlements

There has been a steady drift towards this form of funding internationally but it has proved costly and is being more strictly rationed in a number of countries as the population at risk rises. The classic example here is *Germany*. It introduced a universal social insurance-funded scheme in 1995. All employees and employers have to contribute equally. The total contribution rate was 1% originally but has risen to 2.35% in 2015. Childless employees pay an extra 0.25%. It covers not just older people, but those with other kinds of disability. The unemployed have their contributions paid by the unemployment insurance scheme. There is a maximum contribution. Since 2004, retired people also have to contribute. The tax rate has been regularly reviewed.

A nationally set assessment of need determines service entitlement and the basic level of support that individuals require. This assessment is made by the Statutory Medical Insurance Review Board. The cost of care determined does not include accommodation costs. There is no income test and each level of care attracts a fixed sum. However, if the facility's prices are higher than that sum, the individual or family must pay. Individuals can decide whether to opt for direct service provision or receive cash. The latter is lower – less than half the value of formal provision.

The level of financial support has not kept pace with care prices, so families have to make up the difference. Given that accommodation costs will need to be paid, people are advised to take out private insurance to cover the gap. The Lander public assistance schemes come to the support of those who fall through these various cracks. This scheme has its flaws and is suffering from the rising cost of ageing. However, Caroline Glendinning's (2007) comments still hold:

> Although German long term care insurance may be difficult to sustain in its present form, it nevertheless guarantees a sum for all beneficiaries regardless of region, financial circumstances and, to some extent, the type of support used. Virtually the whole population is covered; this also determines the level of risk pooling, thereby creating a highly efficient regime. Eligibility is determined by a single set of criteria, applicable across the country that is administered relatively consistently and leads to high levels of horizontal equity between people with similar levels of dependency. (Glendinning, 2007, pp 417–18)

Japan explicitly followed Germany at least some way down the same path (Ikegami, 2007). For those aged 65 and over, geriatric health care and long-term care services were merged. On reaching 65, people have the right to be assessed for long-term care needs, along with those aged 40 and over with particular long-term conditions. Seven levels of eligibility are determined and funded up to a capped amount and a care plan worked out.

The cost is divided equally between general taxation and a 'social insurance' payment levied on anyone in employment aged over 40. As in Germany, this payment is split evenly between the employee and the employer. Again, there have been cuts and changes since it was introduced. Charges are now made for accommodation and food and home-help services have been restricted to those living alone and with severe disabilities. There has been a shift from municipal to competing private agencies. The service is now delivered by a range of local for-profit and not-for-profit agencies over which the individual has a choice.

Benefits cannot be taken in cash and used to spend on services; they have to be taken in kind. **Table 8.3** presents a summary of some countries' service organisation and scale.

Table 8.3: Overview of long-term care systems

	Main model	Expenditure (% of GDP)	Financing	% private provision	Private insurance
France	A universal basic insurance scheme but meets limited needs and many costs means-tested	1.8	Diverse actors and sources	> 90%	Widely used as a supplement to limited state-funded provision
Germany	Universal	1.3	Mandatory social health insurance	36% private for-profit	Private insurance for higher-income groups
Italy	Universal	0.6	Tax-funded, fragmented (central, regional, local)	22% for-profit	No reliable estimates
Netherlands	Universal	3.8	Mandatory social insurance	Private but not-for-profit (90%)	Insignificant role
Spain	Universal	0.65	Mandatory central government	70% private not-for-profit	Less than 10%
Sweden	Universal	3.7	Decentralised	23% in 2012	Insignificant role
England	Means-tested	1.1	Decentralised	98% residential care and 92% domiciliary	Insignificant role

Source: Adapted from Costa-Font and Zigante (2014).

In the final chapter, I suggest drawing on some of these international examples to introduce an additional social insurance levy on those who reach the age of 40 or 45. The revenue would be allocated to a fund that would reward those local commissioning agencies that produce acceptable schemes for fully integrated health and long-term care. The effectiveness of these arrangements would be regularly reviewed. Areas would lose these funds if they failed the test. This could go hand in hand with more extensive equity release regulated by the state.

Overview

In conclusion, we have seen that much of the cost of caring is born by families and partners, and disproportionately by women. There has been a trend to merge family care with formal service provision and to give families and individuals more say in deciding what package of care suits them.

This is not an area well suited to voluntary private insurance, which can only operate on any scale if the state agrees to meet potential catastrophic costs. However:

- The historical development of health and social care as separately funded services – one funded nationally the other locally – has made it difficult to provide properly integrated care.
- Some attempts at merging long-term social and health-care budgets are being made in the various parts of England.
- However, they need a more fundamental change in funding to work effectively.

Unpopular features are the means and asset tests that are applied to those receiving state support. They have very low thresholds and many people end up paying significant sums in fees, and some may have to sell their houses as a result:

- An attempt to raise the level at which asset and means testing apply was legislated for in 2014 but implementation has been put off until 2020.
- Changes to the way long-term care is funded have been undertaken with some success in other countries. The time to discuss those and other alternatives is now.
- If health and social care are to be integrated, so must be their finance. This is not a totally sufficient solution, but it is a necessary one.

Questions for discussion

1. If you were advising a new minister in Scotland or England, what would you say were the most important issues in funding social care? What options would you present for future action?
2. What is the best way to increase an individual's control over the services she receives?
3. What are the main sources of market failure in the market for long-term care? Are there any remedies?

4. What might we learn from the reforms that other countries have attempted in the funding of long-term care?

Further reading

For an overview of the economics of long-term care and a guide through that literature, see **Fernandez, Forder and Knapp (2011)**.

For a discussion of recent policy changes in the UK, see **Burchardt, Obolenskaya and Vizard (2016)**.

For official reports on the funding of long-term care, see **Royal Commission on Long Term Care (1999)** and **Dilnot Commission (2011)**.

For a review of foreign experience and its relevance for the UK, see **Comas-Herera et al (2012)**.

Paying for education: schools

Summary

Most economists accept the case for some kind of state support for schooling. Economists differ on what the state's role should be. Some advocate funding state schools. Others favour giving parents the purchasing power to buy at least a basic standard of school education on the market. Recognition of the case for state funding of pre-school care has been much more recent. It is still low in international terms.

- Schooling can produce public 'bads', like class and religious prejudice, as well as public good. Forms of funding can foster or limit such divergent effects.
- There is an economic case to be made for devolving budgetary responsibility to individual schools and permitting parental choice of school. This can also produce less beneficial results.
- Schools in England have been increasingly separated from the control of local education authorities to become 'academies'. Funding for these is received directly from central government. This does not apply to other parts of the UK. Again, there are disputed gains and losses to such a policy.
- School funding systems vary widely between countries.

Some history

England only came to accept the case for free state schooling relatively late in its history. Scotland was using local taxes to support its schools in the 17th century. England was still debating the idea centuries later. It was only in 1944 that free universal *secondary* education was legislated for. The job of *providing* education for the 'lower classes' in the 19th century rested primarily with the churches and mostly female entrepreneurs, who ran 'dame schools'. The National Society (Church of England) and the British and Foreign School Society (Nonconformist) provided elementary education for their respective communities.

The state began supporting these bodies in 1833 but only to help with the building of new schools. Half the funds had to be raised by public subscription. State support began to be extended slowly to cover equipment and a range of other expenses, including teacher training. This complexity was resented and a commission was set up to consider the future role of the state. The Newcastle Commission on the State of Popular Education (Newcastle Commission, 1861) sent investigators abroad to report on other countries' financial support for and provision of schooling. However, the Commission concluded that state schooling was not for England. Pupils' minds should not be tainted by state indoctrination. *Some* financial support was legitimate but should be simplified into one general grant to the managers of individual schools and paid only if the pupils were doing well – 'a system of simply testing by examination and paying by results'.

Yet, any state support for Church of England schools, let alone Roman Catholic ones, was deeply unpopular with Nonconformists. The majority of schools for the poor attracted no state support at all. However, the evidence before the Commission claimed that most children got some kind of education for some period paid for by their parents (West, 1975). There has been a long dispute about the quality of much of this schooling, how many pupils actually attended and for how long. However, West is surely correct in claiming that the coming of free state education later in the century made this sector unviable, except for the rich. His case fits the current neoliberal view that the state has acquired an excessive and unnecessary role in schooling (Tooley, 2008).

The Gladstone ministry, which came shortly afterwards and had strong Nonconformist backing, broke the old pattern. The Education Act 1870 gave locally elected boards of education the power to *provide* elementary school places where the voluntary societies had not been able to. The 1870 Act unleashed the school-building boom of the late 19th century, whose 'Board School Buildings' are still with us. These schools still had to charge fees, as did their voluntary counterparts – up to nine pence a week. Poor children could have their fees paid out of the education rate or, later, by the Poor Law authorities. The scale of income used to decide which families were 'poor' enough to have their school fees paid underpinned Booth's attempt to define a 'poverty line' (Gillie, 1996).

The task of enforcing school attendance while charging fees was finally abandoned in a process that began in 1891 (the fascinating politics of this story are described by Sutherland, 1973).

Secondary education was still not free. Under the 1902 legislation, both state and private institutions that provided more advanced 'academic secondary education' received some state support. In return, they had to offer a few 'scholarship places' – free or at reduced fees. This system lasted until the Education Act 1944 was implemented after the Second World War. Even so, academic grammar school education was only available for those who passed an 11-plus examination. Some private, partially state funded, grammar schools continued until the mid-1970s. They were called direct grant schools. In short, the present 'free at the point of use' school system is of relatively recent origin.

The last decade has seen big changes in the way state schools are funded, again primarily in England. Until 1988 and even later, local authority education departments created by the Conservative government of 1902 possessed wide education responsibilities. They shaped education provision throughout their counties or city boundaries. They funded local authority schools and advised and supported them with expert advice. Their chief education officers were major, respected, even nationally famous figures. Now, these powers and funding are being removed almost entirely in England, as described later. Here, it is important to register what a major change this is.

Another major change has been the state's assumption of wider responsibility for funding pre-school provision. The legal age for beginning formal schooling was set at five in the 1870 Act. Blackstone (1971) traced the reluctant and slow adoption of pre-school provision by the state after that. It was extensive during the Second World War but was then largely dismantled. When Blackstone wrote her PhD thesis, there were only just over six nursery school places for every 100 children aged 2–4. Today, most children of that age are in some form of pre-school provision. Two factors influenced this change: women entering the workforce; and the growing appreciation of the importance of early intellectual development in later life. From 1999, children aged four in England were entitled to financial support for 15 hours of education a week for 38 weeks, with a similar entitlement in Scotland and Wales. The entitlement to free part-time education was extended to three year olds in 2004. In 2015, the proportion of two year olds helped by the state was increased to 40%. Just over half the *provision* of pre-school facilities in England is now in state-run pre-schools, nearly three quarters in Scotland and 90% in Wales. Unlike the story we tell in other chapters of the state withdrawing or scaling back its welfare role, here it has greatly expanded. The worry, and the gap with some other countries, lies in the standard of care that can be provided by the subsidised funding available. See Gambaro et al (2014).

Some economic theory

Not only Adam Smith, but John Stuart Mill, saw a role for the state in at least funding, if not providing, schooling. Mill (1970 [1848]) puts this with his usual clarity:

> There are certain primary elements and means of knowledge which it is in the highest degree desirable that all human beings born into the community should acquire during childhood. If their parents, or those on whom they depend, have the power of obtaining for them this instruction, and fail to do so they commit a double breach of duty, towards the children themselves, and towards the community generally, who are all liable to suffer seriously from the consequences of ignorance and want of education in their fellow citizens. It is therefore an allowable exercise of the powers of government to impose on parents the legal obligation of giving elementary instruction to children. This cannot be fairly done without taking measures to ensure such instruction shall be always accessible to them either gratuitously or at a trifling expense. (Mill, 1970 [1848], p 319)

However, with equal clarity, he went on to argue that the state would probably need to provide schools to meet the needs of those who could not afford schooling, but:

> it is not endurable that a government should ... have complete control over the education of the people.... A government which can mould the opinions and sentiments of the people from their youth upwards can do with them whatever it pleases. (Mill, 1970 [1848], p 321)

This encapsulates much of the debate about funding schools that has gone on for the past century and a half. Economists have elaborated a number of distinct market failures:

- Children are not perfectly informed consumers. Parents' interests may conflict with those of their children. For example, poorer parents have an incentive to encourage children to leave school early to reduce the family's costs and increase family income. This results in a waste of human capital.
- Most parents do have high aspirations for their children but many will not be able to afford to buy the level of education that their children need to develop their full potential.
- Education is, in part, a public good. The community benefits from a well-educated populace. Without it, debate is less informed and social cohesion

and law and order are more difficult to achieve. The wider economy can only operate at a lower level of efficiency with a poorly educated labour force.

• There is no reason for an individual parent to take these factors into account in deciding what to spend on their child's education. This will lead to underinvestment in education.

These arguments have led economists to agree the need for *some* kind of state intervention but they disagree as to what kind. Should the state provide schools or fund parents to enable them to buy schooling themselves?

The second view has a long pedigree (Friedman, 1962; Paine, 1969 [1791/92]; Maynard, 1975; Coons and Sugarman, 1978). There is very little agreement about what 'good schooling' is, these economists argue. Parents have a right to make that judgement and not have it shaped or limited by the state. They should receive a voucher sufficient to purchase an agreed minimum standard of education but should be free to use it at any school that reflects their values. They should be able to add to its monetary value so that what they spend on schooling can reflect their highest ambitions for their child (Pauly, 1974). This would promote higher education spending.

The opposing view is that schooling is not just a private good for an individual child. Rather, its form shapes wider community values and cohesion:

• Education can not only produce *beneficial* spillover effects, but also separate communities and breed hatred and ignorance about fellow human beings. Schools segregated by race, religion or class can promote collective *harm*. Northern Ireland may provide a warning.
• This makes the traditional economic case for unrestrained choice more difficult to sustain.
• Most parents say what they want most is a good local school (Exley, 2014).

Others take a view somewhere in the middle:

• To deny parents any choice will encourage many to desert state schooling, as has happened in the US.
• Competition can be used to raise the standards of poor-performing schools. Where school choice has been introduced, less well-performing schools have been shown to raise their game, much as has happened with hospitals (Le Grand, 2003, ch 8; 2007).
• If children with high preferences for education are removed from a school, this may adversely affect the children who remain. However, choice may still be better overall because it makes the worst schools respond. There is some evidence to this effect from an experiment in Colombia (Bettinger et al, 2010).

- To be effective, the schools market requires new entrants, not just competition between existing state schools.

There are also a set of practical issues that constrain these purely theoretical arguments:

- Working-class parents, in particular, do not see schooling as a market, preferring their children to go to the local school and expecting it to be good. They do not exert their exit power. The middle class do. Hence, this efficiency lever is exerted in ways that benefit the middle class (Gerwitz et al, 1995; Ball, 2002).
- Schools seek to compete for students who will add to their reputation and exam performance. Selecting bright or well-behaved pupils is an easier way to improve school outcomes than improving a school's efficiency (Glennerster, 1991).
- There are insufficient spare places in the state sector for a real market to exist.
- To extend a voucher scheme to parents with children at private schools would mean an increase in public expenditure.

A separate strand of economic literature concerns the virtues of devolving budgets and managerial independence to schools and away from the local authority in the UK or the school board in the US:

- There is a general case for devolving decisions to a level where information is richest and the rewards for doing something about it are greatest (Chubb and Moe, 1990).
- There is also an equity case. In the days when teachers were paid by the local education authority, schools in suburban areas had better-qualified, longer-serving staff. Their salaries were higher. This meant that more resources went to suburban schools, whose educational task was somewhat less challenging. This led the author to argue for devolved budgets that reflected the level of disadvantage with which a school had to deal (Glennerster, 1972). The Inner London Education Authority, with some other authorities, adopted this approach.
- *However*, with such managerial and budget devolution went a strong degree of specialist advice and monitoring by the local authority. This has now largely ceased in England at least by local authorities.

From devolved budgets to academies

When the Education Reform Act 1988 introduced local school management and budgets, it was building on academic evidence and 15 years of local experiment. The Blair government took the process further when it introduced 'academies' (Exley, 2012). Local authority schools could be placed in the hands of an independent body and funded directly by central government. This was only in exceptional cases where the governing body and the local authority had proved themselves incapable of rescuing a failing school over many years. This policy was applied to 203 schools before Labour left office.

A careful review of the outcome (Eyles et al, 2015) suggests that these schools did significantly improve pupil performance, even after taking account of the changed composition of the student body. More academically able children began to attend after the change. However, there was an effect over and above this, often the result of a change of head and curriculum. As a special measure in serious circumstances, this does seem to have worked.

The Coalition government then began a very different policy, albeit with the same name. *Most* secondary schools and some primaries were to become academies. By 2015, 60% of secondary schools and 15% of primaries were academies. This was already a far bigger intervention than the similar Charter School movement in the US or the Swedish experiment with free schools that we discuss later. After the change of government, George Osborne announced in his 2016 Budget speech that *all* schools would become academies. This was later downgraded to an aspiration. There is no evidence that such a move to universal 'academisation' would produce significant academic gains (Eyes et al, 2015). Moreover:

- Local authorities will have to transfer ownership of the land on which the school stands and its playing fields to the body now running the school. It is not clear that this gives a very useful additional power to the schools, but it does remove local authorities' capacity to shape the pattern of local schooling in their area.
- It removes the capacity of a local authority to respond to emerging problems and provide specialist help. Schools can buy in advice but seeking help is not the most obvious characteristic of a failing institution. The semi-commercial 'chains' that have emerged to provide specialist support at a price have no proven track record of success. Nor are they democratically accountable.
- On becoming prime minister in the summer of 2016, Mrs May announced that she intended that all academies and free schools would be able to choose to select pupils – to become grammar schools. The strong balance of evidence from the 1950s onwards suggests that this disadvantages most children. (For recent research on the wider inequality it produces, see Burgess et al, 2014.) It also enables a few schools to which a minority of children go to determine the nature of the whole local system of education. They can turn it from a comprehensive system with no selection to an 11-plus-based system with no capacity for local citizens to make a collective choice.

The cost of schooling

The UK now spends a higher percentage of its total output (GDP) on education (public and private) than most other advanced economies. For many years, the UK hovered around the middle of this ranking. From 2000, spending rose more sharply. By 2012, the UK was spending more on its primary schoolchildren than the Organisation for Economic Co-operation and Development (OECD average – US$10,000 rather than US$8,000 per child per year (OECD, 2015c). It spent the OECD average on secondary schoolchildren, roughly the same sum as on its primary schoolchildren, which is unusual internationally and was the partly result of funding policy changes under the 1997–2010 Blair and Brown governments (for English school funding trends, see *Figure 9.1*). Only Denmark, Sweden, the US, Switzerland and Luxemburg spent more on both levels of schooling. In education, at least, the UK does not lag behind other countries' spending – at least not yet.

Within the UK, identifiable public expenditure on education does not differ a great deal. Spending in Scotland and England is about the same, with Wales spending less and Northern Ireland more. Spending within the English regions varies more. Most is spent in London (£1,703), with the least spent in the South East, the South West and East Anglia (at below £1,400).

State education spending per head 2013/14 was as follows:

- England = £1,458.
- Scotland = £1,459.
- Wales = £1,368.
- Northern Ireland = £1,566.

However, under plans announced by the Conservative government elected in 2015, real school spending per pupil will *fall* by 7.5%, after being constant under the Coalition (see *Figure 9.2*).

One of the reasons for the fall in spending per pupil is that pupil numbers have been rising and spending is not keeping pace. Spending on new school places was slow to materialise under both the Labour and Coalition governments. The birth rate has been rising and more children are staying on. Since 2009, nearly half-a-million more children are attending school, and that will rise to 600,000 by 2021.

Figure 9.1: *Spending per pupil in English primary and secondary schools, 1978–2018 (2015/16 prices, GDP deflator)*

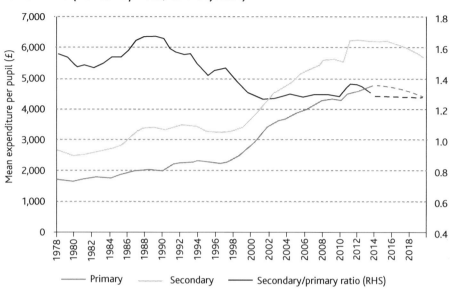

Source: Belfield and Sibieta (2016)

Figure 9.2: *Percentage changes in English school spending and cost factors, 2010/11 to 2019/20*

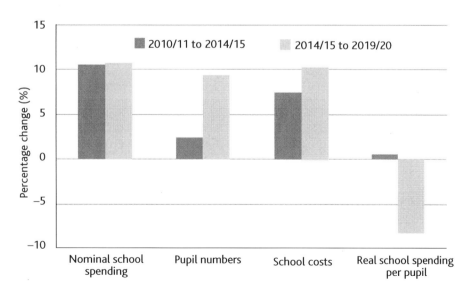

Source: Belfield and Sibieta (2015)

How state school funds are allocated

This currently varies depending on which kind of 'state' school is concerned. The funding mechanisms are under review. England is moving to a common formula funding model. However, historically, there have been major differences.

Voluntary Church schools

In the period before the Second World War, denominational schools were a major constraint on expanding secondary education. It was crucial to include them if post-war governments were to carry through the vast building and staffing programme needed to implement 'secondary education for all'. Under the Education Act 1944, the state would finance all the day-to-day expenses of voluntary Church schools to exactly the same extent as other local authority schools. Central government would give grants to local authorities, which they would match. The local education authority would then fund its own and 'voluntary schools' in its area on the same basis.

Capital spending on new or expanded schools would be shared between the central state and the denomination concerned. This 50–50 split of the capital budget in the 1944 Act gradually got eroded and the state's share grew to 90% by the end of the 20th century. However, the denominations continued to have the right to appoint members of the governing body of voluntary schools and to determine who got places. This could mean applying criteria that gave preference to children whose parents took communion or attended church regularly, for example. This practice varies locally. The Church of England has been concerned about the issue and claims to be moving towards more non-faith criteria for entry (BBC, 2015). Humanists have taken schools to court for applying criteria that could discriminate on social grounds and for other reasons. It has become contested ground.

A number of non-Christian schools have been permitted and funded under this arrangement; 30% of primary schools and 18% of secondary schools are of voluntary status. There are over 4,000 Church of England schools, 1,600 Roman Catholic, 36 Jewish, nine Muslim and four Sikh schools. The bulk of this sector is to be found in England.

It is an arrangement to which many object. The selection of pupils is socially skewed (Gibbons and Silva, 2006). It results in religious separation. However, it permits those with strong religious beliefs to have them reflected in their children's schooling while still being part of a state system with a state-approved curriculum.

Local education authority schools

From the end of the Second World War until 1958, each local education authority received a specific education grant from central government. Central government approved their education budget, after some negotiation, and then awarded the authority so much per schoolchild, plus 60% of the agreed budget, minus an assumed contribution from local revenue.

In 1958 came a big change to local government funding. Central government gave up specific service-by-service support and made a 'general grant' covering a whole range of local services. Local government added its own revenue and decided its own priorities. The size of the grant was related to the authority's population and its relative 'need'. The more children of school age, the more it received. Education needs formed a large weighting in the formula and the 'Standard Spending Assessment for Education' within it provided a guide for local politicians deciding how much to give their schools (Travers, 2000; West et al, 2000).

However, in 2003, the government ran into difficulties that led it to alter the way it funded schools in England. It decided to change the element in the formula.

This caused a political row. As a result, the Labour government introduced the Dedicated Schools Grant in 2006. This went to the local authority, which was then responsible for determining how much each school would get. However, the sum that the government had allocated had to go to schools, not to any other purpose. Some was taken off to fund local authority services to schools – roughly 13% on average. Local authorities could add money from their own council tax funds but only one in 10 did so. Moreover, the sum distributed to schools was heavily constrained. It had to amount to at least a baseline sum – a Minimum Funding Guarantee – plus what extra the local authority decided to pass on to which schools.

The result was that although deprivation formed a significant part of the formula that assigned money to local authorities, councils tended not to discriminate much between schools. The only exceptions were the London boroughs. There was very little variation in the sums that schools received per pupil despite variations in the numbers on free school meals.

The Liberal Democrats wanted to change this and, as a result, the Coalition government:

- Introduced a national pupil premium that gave each school initially £488 for every pupil on free school meals or who was in care. This rose to £1,300 for pupils in primary school and £935 for secondary pupils in 2014/15. Moreover, the measure of deprivation was extended to cover those who had ever been on free school meals in the past six years. This extra money was offset by the loss of small specific grants but it did result in more resources going to more deprived schools.

- A growing number of schools were encouraged – bribed, some would say – to become 'academies' or free schools if they were new schools sponsored by an outside agency like a charity, university, Church or faith group, or parents. Crucially, *their* funding came direct from the central government – the Education Funding Agency for England. This consisted of two grants: one that was meant to replicate how much the school would have received had it continued to be a local authority school (the School Budget Share); and a sum that would enable it to purchase the services that a local authority would have provided (Education Services Grant). This can be used to buy services from the local authority or some private agency. The intention of the Conservative government is that all schools in England eventually become academies, but it has retreated from compulsion.

In 2016, the government consulted on introducing a Schools National Funding Formula to come into operation in 2017 that would cover *all* state-supported schools.

State school funding in England from 2017

There is a case for moving to a single national formula that people could understand and debate and away from the complex muddle that prevailed after 2006. That was made worse by the varied forms of schools with different funding streams the Coalition Government introduced. At one end of the spectrum, per pupil spending was set at about £4,000 in 2015/16 in some authorities and ranged up to £7,000 in others, mostly in London authorities. The great majority of authorities allocated between £4,000 and £5,000 per pupil. However, most of the divergence could be explained by variations in the numbers on free school meals and other measures of social deprivation.

The new schools grant will have four elements:

- A basic sum per pupil graded by age – or more precisely by the number of pupils at each key stage level: numbers in reception class, those at Key Stages 1 and 2, and at Key Stages 3 and 4. The intention is to preserve the ratio of 3:2 for secondary compared to primary school funding.
- Extra funding for 'additional needs'. These include:
  - pupils on free school meals,
  - those with 'low prior attainment' – meaning those who have not achieved expected scores at the appropriate prior key stage assessments,
  - those whose first language is not English,
  - 'mobile' students.

- A sum related to the particular circumstances of the school.
- A factor that takes into account the differential cost of recruiting non-teaching staff.

A series of consultation papers have been issued outlining the proposals (eg DfE, 2016).

In 2017/18 local authorities will receive a schools grant based on this formula but can continue to allocate money to individual schools using their own formula. From 2018/19 the formula will be applied nationally to each school. Areas like London that have had above-average funding are likely to lose out significantly. But reductions in grant are supposed to be limited to 3 per cent over the two-year period as a result of a minimum funding guarantee. Yet these are cash reductions and do not take account of rising costs facing schools such as higher pension contributions.

School funding in Scotland and Wales

School funding in Scotland and Wales is not undergoing significant structural change. State schools are funded by local authorities, who are, in turn, supported by a General Revenue Grant covering a range of services, much as was the case in England before 2004. School building is mostly financed by local borrowing but the Scottish government began a programme of school improvement in 2009 lasting to 2018; 67 schools will be rebuilt or improved under a centrally coordinated and managed programme – the Scottish Futures Trust.

The Scottish government has also created a special fund that targets schools with the highest concentrations of 'pupils living in deprivation'. It is called the Attainment Scotland Fund. The sums involved are quite small – £186 million over four years. Nevertheless, reductions in funding from Westminster and the impact of cuts in local funding have had an impact on the *level* of support schools have received (for more detail, see Accounts Commission, 2014).

There is similar story in Wales, where local authorities fund local schools supported by a General Revenue Support Grant, which meets 80% of the cost. There is also a Pupil Deprivation Fund. Local authorities have their own formulae to distribute money to their schools. (For a comparison of changed funding arrangements in England and little change elsewhere, see West, 2016.)

Private schools

'Independent schools', as the Education Act 1944 designated them, have no direct state funding, though those that are charities attract tax relief. Many of the leading schools are charities. They can reclaim 80% of the local business rate that they would otherwise be liable for. The Independent Schools Council claim that this is worth £100 million a year to such schools. However, they claim, private schools give away £300 million in reduced fee scholarships and save the state £2 billion in expenditure that the state would otherwise have to pay for local state schooling. The reader might like to discuss these claims. Many private schools are not charities though – of those responding to the Independent Schools Census, just 100 were but 280 were not.

In everyday language, people use the term 'public schools' to mean private ones – a highly confusing terminology for foreigners. As the Public Schools Commission (1968, p 23) put it: 'Everyone uses the term "public school" and yet there is no generally accepted definition of these schools'. It reached a view on the leading private schools that it would include (288 of them) and referred to the rest as 'other independent schools'! At the peak of the system are the old established members of the Headmasters Conference.

Many years ago, working for the Public Schools Commission that was set up to advise on the future of such schools, the author and a colleague carried out a survey of independent schools' finances (Glennerster and Wilson, 1970). We estimated that total spending on private schools in 1950 amounted to just under 19% of all school spending. By 1967/68, we estimated that it constituted about 12%. OECD figures suggest that this share is now about the same, at 11%.

The share of the school population attending private schools has fallen from 8% in 1964 to just under 7% in 2015. The fees at these schools have risen sharply. In the period from 1990 to 2014, day school fees rose by 6.2% a year. In the same period, the consumer price index rose by 2.5% a year. As a result, sending one child to a day school would have cost a doctor 19% of her salary in 1990 and 36% in 2014. For a plumber in 2014, it would have cost three quarters of her salary compared to the two fifths it would have in 1990 (Centre for Economics and Business Research, 2014).

What this history suggests is that there are two different, though overlapping, reasons for buying private education:

- The first is that reflected in the standard economic view discussed earlier. Parents want a 'good standard' of education for their children or one that gives a higher priority to education spending than the median voter is prepared to vote for. State schools are not providing the standards that these parents want, so they opt out.
- The second is that at least some parents want to buy academic and social selectivity. They believe that there are good *and* bad spillover effects that come from being educated alongside other children. Being in the same class as 'less bright' children, they believe, can result in a clever child being held back. Being in a class with lower-class children can get them 'bad friends'. The reverse is true if poor children get clever middle-class mates. There is some support for these parental instincts in the educational literature. The least advantaged pupils

who do manage to get to private schools do slightly better in getting into the top universities than similar children in state non-selective schools (Crawford et al, 2014).

• The fact that private schools have so sharply raised their fees as incomes have risen suggests that they are, indeed, trying to ensure that only higher-class, more affluent children attend. That is what they think parents are buying.

There are thus two distinct kinds of market for private education. One is a response to the state not providing good-enough education; the other is a market for socially segregated schools. These markets overlap but the fact that we have seen no big shift to private education in the UK over a long period suggests that the first kind of market has been held at bay while the other has persisted and prospered. Whether the comparative satisfaction of many parents will persist in the face of school budget pressures, only time will tell.

How schools in other countries are financed

The changes to the funding of English schools have their parallels in other countries. The dominant model is still that of state schools being funded out of taxation. There is another model, though: independent, often religious and not-for-profit, organisations running schools with state support. This is the dominant model in some countries that have been divided religiously, culturally or by language. Belgium and the Netherlands exemplify this model. However, choice-based, or neoliberal, arguments have begun to influence funding policies in some unlikely countries, notably, Sweden.

At one extreme, *France* still has the most centralised pattern of funding and organisation. The French Ministry of Education and Culture largely funds all stages of education. Since 1982, the ministry, regional and local government have jointly supervised schools. The ministry determines the major decisions, including the allocation of teachers to schools. It determines the curriculum, the nature of the schools and the national system of testing children in core subjects. This takes place twice in primary school and once at the end of the lower-secondary school. At the end of secondary education are a range of diplomas and awards, including types of baccalaureate. Teachers are centrally paid civil servants. Other parts of the budget and responsibilities vary with the level of education: municipalities for the lowest primary level, the departments for lower-secondary and the region for upper-secondary. Pre-schools are also mainly free and state-provided and are available from three years old up to the school starting age of six.

Most schools are state-run but others are private and under contract with the state. The state pays the teachers and determines the curriculum. Fees are low. Religious schools, including Catholic ones, are private and fee-paying. Thus, overall, France has a much bigger private sector than the UK: 17% of its pupils are in private schools compared to 7% in the UK. Under recent reform proposals, 20% of the national curriculum could be set by the school.

At the other extreme, the *US* resisted any federal role in the finance of schools until the War on Poverty in 1965 included some federal aid to schools with high numbers of poor children. Later legislation with the same purpose took this further. No Child Left Behind, passed in 2001, required states to assess their school pupils annually and take remedial action for those who were 'falling behind'. The states determined what those minimum standards were. There was a large increase in federal funding (more than half in two years) and a requirement to target it more decisively on schools with poor results.

Even so, federal interference was resented, especially by the Republican majority and Republican states, and the successor legislation – Every Student Succeeds Act – took away most federal involvement. States determine how funds will reach schools on what criteria. District School Boards still retain responsibility for funding and administering local school policy. They have to raise a special education levy on property values, gain voter approval for any increase and gain permission to raise capital for school building.

Until two decades ago, US schools remained traditionally administered, with little delegation to school managers and limited school choice. One political response was to create a new type of school outside the school board authority – Charter Schools. The results of a series of evaluations are mixed. Most of the schools are new institutions likely to attract more ambitious or concerned parents. Experimental studies are difficult to set up.

Moreover, from a UK perspective, comparisons with 'academies' are not close, though often quoted. In the UK, most of the freedoms that Charter Schools gained were already available to local authority schools in England after the Education Reform Act 1989. (For a useful weighing of the US evidence on Charter Schools, see Eyles and Machin, 2015.)

The US constitution forbids federally funded religious schools. Income distribution has widened. More parents can afford fee-paying schools and flee the inner-city school. The US now has a tenth of its pupils in private schools – many more in some areas.

Belgium and the *Netherlands* have had a quasi-market in schooling since the Second World War. This sprang from the need to enable the different religious and ethnic groups to have their own schools. A total of 70% of schools in the Netherlands are private. Parents can sign their children into any state-approved school that individuals or religious bodies are able to set up. The school receives a sum of money for each enrolled child from the state. Studying the effect in Belgium, Vandenberghe (1996, 1998) concluded that there was evidence of cream skimming of academically able children but no evidence about improved efficiency.

New Zealand was another country where the state had not permitted parental choice and where local school boards delegated virtually no budgetary control to schools. That provoked a backlash. In 1989/90, zoning restrictions were removed, and in 1991, controls over intake were removed too. Schools received devolved budgets but this did not include teachers' salaries. There followed another backlash. There was evidence of significant cream skimming and widening gaps between better- and worse-performing schools (Fisk and Ladd, 2000; Le Grand, 2003). The original changes had removed all controls on the way schools responded if they were faced with oversubscribed places. In the new regulations, rules were set that governed what criteria schools had to follow. Siblings or those living very near the school got preference – if not, choice was by lottery. That is still the case. The official guidance to parents says: 'children are generally expected to go to the school that is nearest to them'. An experiment in choice has been largely abandoned.

One of the most unlikely places to find school choice prospering is *Sweden*. This country had a particularly low number of pupils in private schools before 1992 when its reform programme began. The figure had remained at just below 1% for many years. Then the government gave parents the choice of sending their children to fee-paying independent schools. Initially, the government would pay a basic sum and the parent could top this up to meet whatever fee the school charged. This was a 'pure' voucher model.

In 1997, with a change of government, local authorities were required to fund these schools at the same level as their own schools and top-up fees were forbidden. However, such schools can only receive government funding if they follow the national curriculum, and they are forbidden from selecting on grounds of academic ability, religion or ethnic origin. No state funding has gone to support the building of new independent schools. Many local authorities have been hostile to the development. There is a wide disparity in its spread. However, after a slow start, there is now about 11% of the compulsory school-age population in such schools – more at post-school level.

Initially, these schools seemed to make little difference. Indeed, during the period of the reform, Sweden saw a decline in its average score in the Programme for International Student Assessment (PISA) rankings. However, more recent work suggests that after 10 years, more positive results began to appear. Areas with more independent schools began to do a little better, even after other possible factors at work were disentangled (Bohlmark and Lindhal, 2012). These authors suggest that ruling out any 'topping up' of fees and 'cream skimming' more able students has forced schools to compete on reputation – doing well with whoever they have. Overall 'not enormous effects but not trivial either' is how the authors put it. There is still room for argument and more work to do, especially in view of Sweden's relative decline in PISA scores during the reform period.

These countries' experiences suggest:

- Parents do welcome some choice of school but electorates become worried if that leads to major cream skimming and social segregation.
- It is possible to constrain choice to prevent this.
- It may produce educational gains but these may not be great.
- It is likely to be popular with some and unpopular with others.

Overview

In conclusion, we have seen that significant changes have been made to the funding of schools in England since 1988. Budgetary control and oversight has passed from local education authorities to schools that are now largely self-governing and increasingly receive money direct from central government. The plan to give individual schools the power to select children on the basis of academic ability takes away from the local community any capacity to determine collectively what kind of school system they want. Schools in Scotland and Wales are not part of this process.

Schools in the UK as a whole have been relatively well resourced, especially primary schools, compared to other countries. However:

- Real-terms reductions in per pupil spending are now likely up to 2020.
- A new 'national' funding formula is being introduced in England and this may have major impacts on funding in some areas, in particular, London and other urban areas.

Private school pupil numbers have remained stable as a percentage of all pupils, mainly because fees have increased sharply. Other countries' experiments with school choice have had varied, and not altogether positive, results.

Questions for discussion

1. What are the major ways in which the funding of English schools differs from that in other countries and other parts of the UK?
2. How far should schools be funded locally or nationally? If nationally, what is the case for a single national formula?
3. What is the case for and against funding parents not schools?
4. What can we learn from other countries' experiences with school funding?

Further reading

For a critique of the neoliberal trend in English education policy, see **Exley and Ball (2014)**.

For an account of UK school spending trends from 1974 to 1996, see **Glennerster (1998)**. For the more recent period, see **Lupton, Thomson and Obolenskaya (2016)**.

For more on UK school funding policy in the recent past, see **West (2016)**.

For the evolving new English school funding formula, follow the Institute for Fiscal Studies commentaries, beginning with **Belfield and Sibieta (2015)**.

ten

Paying for post-compulsory education

Summary

The history of funding post-school education in the UK falls into two very different categories: vocational education and higher education. The first is neglected and the second is complex, being subject to major recent change in England and, as a consequence, very different to Scotland.

- Post-school education can be thought of as an investment by an individual in their future skills, earning power and life satisfaction – their 'human capital'. Capital markets fail to provide an efficient means of financing such investments. Students who cannot provide security for any loan made to them are not a safe risk.
- Employers have an interest in training their own workforce to do things related to their own firm but do not have the same incentive to give a worker general skills that can readily be transferred to other employers.
- In England, higher education remains free at the point of use but the costs are spread over time for the graduate through a special kind of state loan. In Scotland, this route has not been followed. The comparative results remain contested.
- Some attempts to improve the funding of vocational training are about to begin in the UK. It seems doubtful that they will prove sufficient.

Some history

There are two divergent strands to the history of funding post-school education: one relatively neglected; the other subject to considerable recent change.

Vocational training

In the 1890s, only about 4% of English 14 and 15 year olds were in school. By the age of 16 and 17, this fell to 1%. The school leaving age was then increased to 14 in 1918 and to 15 after the Second World War. The ambition was to raise it to 16 as soon as possible and for most young people to continue education part-time until they reached their 18th birthday. In a now-neglected report, the Crowther Committee (1959, para 496) showed that only one in three boys and only 8% of girls who left school at 15 gained entry to day release courses. The great concentration of apprenticeships was in engineering and building. Crowther argued both for raising the school leaving age to 16 and, next in priority, delivering the 1944 Act promise of day release for all school leavers up to 18. This never happened, though the leaving age was raised to 16 in the early 1970s. Apprenticeships in major industries declined, as did those industries. They were not replaced.

Professor Wolfe's more recent report (Wolfe Report, 2011, p 7) on vocational education was even more critical than her predecessor's had been a half-century before: 'The staple offer for between a quarter and a third of the post 16 cohort is a diet of low level vocational qualifications most of which have little to no labour market value'. Compared to the resources devoted to higher education, vocational education has been badly neglected. This may be about to change.

Higher education

The UK, in common with other major economies, has devoted large sums to expanding higher education since the 1960s, albeit in ways that have changed markedly. The University Grants Committee was created in 1919 to help meet the financial needs of individual universities. It was an independent body reporting directly to the Treasury. Grants were made after five yearly – 'quinquennial' – reviews of a university's record and future plans. Until immediately after the Second World War, it had no overarching role in thinking about the university sector as a whole or its role in a changing economy. Although this changed a little after 1946, it still reported to the Treasury, its direct paymaster. Many in the sector and in the Ministry of Education thought this inappropriate. From the mid-1960s, it reported to and consulted with the education ministries in England and their equivalents in Scotland, Wales and Northern Ireland.

Its powers were finally taken over by separate funding bodies for each part of the UK: the Higher Education Funding Council (in England), the Scottish Funding Council, the Higher Education Funding Council Wales and the Department for Employment and Training in Northern Ireland. Throughout, the independence of these bodies from government has been a prized principle. Just how far it may have been eroded is a topic worth more discussion.

The size of the sector has been transformed over the past century. In 1902, 1% of 19 year olds were in full-time education, even fewer were attending universities. Many were in colleges of education that trained school teachers. By the early 1960s, only about 4% of the post-school age group were going to university. However, the proportion of 17 year olds gaining university entrance qualifications (two A levels) had risen from 4.5% to nearly 7% in the 1950s. The post-war changes to schooling were having their impact. Many of those rejected because of the failure of universities to expand came from middle-class, probably predominantly Conservative-voting, families (only 1% of working-class girls went to university in 1961 and only 3% of working-class boys). The then Conservative government appointed Lord Robbins, an economist of impeccable Conservative credentials, to report on the problem.

His committee's fundamental recommendation was that 'All young persons qualified by ability and attainment to pursue a full time course in higher education should have the opportunity to do so' (Robbins Committee, 1963, para 135 [and, slightly differently worded, para 31]). The report then proceeded to estimate how many places would be needed in higher education to accommodate the additional qualified school leavers who would be likely to leave school in the next 20 years. Fulfilling this promise involved creating about 700,000 new higher education places – well over double the previous capacity of universities.

Although this transformed the principle underlying *access*, the committee did not agree to change the means of *funding* universities. They would continue to be financed by central government. Students would continue to receive free tuition and their living expenses would be met from a means-tested student grant given by local authorities that had only recently been made more generous.

Some argued in evidence to the committee at the time that this was unrealistic (Peacock and Wiseman, 1962; Prest, 1962). Students should be able to take out state-backed loans to cover the cost. The critics were proved correct. The government baulked at the rising cost of these expanded places. Moreover, Robbins turned out to have underestimated the growth in the numbers of qualified applicants.

As a consequence, Mrs Thatcher's government refused to expand places in line with qualified demand in the 1980s. Then, faced with frustrated middle-class parents again, the government encouraged universities to take more students but reduced the real value of the grant that universities received for each student by about *half* over a decade (Glennerster, 1998). Successive governments then:

- reduced the generosity of the student grant (1980s on);
- turned it partly into a loan (in 1990);
- began to charge means-tested, low but upfront fees (in 1998);
- made the student maintenance grant repayable through the tax system (in 1998);
- adopted the principle of collecting tuition fees after graduation through the income tax structure (in 2004); and
- tripled the fees that could be charged, eliminating any tuition funding for humanities and social science courses (in 2012).

Some economic theory

- Higher education and training bring external benefits beyond those that accrue to the individual.
- Higher education is not compulsory. Fewer than half of school leavers take this route. Students make what is equivalent to an investment decision. In a pure free market, they could forgo income for a period and borrow enough to pay tuition fees and feed and house themselves. For graduates who, on average, will earn more than other school leavers, this investment would produce an extra flow of money earned over a lifetime. There may be 'non-pecuniary benefits' too – higher job satisfaction. The pecuniary benefits can be expressed as a 'private rate of return' – the financial gain each year expressed as a percentage of the original cost. In addition, society also gains from the higher productivity of the individual plus any wider social gains – a 'social rate of return'. This way of viewing higher education became fashionable in the 1960s – the 'human capital school' (eg Schultz, 1960, 1961). Recent work by the Institute for Fiscal Studies (IFS) shows that while graduates do earn a lot more than non-graduates on average, this 'graduate premium' varies a great deal by subject, socio-economic background and university (Britton et al, 2016).
- This approach was challenged at the time and later. Graduates earned more, critics argued, because employers were using their selection by a university and the student's completion as a *signal* of their capability and application. It was not that the university had taught the student anything useful! This was called the 'screening hypothesis' (Riley, 2001). Most economists agreed that there was something in this view, but only something.
- The capital market has serious imperfections:
  - Students rarely have any secure collateral. They cannot offer a bank their house or other asset that the bank could seize if they default. A rich parent might provide such a security but many students cannot rely on this, causing underinvestment (Friedman, 1962).
  - There are risks – of failing a degree or not getting a high-paid secure job. Knowledge of these lifetime risks is poor. Reluctance to take out a loan

may be high even in the best of circumstances and especially among those from poorer homes (Calendar and Jackson, 2005).

- Knowledge of those risks is asymmetric. The student will be more informed about them than the lender, leading to 'adverse selection', as in health insurance. Lending costs will be high to compensate the lender for this risk.

• In vocational education, employers may be prepared to train their workers free or in return for reduced pay but will do so most readily for skills that are specific to their firm. The more general and transferable the skills, the more reluctant an employer will be to spend resources on training. They will fear that such employees, once trained at their expense, will move to another employer (Becker, 1964). Non-vocational skills of a general kind, like those gained from a degree – the capacity to think and analyse – are also things that cannot be tied to a particular employer, hence the case for state involvement in funding them. What makes no sense is to argue that investment in such skills should be funded by the state if supplied by universities but not by other training agencies.

As a consequence of this analysis, most economists agree that the state should step in and correct the capital market failures. However, as in the case of schooling, they disagree on how to do so:

• The state should provide free tuition and meet the living costs of students, at least from poorer homes. This was the model followed in the UK until the late 1980s and was supported by the Robbins Committee (1963). Critics saw several problems with this model:
  - It suited a world in which very few went to university. However, it was very expensive. That made governments reluctant to expand higher education.
  - It took resources away from schooling and pre-school provision.
  - It largely benefited those from middle-class homes who then went on to earn more – it was regressive in its impact (Glennerster, 1972).

• The state should rectify the key capital market failures:
  - Universities should charge fees but the state should make loans available at the interest rate at which the government can borrow. Fees should reflect the fact that higher education has wider public benefits.
  - Such a scheme should insure the student against the risks of not being able to repay. It can link the scale of repayment to a graduate's future income – 'income-contingent'. It can also limit the period of the loan, cancelling the debt after a period (Barr, 2012a, ch 12; 2016).
  - A more extreme neoliberal idea is that the state gets out of student funding altogether. Individuals make their own lifetime contracts – signing away the right to a share of their future earnings to a bank or insurance

company. This could leverage student finance without the government being involved at all (Del Rey, 2012). Readers might like to think through the possible consequences! Who would find it easy to use such a product? Who would not?

• The state could recover at least part of the cost of higher education by charging graduates a specific 'graduate tax' (Glennerster et al, 1968). This could apply to all graduates for their lifetime or a given period.

Vocational training market failures can be countered by government imposing a levy on employers to require them to pay the costs of such training. However, if the government is prepared to offer loans to university students and subsidise their education for public good or externality reasons, why not do so for those taking vocational courses?

Funding vocational training

Schools, sixth form colleges and further education (FE) colleges all provide post-school qualifications – A levels, Scottish Highers and various vocational courses. All are now funded on a common basis. In the past, school sixth formers were more generously funded and FE colleges less so. Now in England, all are funded at the same level by the same agency. As a result, sixth forms get less for their students aged 16 and 17 than for those aged 14 and 15, less still for 18 and 19 year olds. This was criticised by the Wolfe Report (2011).

The Department for Education in England funds the education of children from age three to 16, as described in Chapter Nine. The Education Funding Agency funds 16–18 provision. Courses for those aged 19 onwards *were* the responsibility of the Department for Business, Innovation and Skills. Since Theresa May assumed the premiership in 2016, the responsibility for teaching in further and higher education has returned to the Department for Education.

Many courses offered in FE colleges have always carried a fee, though in the post-war years, a heavily subsidised one. Now, free courses and student support have been cut back to a minimum core of 'hard cases' in England. Grants from the government meet about a fifth of the costs of an average FE college. Free courses are offered and funded by central government grant for:

• courses teaching reading, writing and basic maths where these are a student's first qualifications;
• training for those on Job Seekers Allowance required to do training as a condition for receiving Universal Credit; and
• 16 and 17 year olds at college and in work.

Bursaries and support are available for living and learning expenses where someone has been in local authority care, is disabled or is on state benefit. Student loans have been extended to 19–23 year olds to cover fees paid for courses at level three and four (A levels and above), as well as at higher levels still for all 19 year olds and above. Thus, the logic of loan finance is being applied beyond university students.

The 2010 Spending Review in England cut the non-school FE budget by 12% in the period up to 2015, including funding for student support. However, partly as a result of the Wolfe Report (2011), the 2017 Budget allocated £500 million a year to fund a much simpler pattern of vocational qualifications – T-levels. From 2017/18, an apprenticeship levy will be imposed on employers. They can either spend the equivalent themselves, and escape the levy, or pay it into a pot that will go to pay for training used by any employer who does not do their own training.

In Scotland, Wales and Northern Ireland, students can still get a means-tested education maintenance allowance to help those from poor families with the expenses of staying in education. Scotland includes those on part-time non-advanced courses under this scheme as from 2016. Full-time students in Scotland pay no fees and they may be waived for some part-time courses.

Funding higher education in the UK

It is here that the most far-reaching changes have been made in England in a series of incremental steps. It is important to distinguish four different kinds of cost of higher education:

- the costs of instruction – teaching, equipment and buildings;
- the costs of research, which also contribute to the quality of teaching, particularly in the case of postgraduate work;
- the opportunity costs that students face in not working, especially when taking full-time courses; and
- the indirect costs of living away from home – food and accommodation.

Each of these types of activity is now funded with different streams of money.

Until the 1980s, universities received a block grant for teaching *and* research. These were considered 'a joint product' – no mutton without wool, as one economist put it. All universities were equally funded to do both. The mix was up to them.

The exception was the funding of particular research projects for definite periods paid for by those who wanted the research done. This could be private firms like pharmaceutical companies or the government through a series of research councils – the earliest being the Medical Research Council, followed by various science research councils or the Economic and Social Research Council. This pattern became fully developed in its modern form in the 1960s. These bodies are to be merged from 2016.

Tuition costs were mainly met out of the grant given by the University Grants Committee (UCG). Students were charged a low, subsidised fee. However, if they were receiving a maintenance grant from a local authority, that paid the student fee. This was a generous arrangement. It was only possible because so few young people went to university. It was particularly beneficial to richer students. Graduates did earn more *and* paid five times as much tax as an unskilled worker but they took 17 times the number of university places (Glennerster, 1972). As higher education expanded, so the ways of funding it changed.

Step changes

The first step came in the 1980s, when the funding of basic research was separated from teaching. Universities had their research 'quality' assessed by panels of leading academics in their field. Departments were graded and a separate element in the overall university grant reflected it. The most recent grading exercise took place in 2014.

The second step came in 1990. Maintenance grants were kept but reduced in size and 'topped up' by a loan that students could take out, provided by an independent government agency – the Student Loans Company. Repayments could be deferred, for example, in times of low income, but still had to be repaid at some point – they were still a mortgage-type loan. The maintenance grant fell in value from 1990 to 1997 so that, by that date, roughly half the total support cost took the form of grant spending and half took the form of loans.

Evidence to the Dearing Committee (1997) on university funding strongly recommended some kind of income contingency for the loan element – repayment linked to capacity to pay. The Dearing Committee recommended that maintenance grants should continue to form half of all government maintenance support.

The third step came when the Labour government accepted Dearing's recommendation and made the Inland Revenue the repayment vehicle for student maintenance loans – a version of a graduate tax but only for student living costs. At the same time, it introduced a means-tested upfront fee for tuition – not something economists recommended. The original top fee was £1,000. It rose with prices over time. It was means-tested on the parents' income. Roughly two fifths of students paid nothing.

The new Scottish Parliament rejected the policy, arguing that it would restrict access. It did not, however, reject the idea of graduates paying something after they had graduated to help repay the maintenance support that they had been given. It was called a 'graduate endowment fee' set originally at £2,000 and was used to contribute to the costs of support for poorer students. That, too, was to be abolished in 2007 by the Scottish Nationalist government with the support of the Liberal Democrats. The Northern Ireland and Wales Assemblies also rejected the upfront fees policy.

The fourth step came after an uncomfortable election for Tony Blair in 2001 in which upfront fees dogged him on the doorstep, or as near as prime ministers get to a doorstep. He also received warnings from leading university vice chancellors that the fee was just too small to materially help their finances. He ordered another major review in which the author was involved. The eventual result was a White Paper (DfES, 2003), legislation in 2004 and new funding arrangements from 2006.

The White Paper argued:

- Upfront fees endangered access. They had to be kept low to minimise this effect and hence raised little income.
- In their place, students should be expected to pay fees after graduation in line with their earnings. This was to be an income-contingent loan collected through the income tax system, which had proved to work in the case of maintenance loans.
- Fees should be capped at £3,000 in real terms until the end of that Parliament – 2010.
- In return for permission to raise fees, universities would be required to minimise the impact on students from poorer homes by providing bursaries. These conditions and access would be monitored by an access regulator.
- The income threshold at which repayment would begin was set at £15,000. Repayments would then be set at 9% of income above this threshold.
- After 25 years, all debt would be written off.
- Students would pay no interest on these loans.
- It was finally agreed, with Organisation for Economic Co-operation and Development (OECD) and Treasury acquiescence, that only those parts of the cost of higher education that would eventually fall on the Exchequer would count as public expenditure. This was called the Resource Accounting Budget adjustment (RAB). This sum, which enters into the Office of Budget Responsibility (OBR) forecasts, includes the projected non-repayment of fees. It counts not as current spending, but as a future cost. This was a crucial breakthrough!

On any measure, this was a big change of policy direction. For a contemporary critique, see Callender and Jackson (2005). They argued that even the distinctive income-contingent student 'debt' would deter the very students that the policy was designed to help. In response, advocates stressed that this was a deliberately modest move – a relatively low fee set at a quarter of tuition costs with conditions designed to minimise impact on access.

The results were fiscally redistributive (Dearden et al, 2008). Students in the lowest part of the income distribution saw a reduction in their lifetime costs of higher education compared to the previous policy. Those in the middle and upper part of the distribution would see their tax contribution rise. Those with caring responsibilities for children, for example, would see their repayments fall because of the 25-year cut-off for repayments.

Long-term application rates were little affected. There was a downward kink in applications in 2006, the first year of the new regime, but after that, trends resumed their past growth – faster in England than in Scotland and Wales, especially so for those from the lowest socio-economic groups in England (Universities and Colleges Admissions Service, UCAS, 2017). This was far from being the end of the story, however.

The fifth step was to follow the 2010 election. Another committee had been set up, with the agreement of both the Conservative and Labour parties, to report after the election. It duly did (Browne Review, 2010). The Coalition government responded with another White Paper from the new department responsible for higher education – the Department for Business, Innovation and Skills (BIS, 2011). In many ways, this built on the previous government's policy, but not in others. It failed to incorporate some of the crucial safeguards that Browne had recommended:

- The fees cap was raised from the £3,375 it had reached by then to £9,000 a year (from 2012).
- The income threshold at which ex-students began to repay was increased from £15,795, which it had by then reached, to £21,000.
- The point at which loans were written off was raised to 30 years after graduation, not 25.
- A variable real interest rate on the loans was introduced.
- There was to be some additional help for students from poorer families with a National Scholarship programme. Student support during study was increased a little.
- The teaching grant that had been made to universities ever since 1919 was abolished in the case of humanities and social science courses, and retained, but cut, in the case of sciences, engineering and maths. This enabled the government to cut *current* public spending on higher education by a significant sum, though, as we shall see, *future* spending to meet non- repayments by students would rise.

Most universities decided to set their fees at or near the new maximum. Universities gained extra money, the Treasury got its paper cuts and everyone, bar students, seemed content.

The sixth step was announced shortly after the 2015 election:

- Universities 'with high-quality teaching' could raise their fees above the £9,000 limit.
- A new system of teaching-quality assessments will match the research assessment exercise described earlier undertaken by an Office for Students.
- Student maintenance grants would end and be replaced by loans.
- Those taking postgraduate courses under the age of 30 would be able to take out loans for sums up to £10,000. The government said that the future public spending cost would be nil because all these loans would be repaid. This looked doubtful.
- The income level at which repayment began was retrospectively frozen at £21,000 until 2020/21.
- The interest rate to be charged would be reassessed to bring it into line with current interest rates, which looked like being lower than the 2.2% at which they were originally set.

The IFS concluded that this set of changes would increase the debt of the 40% lowest-paid graduates to £53,000 – up from £40,000 under the original rules (Britton et al, 2015). This whole story is, therefore, a very good example of how public policy can be changed fundamentally by incremental steps through a 180-degree turn (Streeck and Thelen, 2005).

The right steps?

In the following assessment, the reader should bear in mind that the author was a participant in this process. There were essentially three positions taken in this debate – a neoliberal view, an uncompromising human rights view and a 'relative priorities' view that scarce tax resources should be devoted to those purposes that most help the least advantaged.

The *neoliberal* view is that on efficiency and liberty grounds, state involvement in higher education should be kept to a minimum. Institutions should compete for students and charge competitive fees. Students determine whether courses are good value. The so-called 'wider social benefits' of higher education are largely illusory or, at least, cannot be measured. Individuals can make good judgements about whether to invest in their own futures given access to borrowing. Government can provide access to loans and avoid the student being faced with catastrophic losses. Some authors would not go even as far as this. Banks could be given the power to offer contracts that gave them the right to acquire a percentage of that student's future income (Palacios, 2003).

The Browne Review (2010) embodied much of this reasoning and thus had a coherence to it. However, in the messy coalition politics that followed the 2010 election, the Browne proposals were 'cherry-picked' (Barr, 2012b), with perverse efficiency and equity consequences – perhaps 'rotten-apple-picked' would be more accurate. The following compares the Browne proposals with the government response and assesses the difficulties and benefits:

• Browne argued that the potential losses that the government might incur from low-earning graduates not fully repaying their fees would be limited by requiring universities who charged over £6,000 to pay the government for the loss of income that the government might suffer as a result. A levy was to be charged that could be adjusted as the risks of default became clearer – a 'soft cap' on fee levels:
  – This was never implemented. As a consequence, there was every incentive for universities to charge the maximum fee permitted and leave future governments to pick up the consequences. It increased the scale of future governments' spending and the scale of debt.
  – The government did begin to charge a real rate of interest on the 'loans', as neoliberals advocated, but in a complicated way. Repayments were to be made with an interest rate of 2.2% above the rate of inflation – the government's long-term cost of borrowing. This was varied according to the circumstances of the student and her graduate self. Interest was charged at 3% a year while someone was a student. It was set at nothing if the ex-student was earning below £21,000. Above that, interest was charged at 2.2%, gradually rising with income up to 3%. Although this had equity merits, the complexity has made it more difficult to collect the amounts outstanding, especially from those living abroad. The government originally estimated that 28% of the debt would not be repaid. These estimates subsequently rose to 30%, then 33%, then 35%, then 40%.
• To sweeten the pill politically, Browne recommended raising the income at which graduates would begin to repay to £21,000 and indexing this to average earnings. The government accepted this. However, it lost the government substantial revenue. It was also a bad way to help poorer graduates. It reduced the sums paid by those earning under £21,000 a little, but it reduced the sums paid by those on higher incomes a lot. The Conservative government has now retreated from – reneged on – its promise to raise the threshold with average earnings at least up to 2020.

The *human rights approach* takes access to free higher education to be a basic human right. This was essentially the view of the Robbins Committee (1963). It points to the potential efficiency losses that might occur if the prospect of paying fees, or paying a tax, puts off those who have little experience of handling debt or knowing the value of higher education at first hand.

There *is* US and UK evidence that upfront fees have had this effect (Dearden et al, 2011). (This study included data to 2007, one year after the 2006 post-graduation payment system, and could not properly judge the long-run effect of this change.) Yet, there are objections to this view that can be advanced within that same intellectual tradition:

- Unless politicians are prepared to raise taxes, they will not be able to expand higher education as fast as they would with enhanced revenue from graduates. Yet, a *narrow* entry gate to higher education is a key determinant of *differential* social class access. In Australia, where expansion was funded by the equivalent of a graduate tax, there has been no decline in access by those from the lowest social groups; indeed, their participation seems to have been enhanced as a result, and especially so for women (Cardak and Ryan, 2009; Norton, 2016). In Scotland, it has proved difficult to expand university places without extra fee income. Access by poorer students has been more difficult.
- If there is some politically constrained sum available for public spending on education, how it is apportioned matters. The more a government decides to spend on its universities, the more difficult it is to fund other levels of education. We also know that early childhood experiences have a key influence on later school performance and access to higher education. In the decade after 2000, the English government combined a policy of moderate income-contingent loans with greater funding for pre-schools, especially in deprived areas. It is difficult to assign cause and effect, but in 2010, young people from the most disadvantaged communities in England had a 30% greater chance of entering higher education than the cohort five years earlier. The percentage of those from the lowest socio-economic groups going to university full time rose faster in England from 2006 to 2014/15 than in Scotland, despite two fee increases in England and none in Scotland. (It was, it must be admitted, a *slow* increase in both countries – over 3% in England and 1.8% in Scotland. The UK average entry for this social group is 33%.)

The *relative priorities view* within a human rights perspective is therefore:

- Give first spending priority to measures that raise the *school* attainments of the least-advantaged children.
- Give an equal capital grant to all who reach 18 to subsidise any approved education or training course – an *adulthood life endowment*. Why should free higher education be the only endowment that a young person can gain?
- Charge universities a graduated levy: the more they raise fees above a given sum, the higher the levy. This will compensate the Exchequer for the greater risk of defaults or non-repayments that may result.
- Keep some element of maintenance grant to ease the costs on parents of lower-income families and extend this back to all post-16 education.
- Charge a real interest rate and have a reasonable cut-off point for repayment – say 25 years. This is an efficient redistributive use of public funds.

• Reduce the real income level at which students begin to repay gradually over time.

I advocated such a strategy in the advice I gave to the Blair government prior to the 2004 legislation. (For a fuller technical exposition of these and other options, see Barr, 2016.) For a discussion of the distributional consequences of the 2011 changes see Chowdry et al 2012).

Why not levy a graduate tax?

A tax on graduates, repaying some of the costs of their higher education, was something that I had advocated as a young academic (Glennerster et al, 1968; Glennerster 1972). Why did I change my mind, or at least modify the idea? Such a tax would have been redistributive, raising more tax revenue from those who benefited most from the state's subsidy of higher education. However:

• The money would have gone to the Treasury, not to universities.
• It was a politically naive proposal. The revenue would have accrued to the *next* government – after the first cohort of tax-paying graduates emerged. The political pain would be felt by whoever introduced it. There was no cap on the tax paid. Rich graduates would have been contributing more than the cost of their course.
• The revenue, once spent, would count as public expenditure. It would therefore be subject to all the public spending limits discussed in Chapter Four.

Do governments merely pocket the fee revenue?

This is an entirely legitimate fear and, in some ways, is borne out by experience. In both England and Australia, right-wing governments have followed the introduction of this new revenue stream by cutting government funding and relying on the new fee income to make up the difference. There are two counter-arguments:

• Even if this were entirely the case, such schemes are a more equitable way of raising revenue rather than relying on the average taxpayer to fund better-off graduates.
• However, English universities *have* gained. They did not have to suffer the 12% cuts imposed on the FE budget, for example, or the even larger cuts that other services suffered. English universities now enjoy a relatively high level of funding compared to other countries that rely on tax revenue alone.

Is the present system 'unsustainable'?

Critics point to the high levels of non-payment by graduates forecast by the independent watchdog – the Office for Budget Responsibility (OBR). Changes announced in 2015, coming into effect in 2016/17, were designed to claw back some of that future non-repayment. However, the scope of loans was also extended to postgraduates, increasing the scale of borrowing. The likely outcome was analysed both by the IFS (Britton et al, 2015) and the OBR (2015; 2017).

There is considerable uncertainty about the impact of these changes and future debt estimates, as the OBR admit, but they concluded: 'The net effect has been to push up the peak effect on net debt up to 11.1 per cent of GDP in the late 2030s. By 2066-67 the addition to net debt is projected to fall back slightly to 9.3 per cent of GDP' (OBR, 2017, para 3.94). In 2016/17 net student debt amounted to just over 4.0 per cent of GDP. The OBR put the projected write-off of post-2012 loans at 0.25 per cent of GDP by mid-century.

Is this scale of borrowing sustainable? In principle, it should be. The Australian equivalent (see later), which provides cheap access to university in return for higher taxes later, has been sustained for over 25 years. As we shall see, other countries, for example, New Zealand, the Netherlands and Hungary, all have different versions of income-contingent loans.

Should we be worried by the apparently large 'debt' that this gives rise to? Again, the answer should be 'no' – so long as it is contained in the way in which the Browne Review (2010) suggested. Is it so worrying that 11% of English GDP should have been invested in the human capital of its population over a 30-year period?

The House of Commons Business, Innovation and Skills Committee has raised some serious doubts about the collection of student debt, especially from students overseas, and more generally about the robustness of the whole system: 'The United Kingdom is approaching a tipping point for the financial viability of the student loans system' (House of Commons, 2014, para 56). More steps in this story will follow.

Other international examples

While most countries rely very little on the private funding of schools, private funding of higher education is much more important and varies widely. The US, Japan and Chile rely on fees to finance about two thirds of the costs of tertiary education. It is minimal in Norway and Denmark and very small in France or Germany. With over 40% of its higher education funded privately, the UK is in the top third of countries using this approach. (For a comparative study of student funding, see Callender, 2013.)

In *France*, budget control was devolved from the central state to universities in 2007, though freedom on how to use central state funds is still constrained. French universities are permitted to charge a low enrolment fee and what an English student would consider minimal tuition fees: a maximum BA-level annual fee was €183, and for a master's course €254, in 2016. There are a range of grants to families and students from poorer backgrounds. There is also a system of state-guaranteed loans for students under 28. In the case of default, the state will step in and a graduate can delay payment for a period. The loan has a maximum repayment period of 10 years. A limited number of banks are involved. French students, however, have less teaching and other resources devoted to them than a UK student. The latter receive roughly 60% more teaching resources than their French counterparts (OECD, 2015c).

In *Germany*, it is the Lander, the regional governments, which are the supervising and funding agencies for public universities. They, in turn, receive funding from the federal government. The federal government is supporting an expansion of places up to 2020. The detailed university budgets are approved by the Lander parliaments but this level of control is gradually being relaxed. There is federal and Lander cooperation to promote high-level research institutes and other national priorities.

Lander began to charge tuition fees in a controversial move that was blocked by the Social-Democratic federal government, which made the charging of tuition fees illegal. This law was overturned by the Supreme Court in 2005 but general study-related fees have now gone. Some Lander charge a fee for administering the entrance process and for social facilities that the university provides. Students remaining for long periods and returning for continuing education do pay.

Students from low-income families receive financial support under a federal programme and all families receive a tax allowance if their children under 25 are in education or training. Half of the cash support for living expenses takes the form of a non-repayable grant and the other half takes the form of an interest-free loan. Its repayments are income-contingent and there is a maximum repayment ceiling. Individual Lander have additional support arrangements. The trade-off is that only 19% of German young people under 30 graduate while 33% of that UK age group do so (OECD, 2015c). Again, UK students receive roughly 40% more teaching resources than a German student.

The Netherlands has continued to charge fees, modest by English standards, at roughly €2,000 for a full-time course in 2016. In the past, every student received a basic monthly sum to help with expenses – travel, books and study resources, tuition fees, and medical expenses. This has now ended. Students with poorer parents will continue to receive means-tested support, which they will not have to repay if they graduate within 10 years. Otherwise, interest-bearing loans are available for a 15- to 35-year period, which only become repayable after individuals' income reaches a given point. The repayment is forgiven after

35 years. This has moved the Netherlands nearer to the English model but with much lower fees.

Sweden, on the other hand, has kept to its policy of free university education for Swedes and European Union (EU) students. It has begun charging fees for those from 'third countries' since 2011. Support for students' living costs comes in two parts – a weekly grant (700 kroner in 2016 for full-time students; half that for part-timers) for a maximum of six years. The loan has to be repaid within 25 years and the sum to be repaid increases by 2% each year. However, it can be reduced depending on the individual's circumstances. In addition, Sweden manages to spend not quite as much on its students as the UK but not that much less (OECD, 2015c).

Australia was the first country to adopt the idea of a graduate tax. In order to finance an explosion in the demand for university places, the Labor government introduced what it called a 'Higher Education Contribution' in 1989. This was essentially a flat fee of A$2,000 a year. It was equivalent to about a quarter of the average cost of tuition. Students could pay the fee on entry or while being a student – or their parents could, and get a discount – or they could defer payment and repay it after graduation through the tax system. The sum was linked to later inflation but there was no interest payment. By 1995, the extra revenue was providing 10% of the funding of higher education, and that was rising. The loan facility did not cover maintenance, merely the tuition fee element. An evaluation of the scheme suggested that it had not changed the social class balance of entrants – any disincentives being offset by the effects of expansion (Chapman, 1997).

In 1996, the scheme was changed. Fees were increased from a quarter of the average cost to over a third. They also varied by subject so that students in agriculture paid a quarter of their tuition costs and law students 80%. A separate category of private students was introduced who paid 100% of their tuition costs. These changes were unpopular and led to a major enquiry (Commonwealth of Australia, 1997). It argued that institutions should have the freedom to set fees for the courses they ran but no student should be required to pay fees upfront. Income-contingent loans should be available.

The federal government now supports a number of places in universities. They are allocated to students on a competitive basis depending on their school leaving results. The Commonwealth pays the university a grant for each such place. However, it does not pay the full cost.

Students who fail to get a Commonwealth place can gain a full-fee place. There has been no cap on student places since 2012. A separate loans scheme is available for such students – the FEE-HELP scheme. This carries a 25% addition as an insurance premium against some graduates not repaying in full. The scheme, therefore, differs from that in England in important respects but the two have moved together in some ways. For example, part-time students have been covered in the Australian scheme for a long time. Recently, England made the same move.

The two main disadvantages of the Australian scheme from an economist's point of view are the absence of a real interest rate and the binary nature of the scheme, with no public contribution to tuition costs in one scheme.

New Zealand followed Australia, with important variations. Fees were originally introduced covering a quarter of tuition costs set by individual universities but with no national cap. In 2004, maximum fees were set. A government loan scheme was introduced that covered fees, living expenses and study costs. The loans carried a virtual market rate of interest and repayments were collected through the tax system – originally at 10% of income above a starting level that was below the present English one. A Labour government in 2006 abandoned the interest element for new students after a successful campaign on the issue. That has continued to be the case but the next National government increased the repayment tax level to 12% in 2013. The debt is only written off at death!

The *US* has a wide range of institutions funded in very different ways. There is no national 'system' of funding universities or of student finance apart from the various federal loans explained in the following. At one end of the spectrum are private and largely privately funded universities with international reputations, which attract Federal and private research funding and large donations that go to help support student scholarships. There are a wide range of small liberal arts colleges that exist on the tuition fees they charge.

There are large state universities with significant public funding from their state legislatures. These universities charge low fees to students from within the state. However, higher education costs have been rising faster than US medical costs in the past two decades despite extensive in-college bursary and support schemes. As a result, the costs of college became an election issue in 2016.

The federal government has developed a range of income–contingent loan programmes. They are all based on the idea that students repay a percentage of their income once they have exceeded an income deemed to be a minimum acceptable living standard. The repayment percentage on that 'discretionary income' varies between 10% and 20%. The repayment periods are a maximum of 20 or 25 years (see: https://studentaid.ed.gov). The levels of debt incurred by students became an issue in the US presidential election in 2016. Subsequent debate and possible action by Congress will be worth watching carefully.

Overview

To conclude, most economists agree that the state needs to intervene in the funding of post-school education. However, they disagree on just how to do that:

- A growing number of countries have turned to charging students some level of fee, enabling them to pay these fees from their enhanced later incomes – income-contingent loans. Such schemes vary widely and most have design faults of one kind or another.

- England has shifted from a largely tax-funded university system to one where students have to pay the cost of tuition after graduation in income-related repayments. This varies by subject. There are divergent views about this:
  - The scheme is financially unsustainable because of the size of the debt to government that is not going to be repaid. Poorer students are being deterred from entering.
  - The principles underpinning the current scheme are sound and its recent weaknesses solvable. It has not deterred students from disadvantaged backgrounds. Universities have avoided large cuts and pre-school and school budgets have not had to be raided to support them.
- In the concern with funding universities, the need for better-funded vocational education has been largely ignored. This should now be a major priority for funding. The new apprenticeship levy on employers and the newly funded pattern of vocational courses are two responses.

Questions for discussion

1. Explain why governments have come to be involved in funding or providing higher education.
2. What form should that intervention take? Compare different countries' approaches.
3. What lessons can we draw from the divergent policy paths followed in Scotland and England?
4. How could we stimulate better vocational education and pay for it?

Further reading

For an account of the ideas that led to the English model of income-contingent loans, see **Barr and Crawford (2005)**. For an opposing view, see **Callender and Jackson (2005)**.

For critiques of the large increase in fees in 2010, see **Barr (2012b)** and **Callender (2012)**.

For an assessment of Australia's graduate contribution scheme over time, read **Norton (2016)**.

For a discussion of how to fund vocational training more effectively, read the **Wolfe Report (2011)**.

eleven

Housing

Summary

Housing, or shelter, is one of the most basic human needs, essential for any family to 'fare well'. In the UK, it is provided through the private owner-occupied market, supplemented by not-for-profit organisations, local authorities and a growing private rented sector. The state's role in *providing* housing has declined sharply in the UK in the past three decades. More recently, owner occupation has declined too.

- Nevertheless, the state has continued to play a major role in the regulation and finance of housing:
  - It regulates the standard of housing that can be built or be permitted to remain in use. It sets limits to the level of occupation and minimum amenities provided within dwellings for public health reasons. It determines, through planning controls, where houses can be built and at what density. There are economic costs to such regulation, as well as advantages.
  - It has sought to minimise the cost of housing for poor people by:
    - limiting the rents, or other charges, that can be imposed by private landlords;
    - subsidising the provision of houses for poor households or those in special categories of need; and
    - helping low-income families pay their rents through cash benefits.

- The state, in many countries, has also subsidised the acquisition of owner-occupied dwellings through the tax system. This has benefited higher-income groups especially. Giving tax relief on mortgages was phased out at the end of the 20th century in the UK. However, support for first-time buyers has been reintroduced. Owner-occupiers still have various other tax advantages.
- Rising house prices have opened up a large absolute wealth gap between house-owners and the rest of the population. This is also a generational gap. Young people are now at a major disadvantage in buying houses.

Some history

Shelter may be a basic human need but it is also a consumer product about which households hold very different preferences. For most, the choice of a dwelling, its location in a particular neighbourhood and proximity to a good school are central to their life plans. These preferences put a scarcity value on property and place. This can hinder community integration. There is an unusually difficult tension between public policy goals and individual choice.

Private landlords

The failure of private landlords to provide decent but affordable accommodation for lower-income families led the state to progressively intervene in the rental market during the late 19th and early 20th centuries. This can be seen not so much as altruistic in motivation, but as driven by concerns about public health, the fear of crime and disorder, and the need for a healthy and cheap labour force located in the cities.

During the 19th century, private builders and developers responded to the movement of citizens into the new industrial towns. By the end of the century, 93% of all housing was provided by private landlords. Thus, the market worked, after a fashion, but the lack of sanitation and overcrowding led to epidemics that threatened the whole of urban society. Public health legislation from the 1840s required minimum standards of housing. This essentially put a floor to the private market. Landlords could not make a profit at rents that poor families could afford.

Victorians looked to philanthropy to provide what the market would not. To some extent, it did. Housing associations like the Peabody Trust were founded in the late 19th century but never became major providers until their renaissance in the 1960s was supported by government grants. The First and the Second World Wars produced extreme housing shortages that led governments to set a limit to the rents that private landlords could charge. This reinforced the unprofitable nature of private landlordism.

These 'rent controls' were gradually relaxed after both wars. The decisive move after the Second World War came in 1957 with what was simply called 'The Rent Act'. Where houses had values above a statutory limit, landlords could charge what they wished. When a tenant left a rent-controlled property, it fell into the 'uncontrolled' category. This meant that landlords had a powerful incentive to get tenants to leave through bribes or terror. The landlord could then sell the vacant property or let it at a higher rent. Beginning married life in Notting Hill in 1962, where one landlord, Rachman, specialised in such tactics, my wife and I saw its brutality at first hand. This legislation was repealed by the 1964 Labour government but the process of gradual 'deregulation' continued.

A system of state-regulated renting remains, giving tenants rights to make agreements that last for short periods. During that period, they cannot be evicted without good cause. A new tenancy means a new market rent must be agreed. These tenancies are called Assured Shorthold Tenancies in England and Wales and Short Assured Tenancies in Scotland. Rent limits were set for those in receipt of housing benefit and will be for those on Universal Credit.

Social housing

The Housing of the Working Classes Act 1890 gave local authorities the power to build but not the funding to enable them to subsidise the costs of building. Hence, lower-income groups could not afford the economic rent that local authorities would have had to charge. Some socialist authorities did manage to hold down rents by 'writing down' the book value of the sites they had purchased. This essentially subsidised the cost of the houses they built out of the local rates, which was strictly illegal. By the First World War, only about 24,000 council houses had been built. (The best account of this period and the later rise of state housing is still Merrett, 1979. For its failings, see Power, 1987.)

It was not until after the housing shortage produced by the First World War that interwar governments began to subsidise local authorities' building costs and permit them to subsidise council rents from the local rates. Central grants were later gradually withdrawn as the housing shortage was deemed 'solved' but central subsidies were reintroduced after the Second World War. The 1945 Labour government concluded that local authorities were the only agencies large enough and universal enough to undertake the huge post-war rebuilding programme. They were given priority in the allocation of scarce building resources and built three quarters of all new dwellings in the immediate post-war period.

The state then turned its attention to a massive slum clearance programme, demolishing mostly private landlord property and building new council housing. By the late 1970s, councils and new town development corporations provided nearly a third of all dwellings in England. This was the largest state housing sector outside Eastern Europe.

However, Mrs Thatcher's government in the 1980s reversed this policy. Major changes in social housing policy followed over the next quarter of a century:

- A reduction in council house-building as central government withdrew financial support.
- A right for council tenants to buy their council home.
- A switch to housing associations as the main providers and managers of social housing. They sometimes took over whole council housing estates or these were made over to separate not-for-profit entities.
- An extension of 'the right to buy' to housing association tenants.
- A switch of government financial support to help 'first-time' owner-occupiers and 'buy-to-let' landlords.

In 1918, there were virtually no locally authority tenants. By the beginning of the Second World War, this had risen to about 10%. By 1980, local authority and housing association tenants occupied about a third of the housing stock in England. However, by 2015, this figure had fallen to under a fifth (17.4%). Private rented dwellings constituted nearly a fifth of all accommodation. Local authorities still provided a higher proportion of the total in Scotland and Northern Ireland (see *Table 11.1*). In 1980, council and social housing tenants formed just short of a third of all households in the UK. By 2015, this had fallen to under 18%.

Table 11.1: Dwellings by tenure in England, Scotland, Wales and Northern Ireland, 2015 (percentages)

	Owner-occupied	Private renting	Housing association	Local authority	Total (millions)
England	63	20	10	7	23,543
Wales	69	15	10	6	1,406
Scotland[a]	63	15	10	12	2,534
Northern Ireland[a]	67	17	4	12	767

Note: [a] Data for 2014.

Source: ONS (2016a).

The construction of social housing has been drastically reduced. The current housing crisis for poorer families needs no further explanation than the figures in *Table 11.2*.

The 2016 Autumn Statement did announce an increase in the capital allocation for social housing and a hoped-for 40,000 new starts a year for affordable housing developments.

Table 11.2: Permanent dwellings started in the UK, 1969/70–2015/16

	Housing associations	Local authorities	All dwellings, including owner occupation and private renting
1969/70	10,060	175,550	357,070
1979/80	16,040	67,450	231,590
1989/90	16,460	16,110	209,270
1999/2000	23,300	390	192,900
2009/10	28,030	860	124,170
2015/16	27,000[a]	3,000[a]	171,850[b]

Notes: [a] Estimate. [b] Data for 2014/15.

Source: ONS (2016b).

Owner occupation

Owner occupation began to expand in the 19th century with the invention of building societies. They were originally created from self-help groups – members contributing regularly to a fund from which they would buy or build houses themselves. Its job done, the society was closed down.

It was then realised that the society could continue on a longer-term basis as a 'permanent society'. It could borrow from local savers and lend to local people. Strictly hedged with legislation after various scandals, local building societies became the normal means of collecting small savings to finance house purchases for the working class.

In the low-interest-rate period between the wars, owner occupation boomed in the better-off areas of the South. Societies were given relatively favourable tax treatment compared with other financial institutions but the real tax advantages of owner occupation did not begin until the 1960s. Owner-occupiers were originally small in number and the tax system simply adapted the existing rules for them. They were assumed to be paying themselves rent assessed as the level of rent that other people living in similar houses would pay. They were taxed on that notional rent, just as a private landlord would be. It made good economic sense and was a system followed in many other countries. Both the owner-occupier and the private landlord could also *offset* interest and other costs against their gross income, just like any business. Thus, the owner-occupier received tax relief on the interest paid to buy a house, as well as *paying* tax on the imputed rent. A private landlord would do the same.

This system lasted until 1963. Not having the benefit of weekly economics classes, owner-occupiers could not see the logic of paying income tax on income they never saw. This 'notional income' was set in 1936 values and was never changed after the war because of its political unpopularity. Therefore, the real cost fell, and so did the real value of the revenue that the Treasury received.

As the number of owner-occupiers rose, so political pressure to abolish the tax grew. In 1963, the Conservative chancellor of the day responded. Since the revenue was small, administratively cumbersome to collect and unpopular to boot, he concluded that it could be dispensed with. The Labour Party did not object.

What about the other side of the equity balance – the right to set off the interest paid on mortgages against tax? That was kept. At the time, *all* interest payments could be set against tax, even those that were used to finance consumption, so a case could be made for keeping the arrangement. However, when that general relief was finally abolished in 1974, loans for house purchases were still exempt. By incremental steps, owner-occupiers had acquired a large tax advantage.

A further tax subsidy to owner occupation also arose by accident. The Labour government introduced a capital gains tax in 1965. It was a tax on the difference between the purchase price of a capital asset and its selling price (see Chapter Two). Owner-occupiers were exempt. There was some justification for this. For the most part, someone needs to buy a new house when they sell a previous one. However, it encourages people to 'trade up' – to buy as expensive a house as they can and then sell to buy a larger and more expensive house. It is a way to save without attracting the capital gains tax that would apply if you sold stocks and shares. House ownership thus became a combined form of pension, life assurance and tax avoidance.

By the late 1980s, this tax subsidy had grown in size to the point where it equalled what was spent on the various kinds of assistance that poorer tenants received. The Labour government in 1976 set a limit to the value of the mortgage that could attract tax relief. That was raised by the next Conservative government but once Margaret Thatcher had ceased to be prime minister, the Treasury managed to persuade Chancellor Kenneth Clarke to limit the benefit to standard-rate taxpayers. Gordon Brown finally abolished it altogether in 2000. What had been the largest pro-rich tax relief had been gradually removed over a decade – an unsung achievement!

State housing expenditure

Capital expenditure

Capital expenditure formed nearly half of all state spending on housing in 1990. Local authority rent subsidies and housing benefit in combination were slightly larger. By 2012/13, capital spending had fallen to less than a quarter of the total. Housing benefit paid to private landlords formed by far the largest share. (For a comparison of the various kinds of housing subsidy and state housing capital spending over time, see *Figure 11.1*.)

Figure 11.1: *Public expenditure on housing 1980/81 to 2012/13*

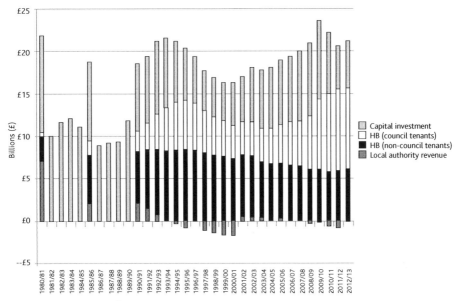

Note: HB = Housing Benefit.

Source: Hills (2007), Table 6.1 (capital expenditure only shown for some years).

There were sound economic reasons that led the Treasury to oppose tax advantages for owner occupation:

- It encouraged savings for investment in housing rather than industrial capital spending. That helped explain the UK's poor investment record. This was an argument advanced by two of the country's leading economists, Tony Atkinson and Mervyn King (1982), and still carries weight today.
- It encouraged the house price boom in the late 1980s from which the economy suffered.
- The cumulative effect of these tax arrangements has given house-owners considerable assistance in accumulating wealth. Housing boosted the wealth of those in the middle of the income and wealth distribution. This equalised wealth somewhat between 1995 and 2005 when other financial assets did less well. However, it made *absolute* differences in wealth much greater, moving the home-owning population far ahead of non-house-owners. It also opened up a gap between the older and the younger generation. (For a detailed discussion, see Bastagli and Hills, 2013, ch 4.)

Helping poor tenants

From the days of National Assistance and before, poor families would receive payments that included help to pay their housing costs. Some received assistance in keeping up their mortgage payments. Local authority tenants were subsidised in many areas not just out of the grants given by central government, but from a subsidy paid out of the general rates. In others, they were helped by a cross-subsidy from other council tenants' 'differential rents'. Similarly, poor tenants in private rented accommodation received no help – especially once rent control had gone. Critics attacked this complexity and unfairness (Nevitt, 1966) and argued for means-tested support for all tenants organised on a national basis through the social security system.

This happened in 1972 with the extension of comparable help to all poor tenants. It took the form of 'rent allowances' to tenants of housing associations and private landlords, and 'rent rebates' to council tenants. Both were combined in the regulations after 1988. The combined support, called 'housing benefit', has increased over the past 20 years to become the largest component of state spending on housing, as shown in *Figure 11.1*. As described in Chapter Six, it is being absorbed into Universal Credit.

Some economic theory

Housing does not fall into quite the same category as the other services covered in the book. There, large-scale market failures exist which may require substantial state funding or provision. In housing, individual preferences are highly varied and unlikely to be satisfied by uniform centralised state provision. Housing markets provide such variety but they also have profound problems:

- There is no reason to suppose that the market for housing will clear (ie match supply and demand) for poor people at a level consistent with public health requirements or morally acceptable standards of shelter. However, once the state steps in to regulate housing standards, it is forced either to subsidise the construction of dwellings and their maintenance or to supplement the incomes of tenants or owners so that they can afford the rental or mortgage costs that result.
- If the state steps in to limit the rents that landlords charge without subsidising them, it removes the incentive they have to supply dwellings. The collapse in the supply of privately rented property in the UK after the Second World War is but one example. It was exacerbated by the state subsidising an alternative form of supply – owner occupation.
- When people buy a dwelling they are purchasing a complex economic asset as well as shelter:

- *An investment opportunity*. Houses last a long time. For many years, their value has risen regularly over time, faster than other assets – not least because of the tax advantages described.
- *A place to live*. People often choose to live, if they can, in neighbourhoods with others of their income or social group. They buy proximity to public transport or a good road network linked to their job. A good school nearby significantly enhances the value of housing, not just in England, but in the US and Paris (Gibbons et al, 2012). An influx of poorer families can do the opposite.

- The annual output of housing is small compared to the total existing stock. The total of new dwellings has recently been around 150,000 in the UK compared to a total stock of 28 million. New entrants to the building market cannot respond to price signals and solve a housing shortage overnight.
- Supply is constrained by planning regulations. Permission to build in 'green belts' around cities is very limited. How many dwellings can be built is constrained by planning density rules and local opposition to high-rise apartments. One school of economists has been calling for a relaxation of such restrictions. It is claimed that economic growth is being held back by such regulations, which raise the price of housing, making it difficult to recruit labour and forcing people to spend longer travelling, among other welfare losses (Cheshire et al, 2015). Others argue that unregulated development produces urban sprawl, leaving city centres underpopulated and crime-ridden. The assets of an urban infrastructure are wasted (Rogers and Power, 2000). This debate goes far beyond the supply of shelter but is critical to it.
- Housing supply is also powerfully determined by government and Bank of England macroeconomic policy on interest rates.

A detailed treatment of housing economics is to be found in Maclennan (1982), brought up to date in O'Sullivan and Gibb (2003).

The cost of housing

The costs of housing are largely borne by households, particularly since the demise of mortgage interest relief. The cost of mortgage repayments, rent, house repairs and maintenance take a large share of people's incomes. This is especially true with young families, as we saw in Chapter One. When a mortgage is repaid, that cost falls away sharply and the house becomes a net asset. In recent years, house price inflation has meant that a house became a net asset almost immediately – it could be sold for a higher price within a few years or months. This may be changing but housing is used by owner-occupiers as a form of insurance against the costs of long-term care and an asset to be cashed in as a pension investment. Thus, housing becomes a kind of mini-welfare state, not just a form of shelter.

National Income and Expenditure data put together by the Office for National Statistics measures owner occupation in two ways. It records how much owner-occupiers pay in mortgage repayments and the costs of housing insurance and repairs. However, it separately calculates what owner-occupiers would be paying in rent ('imputed rent') if they were renting that property. The National Accounts show that, on average, housing costs plus fuel and power take 30% of average household expenditure – 38% for the lowest decile – or that is what it would cost were it not for housing benefit. For total housing costs in 2014, see **Table 11.3**.

Table 11.3: Total housing costs of households, 2014

	£ billion
Rents paid by tenants, gross (before housing benefit)	61.6
Housing benefit	–21.0
Mortgage repayments	63.5
Rents owner-occupiers would have paid (imputed rent)	158.0
Repairs and maintenance	9.7
Furnishings and equipment, 'alterations and improvements'	33.2
All household expenditure	734.4

Note: Family spending in 2014 grossed up to national figures.

Source: ONS (2015c).

Producer or consumer subsidies?

We have seen that if the private market cannot provide decent homes at an affordable price, the state may step in to subsidise it in some way. The choice is then whether to subsidise the construction and improvement of homes (producer subsidies) or to subsidise the incomes of people who are in need (consumer subsidies). There are also issues about how to spread or control who gains from these subsidies. People may need these subsidies for only some parts of their lives but removing them may not be easy or desirable.

Subsidising construction provides the nation with long-term housing assets and a potential rate of return on these assets. It allows the state more control over who benefits – setting its own need priorities for allocating tenancies – and it allows wider control over the use of public assets. If housing demand falls, surplus land can be sold or used for other purposes. On the other hand, a large stock can be mismanaged, especially if tenants have no choice or no voice. There are, some argue, few monetary incentives for tenants to move when they have gained higher incomes. This can make access for the 'new' poor difficult. It is also a rather inflexible system. Housing need may ebb and flow and new housing takes a long time to build. Private landlords or other providers may respond more quickly, converting older property to new uses. Rent levels may rise in favoured areas, generating surpluses that the government may want to claw back and redistribute. There are tensions between a system of national subsidy and local control of housing assets. Some areas have been left well endowed with council properties for historic reasons – others have not.

Subsidising individuals by topping up their regular income in line with their housing needs is more flexible. It can be reviewed to provide subsidy only when a household's income is low. It can also be applied to all tenants, or, indeed, in theory, all households, not just those able to live in a council house. It can move with the tenant if she gains a job in another town. On the other hand, it can result in raising landlords' income without producing more dwellings. The costs of these subsidies have risen sharply in recent years. There are disincentives to work if such benefits are withdrawn too sharply as household income rises. There may be disincentives to buy a house if these subsidies only apply to tenants.

Some of these problems can be mitigated (eg by limiting the time people can live in dwellings constructed with state help). However, attempts to balance the advantages and disadvantages of these two approaches are at the heart of many disputes about funding housing.

For much of their history, local authorities were paid to construct dwellings. Dwellings built at different times each attracted different subsidies. In England, this complexity was swept away by the Housing Finance Act 1972. Poor tenants received financial help to pay their rent whether they were council or housing association tenants or those of private landlords. The English government chose to subsidise consumers. The 1972 Act did not, for the most part, apply to Scotland. The Scottish government continues to subsidise local councils and other providers through its Affordable Housing Supply Programme.

Another form of consumer subsidy continues to be tax advantages given to owner occupation and private renting. Buy-to-let mortgages have enjoyed tax privileges, which were being reviewed in 2016. However, 1.7 million such mortgages had been taken out in the previous 16 years. Constraints put on new council and housing association building curbed the supply of socially rented accommodation, forcing more low-income people to rent privately. High house prices in some urban centres, especially London, forced would-be new owner-occupiers to rent. This trend was accelerated by social and lifestyle factors, leading more people to seek rented property.

Paying for social housing

Housing associations

The end of mass slum clearance, problems with large housing estates and a new approach to 'area renewal' suggested the need for more and more small-scale providers. Not-for-profit housing associations had existed since the Victorian era but catered for specialist needs. Now, they became a more favoured alternative to large-scale local authority provision. The Labour government set up the Housing Corporation in 1974 to fund housing associations to provide new or refurbished accommodation on a much wider scale.

This approach appealed to later Conservative governments. The Housing Act 1988 allowed local authority tenants to choose to transfer their existing homes to another landlord – either an existing housing association or a new one. Tenants had to be balloted before this took place and many associations used the promise of better housing management and repairs to win votes. Some tenants saw this as 'privatisation', believing that housing should remain a local authority service. However, between 1988 and 2008, 1.3 million council houses were transferred to housing association ownership.

There are now 38 arm's length management organisations (ALMOs) managing over half-a-million council homes across 41 local authorities. These are hybrid organisations created after 2002. Local authorities transfer the management of their housing stock, but not the ownership, to a third-party organisation. This also needs tenant agreement. There must be a board of directors that includes tenant representatives, local authority representatives and independent members.

A separate housing association grant was introduced in 1974 to support not-for-profit housing associations, which was based on an entirely new principle. It involved giving associations a capital sum at the beginning of a new scheme sufficient to reduce the loan repayment to such a point that poorer tenants could pay the rent. The grant was called the Housing Association Grant (HAG) and could initially meet around 80% of the costs.

As it turned out, the approach had a fatal flaw. It assumed that the fair rent fixed at the outset would last for the life of the project or at least that it would only be increased sufficiently to meet rising management and maintenance costs. If fair rents were raised in line with market rents elsewhere in the economy, the association would soon make a surplus and this led to attempts by the central government to recover such surpluses or redirect them.

The arrangements were changed in 1988. Grants were fixed as a proportion of the total cost and private loans were meant to cover the rest. There has subsequently been a steady reduction in the share of capital costs met by the government. It had fallen to less than 15% by 2015. Associations now use their housing assets to underpin their strong credit ratings and secure long-term private loans from European capital markets. Some £5.6 billion was raised in 2014 alone to support the sector's building activities. By 2016, there was a total outstanding housing association debt of £63.4 billion.

A further change in 2011 enabled associations to charge 'affordable rents' set at no more than 80% of the local market rent for new homes. This was much less 'affordable' than the previous generally lower rents that associations had charged. Some associations refused to adopt this regime in high-rent local authority areas where even 60% of the local market rent was more than their traditional tenant base could afford.

In 2013, the government also launched the Affordable Housing Guarantee scheme, which offered housing associations and other registered private providers a government loan guarantee on borrowing for newly built 'affordable' homes for either rent or sale. This looks like being a useful way to leverage more private capital into social housing.

However, the government also restricted the length of tenancies for those no longer deemed 'in need' of a subsidy. Previously, tenants had a 'home for life' and could pass on their tenancy to their partner who had lived in the property prior to the tenant's death. These were, until 1989, 'secure tenancies' similar to those of local authority tenants. Thereafter, they became 'assured tenancies' but normally for an indefinite period. However, the Housing and Town Planning Act 2016 introduced a mandatory limit of five years for any new tenants. That applied to both housing association and local authority tenants. The association or local authority must assess whether the tenant still 'needs' the subsidy. If not, she can be forced to move out to private renting (or conceivably owner occupation). In addition, association tenants will have to pay a higher rent if their income rises above a given level.

Finally, associations were required to consider selling higher-value property when it became vacant – thus reducing the cost of maintaining a high-value stock but thereby reducing the standard of housing that the associations could offer. The aim of all these moves was to create more equivalence between social housing and the private market – weaning tenants away from subsidised, more secure tenancies. This is in contrast to the previous emphasis on using the social housing sector to raise the standards and security of poorer tenants.

Local authorities

Ever since 1935, the mechanism through which local authority housing has been funded and audited has been the 'Housing Revenue Account' (HRA). It was a special ring-fenced local authority account whose format was set by central government. It was designed to contain all the financial consequences of a council's housing activity – the ownership of housing property, the repayment of interest charges and its management and maintenance costs. On the income side of the account, it included rent payments, housing benefit income for its tenants and central government subsidies.

This was initially a simple and intuitively clear mechanism but it became more and more convoluted as the government increasingly interfered. Government help to cover a deficit was only given where the reasons were considered legitimate. The government set what it considered to be appropriate spending levels for maintenance and interest. It set rent guidelines and regularly raised them. This resulted in HRAs moving into surplus and losing subsidy.

However, since many tenants were on housing benefit that paid 100% of the rent, housing benefit spending shot up as a result. There was, however, no rational relationship between the rents local authority tenants paid and those paid by housing association tenants. There were also problems with the way 'surpluses' were treated. Until 2004, an authority whose rental income exceeded expenditure on management and maintenance received a reduced 'rent rebate subsidy'. Those authorities that moved into surplus had their surplus removed and redistributed to other authorities.

Following a review initiated by the Labour government, this complex process was wound up by the Coalition government in England. Since 2012, council housing has become self-funding. A one-off financial settlement was made that was intended to allow each English local authority to develop its own 30-year business plan for its housing stock.

Since 136 authorities still had outstanding debt on their housing activities, this was distributed in a way that reduced debts to a level where each council was deemed able to manage its debt without needing central government help. Central government set an overall (and controversial) local authority housing debt cap. Any money raised from the sale of council houses was to be split between central government and the authority (initially 75/25 but then 70/30). An estimate by the House of Commons Library in 2015 suggested that this settlement left 85% of authorities with room to incur more housing debt.

Welsh authorities left the HRA subsidy system in 2015. The HRA remains for those authorities with housing stock but they keep all the revenue they raise from rents and housing benefit. Following a review by the Welsh government, a common policy for rents across all social housing providers (with more than 100 dwellings) was introduced in 2014 and 2015 (see 'Policy for social housing rents', available at: www.cymru.gov.uk). A target rent band is set that gives indicative rent levels for each size and type of social-rented dwelling across Wales. These vary by the location and quality of the dwelling. They are adjusted – 'uplifted' – annually.

Scotland retains a capital grant subsidy system. A capital grant is made for dwellings approved under the Affordable Housing Supply Programme. It applies to all affordable housing providers. The capital sums vary by type of provider, whether the dwellings conform to environmentally friendly 'green' standards and whether the rents are at social rent levels or at 'mid-market' rents (see the 2015 Subsidy Working Group, available at: www.gov.scot).

The right to buy

In 1980, local authority and some other 'secure' tenants of non-charitable housing associations were given the right to buy the dwelling in which they were living if they had been there for two years. This limit was increased to five years in 2005. The longer they had been living there, the lower the price tenants had to pay. Following an initial surge in applications, sales tailed off.

In 2012, the Coalition increased the maximum discount to £75,000, and in 2013, to £100,000 in London, as well as increasing the size of the discount on the value of the house from 60% to 70%. At the same time, a promise was made to replace sales one for one with new social housing homes. Figures for 2015 suggest that one in 10 was what was actually achieved (Gallagher, 2015).

Housing association tenants were given restricted rights to buy on less generous terms from 1996, but in 2015, the housing association movement, under government pressure, entered into an agreement with the government to extend the right to buy to more tenants. Associations were to retain a right to veto and a right to replace homes in most cases.

The Scottish government plans to end the right to buy for all council and housing association tenants. In Northern Ireland, it is possible to buy between 50% and 80% of a property and increase the share over time. A householder pays rent on the part that they do not own. This is called co-ownership.

First-time buyers

The government has begun to creep back into subsidising owner occupation. Pressed by the growing discontent of those unable to get onto the home-owning ladder, the government have introduced a scheme that is supposed to help. Loans are available to those who have a 5% deposit on the value of their first owner-occupied dwelling, though the purchase price must be no more than £600,000. Someone can borrow 20% of the purchase price interest-free for the first five years. There is a limit of borrowing up to 20% of the purchase price – 40% in London.

Section 106 agreements and the Community Infrastructure Levy

Introduced in the Town and Country Planning Act 1990, Section 106 agreements have been of growing importance. Planning authorities can make planning permission conditional on an agreement with the developer to include various amenities and this can include a proportion of affordable housing. It can involve making over a part of the site to a housing association or can include a cash payment. Between 2003/04 and 2007/08, about £2.5 billion a year was contributed to affordable housing as part of these agreements. Almost 60,000 units were provided through this route in 2014/15, according to a freedom of information request (R. Larkin, 20 August 2015, from the Department for Communities and Local Government [DCLG]). This route was supplemented by the Community Infrastructure Levy in 2012. This provides for a tariff to be paid by developers for most new building projects and spent within the local authority area, not restricted to the neighbourhood of the development. Section 106 obligations run in parallel but are restricted to directly mitigate the impact of the proposal.

Housing benefit and the bedroom tax

The amount of benefit is determined by an income test – the household's financial needs after rent. Deductions are made for 'non-dependants' living in the house, who are expected to contribute to the rent. Since 2013, there have also been reductions for any social housing bedrooms deemed 'spare' in relation to the number of people living in the dwelling. This was officially called 'the removal of the spare room subsidy'. It became popularly known as the 'bedroom tax'. Although it mirrored similar restrictions on the eligible rooms rented in the private sector, it lacked the flexibility for social housing tenants to downsize in order to avoid the 'tax'. Tenants who had legitimate need for an extra bedroom – the equipment or space for a disabled member of the family, for example – were often not recognised and hence penalised.

A number of changes have been introduced from 2008 aimed at controlling the scale of the housing benefit budget. The first was a 'Local Housing Allowance', which capped the amount of housing benefit paid in the private sector to the local median (middle) rent in the private sector in that area. It was intended to curb the exploitation of the benefit system. That limit was reduced by successive governments. By 2013, it had been reduced to the 30th percentile of local rents – the bottom third. These rent limits were then raised in line with the consumer price index – less than the retail price index and less than the rise in rents in many areas. This meant that a progressively smaller part of the private sector market would be subsidised.

The Housing White Paper (Cm 9352, DCLG, 2017) concluded that the housing market, especially for owner occupation, was 'broken'. It saw the main culprit as the planning system which restricted development or slowed it down unnecessarily. Government would encourage local authorities to foster development, raise housing densities and, if necessary, release land in the green belt. Money would be put into an infrastructure fund to make new sites available.

Rents in social housing had, until 2015, been considered to be fixed at reasonable rent levels since they were subject to government rules about 'excessive' spending. As from 2018, rents for social housing tenancies that began after 2016 will be subject to the same rules as the private sector. This will further restrict benefit spending and particularly affect social housing tenants in higher-rent and higher-quality homes.

Housing plus

Those who find their way into social housing may often have social needs far beyond 'shelter'. Many housing associations pioneered community care solutions when large hospitals for long-term mental illness and 'handicap' were closed in the 1960s and 1970s. They often draw upon a charitable heritage that leads them into community development and supporting their tenants to address social, economic and personal problems. This approach is sometimes called 'housing plus'. It involves providing job clubs, day care centres, youth services, community space for older people and other community facilities and events.

The finance of housing in other countries

All advanced economies have invented ways to assist those unable to afford decent shelter for the same reasons as the UK. However, in Europe, the agencies that have evolved have been private, mostly not-for-profit, organisations supported in some way by the state.

Germany deliberately tried to avoid what were seen as Britain's housing failures but drew on the cooperative housing models that came from Britain. These were given a legal framework with limits to the scale of dividends that they could distribute. These grew in scale during the interwar period. Afterwards, a huge housing programme was carried through, largely engineered by tax policy, not direct subsidies (Power, 1993).

Private landlords could write off the capital costs of new building against tax over eight years. They could do the same with the current costs of maintaining and managing the property. This encouraged both high levels of building and high standards of maintenance. Social housing landlords received a subsidy from the government in the form of low-interest loans and, in return, had to accept nominated tenants in housing need.

The government also encouraged owner occupation from the mid-1950s through a series of low-interest loans and guarantees. Tax incentives encouraged owner-occupiers to build a house with a rental flat attached or forming one floor of the building. This both reduced the costs to the owner and widened the rental market for new couples, students or single people. Local authorities are funded by Lander governments to subsidise social landlords.

As rents were increasingly freed from controls, a system of means-tested housing allowances was introduced in the 1960s. Despite the diversity of provision and the high standard of much German housing, it has not escaped the problem of estates becoming the refuge of the most disadvantaged and of immigrants.

France developed a pattern that shared some of the same characteristics. The French state never saw its role as including the provision of housing. Some liberal employers took an early lead in providing 'model' housing communities – as happened in the UK too. However, the decisive move came in 1912 with a law gave local municipalities and 'departments' the power to create arm's-length housing organisations to provide low-cost housing with state subsidies. Little use was made of these powers initially, but with the growth of shanty towns around some of the country's large cities, the French state began to use this mechanism to begin a large building programme that outdid many of the UK's errors of the 1960s.

These *habitations à loyer modéré* (HLMs) have become the main vehicles for French social housing. They receive separate streams of funding to meet the costs of renovating old property, grants, subsidised loans and rental income. Representatives of the nation-state, local employers and communities have the right to nominate families for tenancies. Owner-occupiers were encouraged by making the housing allowance available to them as well as tenants. The government also subsidised low-cost homes for sale.

In *Scandinavia*, housing similarly relies heavily on social housing companies sponsored by local authorities. Tenants' capacity to pay rent is supported by a system of housing allowances.

The US has never had a significant public or social housing sector, while, at the same time, giving massive tax support to owner-occupiers. As it once did in the UK, this goes disproportionately to higher-income groups. A small scheme of housing vouchers, not that different from housing benefit in the UK, was introduced during the Clinton administration.

The relaxation of rules governing mortgage lending in the 1990s, plus abundant credit in later years, led to those with low, or minimal, incomes being sold mortgages that they could not repay – 'sub-prime' loans. There could be no clearer evidence of the limits to viable owner occupation.

Overview

In short, the state's role in the housing market has changed profoundly over the past century. It moved from merely setting minimum housing standards to becoming a major provider of housing for the working class by the 1960s. It then retreated from this role. Council house tenants were given the right to buy their house under certain conditions. Housing associations took over much of local authorities' previous functions, especially in England. Local authority homes are more numerous in Scotland and Northern Ireland.

Their management has frequently been hived off to separate organisations. Major funding issues now face housing:

- England has greatly reduced the scale of funding for new social housing construction.
- Taken together with some unhelpful planning restrictions, this is causing a crisis in housing supply.
- The state gave important mortgage tax advantages to owner occupation from the 1960s and then withdrew them. Owner occupation retains tax advantages in relation to capital gains tax.
- This leads to it being treated as a privileged savings vehicle, thus increasing the cost of housing. The government has stepped in to provide some financial support to first-time buyers. This may merely boost the price of housing further.
- Other countries show how a more varied pattern of housing finance can work.

Questions for discussion

1. What have been the state's most important interventions in the housing market since 1914 and what have been the consequences?
2. Why did the state shift from subsidising producers of housing to subsidising consumers? What has been the effect?
3. How does the UK's system of housing finance vary within the UK and between it and other countries?
4. What changes would you make to the housing benefit system?

Further reading

For a review of the history of the state's role in housing in the UK, see **Merrett (1979)**, and for Europe, see **Power (1993)**.

For a view of the way forward for funding social housing, see **Williams and Whitehead (2015)**.

For an account of the way in which housing wealth has accumulated for some, but not others, read **Bastagli and Hills et al (2013, ch 4)**.

For a comparison of housing finance and provision internationally, see **Fahey and Norris (2013)**.

Part Three
The future

twelve

The future

Summary

I began this book by arguing that the costs of sustaining our well-being as individuals and families take a large share of our incomes, whether we do so through the public purse or otherwise. Indeed, because there are failures in the private insurance and health markets, private costs are larger than public ones, and, in some cases, private insurance markets do not work at all. All advanced economies, and many industrialising countries too, are now facing big demographic transitions. In the UK, we are experiencing not just a steady rise in the age to which we live, but a bulge in the numbers of older people that is an inevitable consequence of the baby boom that followed the Second World War.

We have all been reluctant to fully face up to this phenomenon. The UK, along with other advanced economies in Europe, has not been prepared to tax its population sufficiently to finance its existing social policy goals:

- There are two possible responses to this problem:
    - Reduce the scope of social policy and the role of the state, thus transferring responsibility for funding such services back to the individual household purse.
    - Persuade the electorate to increase the scale of taxes most people pay. For this to be possible, the tax system has to be seen to be fair and the extra taxes securely tied to improved services.

- The need to persuade the population to pay more taxes was made more difficult by the consequences of leaving the European Union (EU). A period of economic uncertainty was not conducive to raising higher taxes. That does not make the central problem go away. The alternative is to require households to shoulder more of the costs of welfare themselves and restrict their other purchases and lifestyles.
- A feasible set of measures could be taken to increase government revenue in the medium term, however.

A long-run reluctance to pay

It is time to draw together the major themes of this book. I began by defining welfare in its traditional English sense of 'remaining in good health and sufficiency' throughout a lifetime. Yet, life brings risks. Most of us will pass through periods of sickness and old age, many through periods of joblessness, and some through long periods of disability. All of us will be dependent on parents or partners for part of our lives, and we shall need to invest in some kind of training or advanced education not just early in our lives, but increasingly throughout them.

It might be possible, if we are lucky, to survive such adversity by insuring ourselves during our working lives, or it might be possible to borrow to meet temporary needs. However, both are expensive. The costs fall heavily on families during periods when they are also trying to bring up children. Moreover, private insurance and capital markets do not work well for these purposes, if at all in some cases.

As a consequence, virtually all modern advanced economies have evolved ways to spread the costs of meeting these risks over lifetimes and across income groups. I have described how they do so in this book. The costs have increased as populations have come to live longer and taken longer to be fully educated and trained. Families have come to demand higher standards of care for themselves and their older parents.

The state has therefore been drawn into meeting such needs on an increasing scale. This is true in all modern economies. As we saw in Chapter One, in 1950, the UK devoted about 10% of its gross domestic product (GDP) to collective social welfare provision. By 2010, this reached 30% at the peak of the economic crisis. This share has fallen back to just over a quarter in 2016 but is still a significant share of the population's income, and it is set to increase as the share of the population over 65 rises sharply during the next two decades.

The share of total national income paid in taxation has been relatively stable for nearly a quarter of a century. The pressure on families to consume new products and services is powerful and unrelenting. So, electorates' reluctance to permit governments to take more of their incomes in taxation is understandable. Social services have managed to survive reasonably well only because governments have reduced the relative scale of spending on *other* items. First came reductions in the share taken by defence expenditure. Then came transport, road building and the police, though house building also took a big hit, as we have seen.

In 1951, just after the welfare state in its modern form was founded, the social services discussed in this book absorbed just over a quarter (27%) of all state spending. Now, that figure is two thirds. This rising share cannot continue indefinitely for purely arithmetical reasons. The country would have to give up its armed forces, its roads and railways, or abandon any attempt to counteract global warming. The trick we have pulled off over the past three decades will not work anymore. Moreover, in the aftermath of the banking crisis, the expected total public debt has risen from a figure equivalent to 40% of GDP to nearly 90% by 2020. Any government will aim to reduce that share and relieve the Exchequer of the interest burden that will be involved in normal times.

The question therefore remains – will modern capitalist societies 'be able to do what is required for the future viability of their increasingly unstable, fragile and disorganised societies' (Streeck and Mertens, 2013)? That question has increasing salience in the aftermath of the UK's decision to leave the EU and the threat that we may have to pay more for our own defence, relying less on the US. We must also come to terms with the costs of climate change and the need to reduce our national debt. The answer to Streeck and Mertens' question addressed to the UK therefore looked distinctly uncertain at the point of writing this book at the end of 2016. The one certain feature of our future is that we are experiencing a major change in the age structure of our population.

Demography

Ageing

The consequences of an 'ageing population' are considerable and wide ranging, as we have seen throughout this book. It has implications for virtually every aspect of public policy, as a House of Lords cross-party committee forcefully concluded (House of Lords, 2013). That report was followed by an independent assessment by the Government Office for Science (2016) that is well worth reading, for it sets out not just the figures, but the implications of them, for a wide range of policy areas:

- In 2016, those aged 65 and over constituted 18% of the UK population. By 2025, they will make up 20%, and by 2035, nearly 24%.
- By 2025, there will be 18% more people over the age of 65, and by 2035, 29% more.

- In 2016, less than 5% of the population were over 80. By 2025, that will be nearly 6%, and by 2035, nearly 8%.
- Over 70% of the UK population growth between 2014 and 2039 will be in the age group over 60. Those numbers will rise from 14.9 to 21.9 million people.

These changes are occurring for two quite different reasons – one long-term the other more temporary. First, people are living longer; second, we are experiencing the consequences of a significant change in the shape of our population after the Second World War. There was first a sharp rise in births for two decades and then a fall. Those born in the post-war 'bulge' are now retiring and reaching the ages at which service demands rise. However, the size of the population now at work and born in the later decades fell. There are fewer British-born workers and more old people to look after. This 'post-war effect' will sharpen the longer-term ageing trend in the next 30 years. This impact would have been significantly worse without the rise in working-age immigration that has occurred, whatever other impacts it may have had.

As Chapter Five showed, the state pension age has been raised and may rise further. The number of people over the current state pension age, for every thousand people of working age, will *fall* from 310 in 2014 to 284 in 2020 as a result of recent changes made to that age. The numbers per thousand population over pension age would then rise again to 370 in 2039. That age is under regular review. In October 2016, the then current review team published its interim report (Independent Review of the State Pension Age, 2016). The full report is expected in 2017.

Demography is not the only factor at work here, though. As we saw in Chapter Six, state pension recipients have been treated relatively generously compared to those of working age receiving benefits. The 'triple lock' has meant that pensioners have received a guaranteed rise in their state pension. Those of working age have had their benefits capped, resulting in a real decline in their benefit payments. This reinforces the impact of 'ageing' on the public purse. What the response should be is already dividing opinion – end the triple lock or change policy on working-age benefits, or both.

That structure varies considerably between parts of the UK. Giving evidence to the House of Lords Committee on Demographic Change (House of Lords, 2013), the permanent secretary of the Welsh government commented:

> The impact of demographic change will have particular significance for Wales, which has the highest concentration of older people within the UK nations … [the proportion reaching 85] has doubled since 1983 and will double again by 2033 … some 5 per cent of the total population. [In the UK as a whole, the figure is projected to be 3.2%.] (House of Lords, 2013, p 19, fn 25)

None of this should lead us to overlook the positive features of ageing. Older people are making a large contribution to caring, unpaid work and being around for their grandchildren, as I hope my wife and I have shown! Older people do more caring for each other and their grandchildren than they did precisely because they are healthy and more active. There has been a delay in the onset of disability. If the decreasing trends in disability continue, the increase in numbers suffering from long-standing illness could fall by 2050 despite a continuation of ageing (see evidence by Professor Rees to the House of Lords Committee; House of Lords, 2013, p 22). People are extending their working lives and will be healthier as a result. However, adapting to this new population structure has financial consequences for all of us.

More children too

Relatively forgotten in this debate is the fact that more children are being born each year. Happily for the long term, the UK, and especially the English, birth rate has been rising, unlike some other European countries. In 2001, the number of births was 670,000. This number continued to rise steadily so that by 2012, it had risen to 813,000, the highest figure for 40 years. There has been a slight fall since but the number of children entering school and needing day care is of a different order from the recent past. A quarter of those born were to mothers not themselves born in the UK.

Net migration

Another change to our population has been increased immigration. This was partly a deliberate decision by the Labour government in the early years of this century to keep the UK open to workers from the new EU member countries precisely because the UK's labour force was declining. Partly as a result, the UK is projected to have the fourth-fastest growth in its population of any country within the EU. Not only was there an unprecedented rise in net inward migration, but newcomers had a higher fertility rate.

In 1992, there was effectively *no* net inward migration – the numbers leaving the UK roughly matched the numbers coming in. By 2015, this figure had reached 323,000. More immigrants are of working age and contribute more not just financially, but in terms of the jobs they do, not least in the social services and health care. However, more children need more school places, and more people, whatever their age, will need more hospital places and more GPs. That would be just as true if the children were born of native–born English!

Resource implications

The Office of Budget Responsibility (OBR) regularly makes estimates of how much the country needs to spend simply to sustain existing service standards given the changing age structure of the population. In the past, this analysis has provided a useful marker. However, the OBR has to take as given government spending targets for the period 2015–20. That has involved assuming a reduction in the share of GDP devoted to the National Health Service (NHS), for example. Given what we know of the NHS's current financial difficulties, its spending base for 2020 looks unrealistic. As explained in Chapter Six the OBR re-assessed the long-run rising cost of health care in 2016, and their 2017 projections conclude that on existing policies (OBR, 2017):

- state health care expenditure would rise from 6.9% of GDP in 2020/21 to 9.1% in 2036/37 and 12.6% in 2066/67. This is their central projection. Their 'higher cost pressure' alternative reaches 15% in 2066;
- long-term care costs rise from 1.1% in 2020/21 to 1.6% in 2036/37 and 2.0% in 2066. Here the cost pressures that arise from a rising living wage are left out;
- the share taken by education remains relatively stable despite a higher birth rate because much of higher education has been counted as private expenditure – a 'financial transaction with students'. Yet the government debt that that implies rises to 11% of GDP by the 2030s;
- the cost of state pensions rises from 5.0% in 2020/21 to 6.2% in 2036/37 and to 7.7% in 2066.

Age-related spending on its own thus rises from 19.8% of GDP in 2021/22 to 23% in 2036 and 28% in 2066.

Costs of reducing child poverty to Scandinavian levels or having free long-term care or improved early years education are all goals that would cost substantially more. The King's Fund estimated that the NHS and long-term care services combined will need between 11% and 12% of GDP by 2025. It looks as if the combined spending on these services will not be much more than 8% by that point. This suggests that to meet population ageing and to remedy glaring quality deficiencies, the two services will require *3% more* of GDP over the next decade.

Given the squeeze on real per pupil spending discussed in Chapter Nine, the schools budget will need to increase to cope with a rising school population in the next few years. Any attempt to freeze or reduce the university fee levels, let alone abolish them, would cost a great deal more. The costs of meeting the non-repayment of fees by ex-students will soon start to add to the public finances. There has been serious underspending on social housing, which the government is now beginning to address.

In short, it is impossible to avoid the conclusion that the electorate will soon have to face a choice – keep the kind of services you have been used to and agree to pay more in taxation, or keep taxes as they are and prepare to pay a good deal more in private school fees and private health insurance, and be prepared to devote the capital value of your house to your care in old age. Do any of the political parties properly address this choice?

Alternative futures

A likely Conservative future

A pure neoliberal future of the kind outlined in Chapter One of this book sees no role for the state in providing social welfare apart from a low citizen's income, with citizens then being told to fend for themselves. This looks an unlikely scenario, at least for now, for all the reasons discussed in the first two chapters of this book.

During the past decade, however, mainstream Conservative opinion has evolved a more moderate strategy. It contains, but keeps, the state's role in some areas and sharply reduces it in others. It diversifies the modes of state intervention. It nudges individuals to save for their own retirement. It requires people to spend money on private sector pensions or nudges them heavily to do so. It shifts more of the financial burden onto employers, requiring them to pay higher wages or contribute to retirement plans. This approach may be extended to long-term care and even health care. This is hidden taxation rather than less taxation but it may be more politically acceptable.

The more detailed strategy may be summarised as follows:

- *Core universal services 'protected' but gradually privatised.* Funding for schools and health care remain a *national* (ie Westminster-based) responsibility. This trend has been gradual but effective. In 1979/80, the share of 'welfare activity', as defined in this book, that was financed *and* provided by the state formed about 58% of the total. By 2013/14, it had fallen to 44% (Burchardt and Obolenskaya, 2016). Gradually, responsibility for the delivery of services has been hived off to separate non-state institutions. A mix of not-for-profit and private for-profit hospitals will grow. Education 'chains' or private organisations provide schools with common services, not local authorities. Schools responsible to independent governing bodies may come to have no political or parental representatives. The actual sums made available to these institutions will be set by central government and squeezed in real terms, gradually reducing their share of GDP as GDP grows. Parents will increasingly be called upon to make up the difference or migrate to the private sector perhaps encouraged with a subsidy to the school set at the level of that state school grant.

- *Private finance of welfare grows.* As families' ambitions for their children keep rising, so local schools are unable to keep pace and meet these aspirations. The same holds for other services. This process may be gradual but profound. In 1979/80, private funding of private welfare provision stood at £54 billion in 2014/15 prices. In 2013/14, it stood at £260 billion – a near fivefold increase. In the same period, public funding of publicly provided serves rather more than doubled, from £118 billion to £276 billion (Burchardt and Obolenskaya, 2016).
- *Higher education ceases to be funded out of general taxation.* Students now pay deferred fees collected through the income tax system – a capped 'graduate tax'. This was introduced during the Blair administration in 2006 but has been substantially extended since.
- *Funding and providing for long-term care in old age becomes an individual responsibility.* The state will meet the costs of those who are poor and have no, or few, assets but the bulk of the population will be required to plan and fund their long-term care themselves. Local authority support for families is already confined to extreme cases. The state will only step in to meet long-term care costs when they become 'catastrophic'. The *provision* of long-term care and most other services for elderly and disabled people has been mostly handed over to the private sector from the 1980s onwards.
- *The state's responsibility for pensions will be confined to providing a flat-rate pension set just above the poverty line.* Responsibility for 'income smoothing' between work and retirement has passed to the individual. People will be 'nudged' or encouraged to participate in employer-based pension schemes with some tax advantages and automatic enrolment from which they can exit. In practice, perhaps a third of pensioners will not get a pension above the 'poverty line', at least for a long time.
- *The age at which people will be able to draw such a pension will rise in line with life expectancy.* This implies raising the pension age from what was 65 to 68 – already in train – and then to 69 and 70 if present trends continue.
- *Cash benefits for the working-age poor will be cut* – especially tax credits that supplement low wages. Employers will be required to increase their minimum wages.
- *Benefit sanctions are more vigorously applied where recipients fail to meet work-search conditions.* As a result, a small but growing number of people have no legal right to the social safety net.
- *The scale of public and state-supported not-for-profit housing has been massively reduced and will remain small despite more funding announced in 2016.* In 1980, capital spending on new social housing amounted to 2.4% of GDP. By 2015, it amounted to only 0.3%. This was to be increased following the 2016 Autumn Statement but not by very much – enough to finance 40,000 new affordable housing starts by 2020. Public subsidies to private landlords have risen, though, from 0.6% of GDP to 1.5%.

It is possible to disagree with some or all of these goals but they do represent a coherent long-term strategy to reduce the state's direct spending role. It shifts the emphasis to the state pressing others to pay for its policies. This raises some fundamental questions of accountability. Are hidden taxes and nudges a good way to deliver?

There are some major practical difficulties too. The Osborne family example in Chapter One showed that even for a reasonably well-off family, these can be expensive options. For a poorer family, the costs are very serious. Costs will fall on employers. There are severe limits on the extent to which this can be done without having an impact on employment. It will also affect the costs of public sector employers or those who provide the state with services, not least long-term care. Employers' pension schemes are already a major worry. Unfunded deficits in company pension schemes for 2016 amounted to £937 billion (Somerset Webb, 2016). In short, shifting the cost burden onto employers and families has its limits every bit as much as taxation.

A different feasible future

The UK has been devoting at least 40% of its GDP to public purposes for many years. The government are proposing to reduce that share by 2% by 2020. However, as I have shown already, some authoritative work suggests that the NHS and long-term care will need to take an *additional* 2–3% of GDP in the next decade. To aim for a public spending share within a decade that was nearer to that in Germany or Sweden (44% or so) would not be *economically* impossible. These are not economic basket cases after all.

There are some expenditure savings and productivity gains that can be made – doing things better. Moreover, the government could reduce the generosity that it is showing to older people – ceasing to raise pensions faster than working-age benefits (the triple lock), for example. It could abolish benefits given to older people regardless of financial need – from free fares to free TV licenses. However, it cannot forever go on reducing working age benefits compared to the general standard of living.

The government could improve the productivity of health and care providers. There are better ways to organise local health and care services. It could continue to raise pension ages. It could continue to encourage a higher level of labour market participation. However, this is already high compared both to the past and to many other countries. In short, it could build on some of the more sensible measures already taken to adapt state social welfare provision to the new demographic reality. None of this will be enough, though. The UK, and above all its devolved parliaments, have to come to grips with the need to raise the total level of taxation if it wants a different future to the one outlined earlier. That is the case that non–Conservative parties have to make and show how they can do it. Muttering incantations about 'anti-austerity' will not suffice. That is especially true for devolved administrations who aspire to provide the standard of services now found in Scandinavian countries. That requires Scandinavian levels of tax.

Fair taxation

No significant increase in tax revenue is possible unless the whole tax system is seen to be 'fair'. Fairness can mean many different things but a tax regime that takes away the same or even a higher share of poor people's income than that taken from higher-income groups, which I described in Chapter Three, must surely count as 'unfair':

- In the tax year ending in 2015, the total of direct taxes – income, council tax and social security contributions – reduced the disposable income of the poorest fifth of households by just over 10%. The richest fifth paid 23% of their incomes in such taxes. However, the poorest fifth paid about 30% of their disposable income in *indirect* taxes – VAT, taxes on alcohol, tobacco and fuel, for example. The richest fifth paid only 15% of their disposable incomes in that way. It is hardly surprising that poor families are resistant to more taxation. Any recasting of the tax structure would have to rebalance the direct and indirect burden and the type of indirect taxes charged.
- The combined top marginal tax rates for income and social security taken together are over 50%. Work on taxpayer responses to such marginal rates suggests that there is not much room to raise that rate and gain substantial revenue, as explained in Chapter Three. However, it will be difficult to raise the taxes for the average person without asking more of those at the top of the income chain. This could be done by charging social security contributions all the way through the income range, with no age ceiling. Merging social security and income tax could have the same effect. A marginal rate tax of 50% or more might make sense in that context.
- Chapter Three examined the scale of tax reliefs. They disproportionately benefit the highest-income groups. Their total cost recently amounted to over £300 billion. A major strand of tax reform has to be a root-and-branch cull of tax reliefs, including tax relief on pension contributions. This was once envisaged by Chancellor Osborne and then abandoned. In contrast, recent changes to pension tax law have increased the ways to avoid inheritance tax.
- A major weakness of the present tax system is its failure to tax wealth effectively. It is minimally taxed and at a rate far lower than in the 1940s. A range of possibilities exist to tax wealth (Hills and Glennerster, 2013):
  - Roughly half of all wealth takes the form of land or property ownership. A site-value tax – a percentage tax on the value of all sites – would reap

for the community some of the benefits that private individuals now gain from public transport developments, good schools and other public activity.

- Council tax is levied on property values 30 years out of date, during which time house prices have risen massively, especially in some areas. At the very least, extra top bands could be added and the values updated.
- *Recipients* of wealth gained from inheritance or otherwise could be taxed – as Atkinson (2015) has advocated.
- A global tax on wealth (Picketty, 2013) may be further away but should not be dismissed as a goal. Cooperation between countries to track and tax wealth and tax havens would have to be developed. A tax on capital transfers again needs international agreement to work effectively. High stamp duty is a poor alternative.
- Just as there are public goods, there are also public 'bads'. The tax system can be used to deter actions that harm the public good and harm individual health and well-being. Environmental taxes can serve a double purpose.

In short, there is no lack of a menu for possible tax reform.

Taxation and trust

The need to raise more revenue coincides with an unprecedented loss of trust in politicians. There are four ways in which this might be restored, in part:

- If voters see leading figures or firms getting away with cheating the tax authorities, it undermines their readiness to vote for the taxes they have to pay. A major boost to the Inland Revenue's capacity to chase tax avoidance is a necessary building block for regaining trust.
- The UK has the most centralised tax system of any major economy. It is not surprising that voters find it difficult to link taxes paid to local service benefits. Taxing powers are now being devolved to some parts of the nation but on nothing like the scale needed. Local taxation needs a thorough overhaul. Council tax is both outdated and regressive. A dwelling service charge could replace it. A local income tax is now technically feasible. Regular revaluations are also feasible using national computerised information on property values.
- Although there are good grounds for not charging separate tax rates for each public service, a new specific tax to fund health and long-term care for elderly people can be justified. The present separate funding mechanisms for each service are damaging in their effects. They perpetuate and reinforce separate services for what should be a highly integrated single service. Such a response should include specialist housing and housing adaptation, as well as carer support. Other countries have introduced a distinct tax to fund such activities. The UK faces a rapid increase in the need for specialist integrated

care for exceptional demographic reasons that people can understand. If they are convinced that any extra taxes they pay will go to solve this problem, they might well agree to such a charge:

- A tax could take various forms. It could be an addition to the social security contribution paid across the whole of an individual's income, not just up to the present limit. It could be an addition to income tax. It could be paid by adults of all ages, that is, including in retirement. It could be paid only on reaching the age of 40 or 45, when family costs are reduced and when it begins to dawn on people that they may need looking after at some point.
- The revenue would have to go into a separate visible pot. The way it is spent each year would be published and monitored by the National Audit Office.
- It could be allocated only to those bodies that had devised an acceptably integrated pattern of care for older people – integrating geriatric, long-term health and social care with good support to those living at home, as well as in residential and nursing home care. People should be able to die at home if they so wish. An 'integrated care authority' would have to produce an annual report. Such is the high-profile nature of these services that such revenue would not be 'stolen' for other purposes as it is sometimes claimed that it would be – the example of the vehicle licence tax is often quoted.

• The basic idea of a graduate tax (partial fees repaid through the tax system) is a good example of the way in which electorates can be convinced to pay more tax if they know it is going to a purpose of which they approve and from which they benefit. The case for this approach was argued in Chapter Ten. It is therefore particularly irritating that this 'tax' has been so badly handled since 2010. There is a public benefit to be gained from all good graduate education and all graduate courses should receive some public support if they are of proven quality. However, such support should not be confined to university education. Further education and training, not just for apprentices, needs some form of comparable funding. The levy on employers to fund training is justified and could be extended.

Indirect taxation

We have seen how regressive much indirect taxation can be. On the other hand, it has the virtue of being difficult to avoid. The Scandinavian countries, despite their more egalitarian stance, do levy higher levels of VAT than the UK. This helps to fund more generous welfare and care systems. The 'emergency' rise in VAT after the banking crisis has stuck. A further rise over a decade would bring the UK more in line with Scandinavian levels. Announcing a first step, delayed for a year, might stimulate spending in the short term.

Taxing 'bads'

There are strong grounds for taxing activities that impose costs on the wider population – pollution, congestion, air travel, fatty foods, sugar consumption and excessive salt or alcohol, for example. Some taxes may pose difficulties where they fall excessively on poor families. However, it is possible to counter such effects.

Charging

A frequently mentioned 'solution' for funding the NHS is to introduce charging. Opinion and evidence differs on precisely how far charging might deter people from going to see their GP, or delay doing so, which is discussed in Chapter Seven. However, the political reality is that it would be very difficult to justify large charges that fell largely on the old or long-term sick. In practice, most charges would be excused in such cases on political grounds. Prescription charges only apply in less than 20% of cases and they are much lower than charges contemplated for attending the GP or for hospital care. The administrative costs would be high and disrupting to a local surgery that has enough to do without introducing a charging regime at the front desk. 'Hotel' charges for hospital care fall into the same category. Few stay long in hospital now and those who do are mostly poor or old.

Charging for long-term care will no doubt continue, especially for the housing element in the costs, and it should do so. A contribution could be made to long-term nursing care too. That could be paid for by residents drawing on their housing capital. However, for the most part, charging is likely to be no more than a token answer to raising revenue.

Social investment

This all needs to go alongside more social investment to increase the capacity and efficiency of the wider economy, as we argued in Chapter One.

Politics

The eventual mix of these strategies are a political matter. However, there is a straight choice with which to face the electorate. Pay some more to sustain and improve the quality of your schools and your health and long-term care over your longer lifetime, or run much greater financial risks or pay more out of your own pocket in private insurance to mitigate those risks. This really is a political choice.

Overview

In conclusion, we have argued that the UK has largely sought to pay for its social policies in the recent past by reducing spending on other things. This approach is no longer feasible. Recent governments in Westminster have evolved a strategy that has involved reducing the state's role, especially in providing less social housing and reducing support for families of working age. It has failed to increase funding for the NHS or long-term care in line with rising demands and demographic change. This ultimately leaves families to face more of the risks that life brings from their own resources.

The alternative is to increase the level of overall taxation. This requires people to feel that the overall burden is fairly distributed. That involves:

- reducing the scale of tax evasion;
- culling the extent of tax reliefs that mainly benefit higher-income groups;
- raising the top rate of tax sufficiently to make people feel that the rich are paying their fair share;
- taxing wealth more effectively in a variety of ways;
- giving local authorities greater taxing powers over site values and income; and
- improving the efficiency with which services are delivered.

However, none of this will be enough:

- A new specific tax or the adaptation of National Insurance Contributions to fund health and long-term care for older people is needed.
- Such revenue should be explicitly tied to integrated health and care services for older people and its success reviewed bi-annually to see that the funds are being used to provide effectively integrated services.
- Higher VAT and a higher standard rate of tax may both be needed over the next decade – possibly at 22% for both.
- The more successful governments are with items in the previous list of options, the lower such rates can be.

Questions for discussion

1. What general conclusions do you draw from your reading of this book? What would your spending priorities be and how would you finance them?
2. Appraise the right-of-centre response. How does it compare to other possible and actual responses?
3. How far can these dilemmas be met by an 'anti-austerity programme'?
4. Draw up your own priorities for tax reform.

Further reading

The more general long-term case that Western welfare states have not been able to fund their promises is made in **Streeck and Mertens (2013)**.

For a more positive view read **Gamble (2016)**.

For a critical account of recent tax policy from a social policy perspective, see **Ruane and Byrne (2014)**.

For the best economically informed summary of tax reform, see the last chapter of the **Mirrlees Review (2011)**.

References

Acemoglu, D. and Robinson, J.A. (2006) *Economic dictatorships and democracy*, Cambridge: Cambridge University Press.

Accounts Commission (2014) *School education*, Edinburgh: Audit Scotland.

Adema, W., Fron, P. and Ladaique, M. (2011) *Is the European welfare state really more expensive? Indicators on Social spending, 1980–2012*, OECD Social, Employment and Migration Working Paper No 124, Paris: OECD.

Akerlof, G.A. (1970) 'The market for "lemons": qualitative uncertainty and the market mechanism', *Quarterly Journal of Economics*, vol 84, pp 488–500.

Alcock, P. (2013) 'A new role for the third sector', in S. Griffiths, H. Kippin and G. Stoker (eds) *Public services: A new reform agenda*, London: Bloomsbury.

Alcock, P., Glennerster, H., Oakley, A. and Sinfield, A. (eds) (2001) *Welfare and wellbeing: Richard Titmuss' contribution to social policy*, Bristol: The Policy Press.

Alcock, P., Haux, T., May, M. and Wright, S. (eds) (2016) *The students' companion to social policy*, Oxford: Wiley Blackwell.

Arrow, K. (1951) *Social choice and individual values*, New York, NY: Willey.

Atkinson, A.B. (1999) *The economic consequences of rolling back the welfare state*, Cambridge, MA: MIT Press.

Atkinson, A.B. (2015) *Inequality: What can be done?*, Oxford: Oxford University Press.

Atkinson, A.B. and King, M.A. (1982) 'Housing policy taxation and reform', *Midland Bank Review*, Spring, pp 7–15.

Ball, S.J. (2002) *Class strategies and the education market: The middle classes and social advantage*, London: Routledge Farmer.

Barr, N. (2001) *The welfare state as piggy bank: Information risk and uncertainty and the role of the state*, Oxford: Oxford University Press.

Barr, N. (2012a) *Economics of the welfare state* (5th edn), Oxford: Oxford University Press.

Barr, N. (2012b) 'The higher education White Paper: the good, the bad, the unspeakable – and the next White Paper', *Social Policy and Administration*, vol 46, no 5, pp 483–508.

Barr, N. (2013) *Swedish pensions*, Report to the Swedish Ministry of Finance, Stockholm: Ministry of Finance.

Barr, N. (2016) Milton Fiedman and the finance of higher education in R. Cord, J. D. Hammond, (eds) *Milton Fiedman's contribution to economics and public policy*, Oxford: Oxford University Press.

Barr, N. and Crawford, I. (2005) *Financing higher education: Answers from the UK*, London: Routledge.

Barr, N. and Diamond, P. (2008) *Reforming pensions: Principles and policy choices*, Oxford: Oxford University Press.

Barr, N. and Diamond, P. (2010) *An overview of reforming pensions: Principles and policy choices*, Oxford: Oxford University Press.

Barr, N. and Diamond, P. (2016) 'Reforming pensions in Chile', *Polityaka Spoleczna*, no 1, pp 4–9.

Bastagli, F. and Hills, J. (2013) Wealth accumulation, aging, and house prices in J. Hills, F. Bastagli, F. Cowell, H. Glennerster, E. Karagiannaki, and A. McKnight (eds) *Wealth in the UK: Distribution, accoumulation and policy*, Oxford: Oxford University Press.

British Broadcasting Corporation (BBC) (2015) BBC News website, 6 May 2015.

Becker, G.S. (1964) *Human capital. A theoretical and empirical analysis with special reference to education*, Chicago, IL: University of Chicago Press.

Becker, G.S. (1976) *The economic approach to human behaviour*, Chicago,Il: Chicago University Press.

Belfield, C. and Sibieta, L. (2015) *English schools will feel the pinch over the next five years*, Observations, 21 October, London: Institute for Fiscal Studies.

Belfield, C. and Sibieta, L. (2016) *Long run trends in school spending in England*, IFS Report R115, London: Institute for Fiscal Studies.

Bell, D. and Bowes, A. (2006) *Financial care models in Scotland and the UK*, York: Joseph Rowntree Foundation.

Bell, D., Bowes, A. and Dawson, A. (2007) *Free personal care in Scotland: Recent developments*, York: Joseph Rowntree Foundation.

Bettinger, E., Kremer, M. and Saavendra, J. (2010) 'Are education vouchers only redistributive?', *The Economic Journal*, vol 120, pp F204–F228.

Bevan, G., Karanikolos, M., Exley, J., Nolte, E., Connolly, S. and S. Mays, N. (2014) *The four health systems of the United Kingdom: How do they compare?*, London: The Health Foundation and Nuffield Trust.

Beveridge Report (1942) *Social insurance and allied services*, Cmd 6404, London: HMSO.

Billis, D. and Glennerster, H. (1998) 'Human services and the voluntary sector: towards a theory of comparative advantage', *Journal of Social Policy*, vol 27, part 1, pp 79–98.

BIS (Department for Business, Innovation and Skills) (2011) *Students at the heart of the system*, Cm 8122, London: The Stationery Office.

Blackstone, T. (1971) *A fair start: The provision of pre-school education*, London: Allen Lane.

Bloom, N., Cooper, Z., Gaynor, M., Gibbons, S., Jones, S., McGuire, A., Morreno-Serra, R., Propper, C., Van Reenen, J. and Seller, S. (2011) 'In defence of our research on competition in England's National Health Service', *Lancet*, vol 378, no 9809, pp 2064–5 (see also the same authors' longer *A response to Pollock et al* (2011), available at: www.bristol.ac.uk).

Bloom, N., Propper, C., Seiler, S. and Van Reenan, J. (2015) 'The impact of competition on management quality: evidence from public hospitals', *Review of Economic Studies*, vol 82, no 2, pp 457–89.

Blundell, R. (2000) 'Work incentives and "in work" benefit reforms: a review', *Oxford Review of Economic Policy*, vol 16, no 1, pp 27–44.

Bohlmark, A. and Lindhal, M. (2012) *Independent schools and long run educational outcomes: Evidence from Sweden's large scale voucher reform*, Stockholm: Institute for the Study of Labour.

Bolderson, H. and Mabbett, D. (2001) 'Non-discriminating social policy? Policy scenarios for meeting needs without categorisation', in J. Classen (ed) *What future social security? Debates and reforms in national and cross national perspective*, Bristol: Policy Press, pp 53–67.

Bonoli, G. (2013) *The origins of active social policy*, Oxford: Oxford University Press.

Bradshaw, J. and Wakeman, I. (1972) 'The poverty trap updated', *Political Quarterly*, vol 43, no 4, pp 459–69.

Brewer, M., Saez, E. and Shephard, A. (2010) 'Means testing and tax rates on earnings', in J. Mirrlees, S. Adam, T. Besley, R. Blundell, S. Bond, R. Chote, M. Gammie, P. Johnson, G. Myles and J. Poterba (eds) *Dimensions of tax design* (papers prepared for the Mirrlees Review), Oxford: Oxford University Press and Institute for Fiscal Studies.

Brien, S. (2009) *Dynamic welfare that works*, London: Centre for Social Justice.

Britton, J., Crawford, C. and Deardon, L. (2015) *Analysis of the higher education funding reforms announced in Summer Budget 2015*, London: Institute for Fiscal Studies.

Britton, J., Deardon, J., Shephard, N. and Vignoles, A. (2016) *How English domiciled graduates' earnings vary with gender, institution attended, subject and socio economic background*, London: Institute for Fiscal Studies.

Browne Review (2010) 'Securing a sustainable future for higher education'. Available at: www.independent.gov.uk/browne-report

Buchanan, J.M. (1975) *The limits of liberty: Between anarchy and Leviathan*, Chicago, IL: University of Chicago Press.

Bulmer, M. (1986) *Neighbours: The work of Philip Abrams*, Cambridge: Cambridge University Press.

Burchardt, T. and Obolenskaya, P. (2016) 'Public and private welfare', in R. Lupton, T. Burchardt, J. Hills, K. Stewart and P. Vizard (eds) *Social policy in a cold climate: Policy, poverty and inequality in England 2008–2015*, Bristol: The Policy Press.

Burchardt, T., Hills, J. and Propper, C. (1999) *Private welfare and public policy*, York: Joseph Rowntree Foundation.

Burchardt, T., Obolenskaya, P. and Vizard, P. (2016) 'Adult social care' in R. Lupton, T. Burchardt, J. Hills, K. Stewart and P. Vizard (eds) *Social policy in a cold climate: Policy, poverty and inequality in England 2008–2015*, Bristol: The Policy Press.

Burgess, S., Dickson, M. and Macmillan, L. (2014) *Selective schooling systems increase income inequality*, Working Paper No 14-09, London: Institute of Education, London University, Department of Quantitative Social Science.

Buss, R. and Blumel, M. (2014) 'German health system review'. Available at: www.eurowho.int

Cardak, B.A. and Ryan, C. (2009) 'Participation in higher education in Australia: equity and access', *Economic Record*, vol 85, no 271, pp 433–48.

Calabresi, G. and Bobbitt, P. (1978) *Tragic choices*, New York, NY: Norton.

Callender, C. (2012) 'The 2012/3 reforms of higher education in England: changing student finances and funding', in M. Kilkey, G. Ramia and K. Farnsworth (eds) *1972–2012: Social policy review 24: Analysis and debate in social policy, 2012*, Bristol: The Policy Press.

Callender, C. (2013) *Student financing of higher education. A comparative perspective*, London: Routledge.

Callender, C. and Jackson, J. (2005) 'Does fear of debt deter students from higher education?', *Journal of Social Policy*, vol 34, no 4, pp 509–40.

Centre for Economics and Business Research (2014) *Killik private education index*, London: Killik.

Chapman, B. (1997) 'Conceptual issues and the Australian experience with income contingent loans for higher education', *Economic Journal*, vol 107, May, pp 738–51.

Cheshire, P., Nathan, M. and Overman, H. (2015) *Urban economics and urban policy: Challenging conventional policy wisdom*, Cheltenham: Edward Elgar.

Chief Medical Officer (2014) *Annual report of the Chief Medical Officer 2013. Public mental health provision: Investing in the evidence*, London: Stationery Office.

Choi, J., Laibson, D., Madrian, B. and Metrick, A. (2004) 'For better or for worse: default effects and 401K savings behaviour', in D. Wide (ed) *Perspectives on the economics of ageing*, Chicago, IL: Chicago University Press, pp 81–121.

Choi, J., Laibson, D., Madrian, B. and Metrick, A. (2006) 'Savings for retirement on the path of least resistance', in E. McCaffrey and J. Slimrod (eds) *Behavioural public finance: Towards a new agenda*, New York, NY: Russell Sage Foundation, pp 304–51.

Chowdry, H., Dearden, L., Goodman, A. and Jin, W. (2012) 'The distributional impact of the 2012–3 higher education funding reforms in England', *Fiscal Studies*, vol 33, no 2, pp 211–36.

Christie, I. and Leadbeater, C. (1998) *To our mutual advantage*, London: Demos.

Christie, A. and Swales, J.K. (2010) 'The Barnett allocation mechanism: formula plus influence,' *Regional Studies*, vol 44, no 6, pp 761–75.

Chubb, J.E. and Moe, T.E. (1990) *Politics, markets and American schools*, Washington, DC: Brookings Institution.

Clark, G.L., Munnell, A.H. and Orzag J.M. (2006) *The Oxford handbook of pensions and retirement income*, Oxford: Oxford University Press.

Cmnd 2764 (1965) *The national plan*, Cmnd 2764, London: HMSO.

Comas-Herrera, A., Butterfield, R., Fernandez, J.-L., Wittenberg, R. and Wiener, J.M. (2012) 'Barriers and opportunities for long-term care insurance in England: what can we learn from other countries?', in A. McGuire and J. Costa-Font (eds) *LSE companion to health policy*, Aldershot: Edward Elgar.

Commonwealth of Australia (1997) *Learning for life: Review of higher education financing and policy*, Canberra: AGPS.

Coons, J. and Sugarman, S. (1978) *Education by choice: The case for family control*, Berkley, CA: University of California Press.

Cooper, Z., Gibbons, S., Jones, S. and McGuire, A. (2011) 'Does hospital competition save lives? Evidence from NHS patient choice reforms', *Economic Journal*, vol 121, pp 228–60.

Cooper, Z., Gibbons, S., Jones, S. and McGuire, A. (2012) *Does competition improve public hospital efficiency? Evidence from a quasi-experiment in the English NHS*, CEP Discussion Paper 1123, London: LSE, Centre for Economic Performance.

Costa-Font, J. and Zigante, V. (2014) *Long term care coverage in Europe: A case for 'Implicit Insurance Partnerships'*, Working Paper No 37, London: LSE Health.

Crawford, R. and Tetlow, G. (2016) *The new (not yet flat rate) state pension*, Observations, 6 April, London: Institute for Fiscal Studies.

Crawford, R., Emmerson, C. and Tetlow, G. (2009) *A survey of public spending in the UK*, IFS Briefing BN 43, London: Institute for Fiscal Studies.

Crawford, R., Keynes, S. and Tetlow, G. (2013) *A single tier pension: What does that really mean?*, Report R. 82, London: Institute for Fiscal Studies.

Crawford, C., Macmillan, L. and Vignoles, A. (2014) *Progress made by high attaining children from disadvantaged backgrounds*, London: Social Mobility and Child Poverty Commission.

Cribb, J. and Emmerson, C. (2016) *What happens when employers are obliged to nudge. Automatic enrolment and pension saving in the UK*, London: Institute for Fiscal Studies.

Crowther Committee (1959) *15 to 18: A report of the Central Advisory Council for Education (England)*, London: HMSO.

Curchin, K. (2016) 'From the moral limits of markets to the moral limits to welfare', *Journal of Social Policy*, vol 45, part 1, pp 101–18.

Daunton, M. (1995) *Progress and poverty: An economic and social history of Britain 1700–1850*, Oxford: Oxford University Press.

Daunton, M. (2001) *Trusting leviathan: The politics of taxation in Britain 1799–1914*, Cambridge: Cambridge University Press.

Daunton, M. (2002) *Just taxes: The politics of taxation in Britain 1914–1979*, Cambridge: Cambridge University Press.

Davies, B. (1968) *Social needs and resources in local services*, London: Michael Joseph.

DCLG (Department for Communities and Local Government) (2017) *Fixing our broken housing market*, Cm 9352, London: The Stationery Office

Deakin, N. and Parry, R. (2000) *The Treasury and social policy: The contest for control of welfare strategy*, London: Macmillan.

Dean, H. (2010) *Understanding human need*, Bristol: The Policy Press.

Deardon, L., Fitzsimonds, E., Goodman, A. and Kaplan, G. (2008) *Higher education funding reforms in England: The distributional effects and the shifting balance of costs*, London: Centre for the Economics of Education, LSE.

Deardon, L., Fitzimons, E. and Wyness, G. (2011) *The impact of tuition fees and support on university participation in the UK*, Centre for Economics of Education Discussion Paper 126, London: LSE, Centre for Economic Performance.

Dearing Committee (1997) *Higher education and the learning society. Report of the National Committee*, London: HMSO.

Deeming, C. and Smyth, P. (eds) (2017) *Reframing global social policy: Inclusive growth and the social investment perspective*, Bristol: The Policy Press.

Del Rey, E. (2012) 'Deferring higher education fees without relying on contributions from non-students', *Education Economics*, no 5, pp 510–21.

Department for Education (2016) *Schools National Funding Formula; Consultation Response*, London: Stationery Office.

Department for Work and Pensions (2015) *National Insurance Fund 2015: Receipts and payments account*, London: Department for Work and Pensions.

Department for Work and Pensions (DWP) (2010) *Universal Credit: Welfare that works*, Cm 7957, London: The Stationery Office.

Department of Health (1988) *Community care agenda for action*, London: HMSO.

Department of Health (2003) *Report of an enquiry by Lord Laming*, London: The Stationery Office.

Department of Health (2011) *Resource allocation: Weighted capitation formulas. Seventh edition*, London: Department of Health.

Department of Health (2016) *Department of Health Annual Report 2015/16*, London: The Stationery Office.

Department of Health and Social Security (1976) *Sharing resources for health in England: Report of the Resource Allocation Working Party*, London: HMSO.

DfES (Department for Education and Skills) (2003) *The future of higher education*, Cm 5735, London: The Stationery Office.

Dilnot, A.W., Kay, J.A. and Morris C.N. (1984) *The reform of social security*, Oxford: Oxford University Press.

Dilnot Commission (2011) 'Fairer care funding: the report of the Commission on Funding of Care and Support'. Available at: http://webarchive.nationalarchives.gov.uk

Disney, R. (2000) 'Crises in public pension provision in OECD: what are the reform options?', *The Economic Journal*, vol 110, no 1, pp 70–94.

Doyal, L. and Gough, I. (1991) *A theory of human need*, London: Macmillan.

Dunleavy, P. (1991) *Democracy, bureaucracy and public choice*, Hemel Hempstead: Harvester Wheatsheaf.

Emmerson, C., Johnson, P. and Miller, H. (2014) *IFS Green Budget, 2014*, London: Institute for Fiscal Studies.

European Observatory on Health Care Systems (2002) *Health care systems in eight countries: Trends and challenges*, London: London School of Economics.

Exley, S. (2012) 'The politics of education policy making under New Labour: an illustration of shifts in public service governance', *Policy and Politics*, vol 40, no 2, pp 227–44.

Exley, S. (2014) 'Are quasi markets in education what the British public wants?', *Social Policy and Administration*, vol 48, no 1, pp 24–43.

Exley, S. and Ball S. (2014) 'Neo liberalism in English education', in D. Turner and H. Huseyin (eds) *Neo liberal educational reforms: A critical analysis*, London: Routledge.

Eyles, A.E. and Machin, S. (2015) *The introduction of academy schools in English education*, CEP Discussion Paper No 1368, London: Centre for Economic Performance, LSE.

Eyles, A.E., Machin, S. and Silva, O. (2015) *Academies 2: The new batch*, CEP Discussion Paper 1370, London: Centre for Economic Performance, LSE.

Fabian Commission on Taxation and Citizenship (2000) *Paying for progress: A new politics of tax for public spending*, London: Fabian Society.

Fahey, T. and Norris, M. (2013) 'Housing', in F.C. Castles, S. Leibfried, J. Lewis, H. Obinger and C. Pierson (eds) *The Oxford handbook of the welfare state*, Oxford: Oxford University Press.

Fernandez, J., Forder, J. and Knapp, M. (2011) 'Long term care', in S. Glied and P.C. Smith (eds) *Oxford handbook of health economics*, Oxford: Oxford University Press.

Finch, D., Corlett, A. and Alekson, V. (2014) *Universal Credit: A policy under review*, London: Resolution Foundation.

Fisk, E.B. and Ladd, H.F. (2000) *When schools compete: A cautionary tale*, Washington, DC: Brookings Institution.

Forder, J. and Fernandez, J.-L. (2011) *What works abroad? Evaluating the funding of long term care: International perspectives*, PSSRU Discussion paper 2794, Canterbury: PSSRU.

Foster, R. and Fender, V. (2013) *Valuing informal adult care in the UK*, London: Office of National Statistics.

Friedman, M. (1962) *Capitalism and freedom*, Chicago, IL: Chicago University Press.

Gallagher, P. (2015) 'Government forced to admit that right to buy scheme hasn't hit its targets' *Independent*, 25 February 2015.

Gambaro, L., Stewart, K. and Waldfogel, J. (eds) (2014) *An equal start? Providing quality early education and care for disadvantaged children*, Bristol: Policy Press.

Gamble, A. (2016) *Can the welfare state survive?*, Cambridge: Polity Books.

Gaynor, M., Morreno-Sera, R. and Propper, C. (2013) 'Death by market power: Reform, competition and patient outcomes in the National Health Service,' *American Economic Journal: Economic Policy*, vol 5, pp 134–66.

Gerwitz, S., Ball, S.J. and Bowe, R. (1995) *Markets, choice and equity in education*, Buckingham: Open University Press.

Gibbons, S. and Silva, O. (2006) *Faith primary schools: Better schools or better pupils?*, Centre for the Economics of Education Discussion Paper, London: LSE.

Gibbons, S., Machin, S. and Silva, O. (2012) *Valuing school quality using boundary discontinuities*, CEP Discussion Paper 132, London: CEP/LSE.

Gilbert, B. (1966) *The evolution of National Insurance in Great Britain*, London: Michael Joseph.

Gillie, A. (1996) 'The origin of the poverty line', *Economic History Review*, vol 49, no 4, pp 715–30.

Gilson, L. and McIntire, D. (2005) 'Removing user fees for primary care in Africa: the need for careful attention', *British Medical Journal*, vol 331, pp 762–5.

Glendinning, C. (2007) 'Improving equity and sustainability in UK long term care finance. Lessons from Germany', *Social Policy and Society*, vol 6, no 3, pp 411–22.

Glennerster, H. (1972) 'Education and inequality', in P. Townsend and N. Bosanquet (eds) *Labour and inequality*, London: Fabian Society.

Glennerster, H. (1983) *Planning for priority groups*, Oxford: Blackwell.

Glennerster, H. (1985) *Paying for welfare*, Oxford: Blackwell.

Glennerster, H. (1991) 'Quasi-markets for education?', *Economic Journal*, no 408, pp 1268–76.

Glennerster, H. (1998) 'Education: reaping the harvest?', in H. Glennerster and J. Hills (eds) *The state of welfare: The economics of social spending*, Oxford: Oxford University Press.

Glennerster, H. (2012) 'Why was a wealth tax for the UK abandoned? Lessons for the policy process and tackling wealth inequality', *Journal of Social Policy*, vol 41, no 2 pp 233–49.

Glennerster, H. (2013) 'Financing future welfare states: a new partnership model', in S. Griffiths, H. Krippin and G. Stocker (eds) *Public services: A new reform agenda*, London: Bloomsbury.

Glennerster, H. (2014) *Richard Titmuss: 40 years on*, CASEpaper 180, London: LSE/CASE.

Glennerster, H. (2015a) 'A wealth of options', in D.-R. Srblin (ed) *Tax for our times: How the Left can reinvent taxation*, London: Fabian Society.

Glennerster, H. (2015b) 'The coalition and society (III): health and long term care', in A. Seldon and M. Finn (eds) *The Coalition effect 2010–2015*, Cambridge: Cambridge University Press.

Glennerster, H. and Evans, M. (1994) 'Beveridge and his assumptive worlds: the incompatibilities of a flawed design', in J. Hills, J. Ditch and H. Glennerster (eds) *Beveridge and social security: An international retrospective*, Oxford: Oxford University Press.

Glennerster, H. and Le Grand, J. (1995) 'The developments of quasi-markets in welfare provision in the United Kingdom', *International Journal of Health Services*, vol 25, no 2, pp 203–18.

Glennerster, H. and Lieberman, R.C. (2011) 'Hidden convergence: Toward a historical comparison of US and UK health policy', *Journal of Health Politics, Policy and Law*, vol 36, no 1, pp 5–31.

Glennerster, H. and Wilson, G. (1970) *Paying for private schools*, London: Allen Lane.

Glennerster, H., Merrett, S. and Wilson, G. (1968) 'A graduate tax', *Higher Education Review*, vol 1, no 1, pp 26–38.

Glennerster, H., Hills, J. and Travers, T. (2000) *Paying for health, education and housing: How does the centre pull the purse strings?*, Oxford: Oxford University Press.

Glennerster, H., Bradshaw, J., Lister, R. and Lundberg, O. (2009) *Reducing the risks to health: The role of social protection*, CASEpaper 139, London: LSE.

Goodhart, C., Pratham, M. and Pradesh, P. (2015) *Could demographics reverse three multi decade trends?*, London: Morgan Stanley.

Goodin, R. and Le Grand, J. (1987) *Not only the poor: The middle classes and the state*, London: Allen and Unwin.

Gorsky, M. and Sheard, S. (2006) *Financing medicine: The British experience since 1750*, London: Routledge.

Government Office for Science (2016) 'Future of an ageing population'. Available at: www.gov.uk/government/publications/future-of-an-ageing-population

Grace,C., Pope, T. and Roantree, B. (2015) *A survey of the UK tax system*, London: Institute for Fiscal Studies.

Gregg, P. and Corlett, A. (2015) *An ocean apart: The US–UK switch in employment benefit receipt*, London: Resolution Foundation.

Gregg Report (2008) *Realising potential: A vision for personalised conditionality and support*, London: Department for Work and Pensions.

Grogan, C.M. and Andrews, C.M. (2015) 'Medicaid', in D. Bleland, C. Howard and K. Morgan (eds) *The Oxford handbook of US social policy*, Oxford: Oxford University Press.

Hancock, R., Wittenberg, R., Hu, B., Morciano, M. and Comas-Herrera, A. (2013) *Long term care funding in England: An analysis of the costs and distributional effects of potential reforms*, PSSRU Discussion Paper 2857, Canterbury and London: Kent University and LSE.

Hansmann, H. (1980) 'The role of non-profit enterprise', *Yale Law Journal*, vol 89, pp 835–901.

Hansmann, H. (1987) 'Economic theories of non-profit organisation', in W.W. Powell (ed) *The non-profit sector: A handbook*, New Haven, CT: Yale University Press.

Hatton, C. (2004) 'Choice', in E. Emmerson, C. Hatton, T. Thomson and R. Parmenter (eds) *The international handbook of applied research on intellectual disabilities*, London: Wiley.

Hayek, F.A. (1944) *The road to serfdom*, London: Routledge.

Heald, D. and McLeod, A. (2003) *The laws of Scotland, Stair memorial encyclopaedia: Public expenditure*, London: Butterworths.

Health and Social Care Information Centre (NHS Digital) (2015) *Personal Social Service Expenditure and Unit costs 2013-4*, London: The Stationery Office.

Heclo, H. and Wildavsky A. (1974, 2nd edition 1981) *The private government of public money*, London: Macmillan.

Hemerijck, A. (2013) *Changing welfare states*, Oxford: Oxford University Press.

Hemerijck, A. (ed) (2017) *The uses of social investment*, Oxford: Oxford University Press.

Hill, M. (1993) *The policy process: A reader*, London: Harvester Wheatsheaf.

Hills, J. (2007) *Ends and means: The future roles of of social housing in England CASEreport 34*, London: London School of Economics.

Hills, J. (2015) (second edition, 2017) *Good times, bad times: The welfare myth of them and us*, Bristol: Policy Press.

Hills, J. and Glennerster, H. (2013) 'Wealth and policy: where do we go from here?', in J. Hills, F. Bastagli, F. Cowell, H. Glennerster, E. Karagiannaki and A. McKnight (eds) *Wealth in the UK: Distribution, accumulation, and policy*, Oxford: Oxford University Press.

Himmelstein, D.M., Jun, M. and Busse, R. (2014) 'A comparison of hospital administrative costs in eight nations', *Health Affairs*, vol 33, no 9, pp 1586–94.

Hirsch, D. (2015) *Could a citizen's income work?*, York: Joseph Rowntree Foundation.

Hirschman, A.O. (1970) *Exit, voice and loyalty: Responses to decline in firms, organisations and states*, Cambridge, MA: Harvard University Press.

HM Treasury (1961) *Control of public expenditure: The Plowden Report*, Cm 1432, London: The Stationery Office.

HM Treasury (2015a) *Public expenditure statistical analyses 2015*, London: HM Treasury.

HM Treasury (2015b) *Spending Review and Autumn Statement*, London: HM Treasury.

HM Treasury (2015c) *Strengthening the incentive to save: A consultation on pensions tax relief*, Cm 9102, London: The Stationery Office.

HM Treasury (2016a) *Public expenditure and statistical analyses 2016*, London: HM Treasury.

HM Treasury (2016b) *2016 Autumn Statement*, London: HM Treasury.

HM Treasury and the Greater Manchester Combined Authority (2015) *Greater Manchester Agreement: Devolution to the GMCA & transition to a directly elected mayor*, London: HM Treasury.

Hochman, H.M. and Rodgers, J.D. (1969) 'Pareto optimal redistribution', *American Economic Review*, vol 59, pp 542–7.

Hodge, M. (2016) Called to account: How corporate bad behaviour and government waste combine to cost us millions, London: Little Brown.

Holland, W. (2013) *Improving health services: Background, method and applications*, Cheltenham: Edward Arnold.

Holloway, S. and Tamplin, S. (2001) 'Valuing informal child care in the UK', in *Economic trends*, September, London: The Stationery Office, pp 51–60.

Hood, C., Heald, D. and Himax, R. (eds) (2014) *When the party's over: The politics of fiscal squeeze in perspective*, Oxford: Oxford University Press and The British Academy.

House of Commons (2014) *Report of the House of Commons Business, Innovation and Skills Committee, third report 2014/5: Student loans*, HC 558, London: Stationery Office.

House of Lords (2009) *Report of the Select Committee of the House of Lords on the Barnett Formula*, HL 139 Session 2008/9, London: Stationery Office.

House of Lords (2013) *Ready for ageing? Report of the Select Committee on Public Service and Demographic Change*, HL Paper 140, Session 2012–13.

House of Lords (2015) *Fractured union: The implementation of financial devolution to Scotland*, First Report, HL Paper 55, Session 2015–16.

IFS (Institute for Fiscal Studies) (2016) 'The (changing) effects of universal credit', in IFS (ed) *IFS green Budget*, London: IFS.

Ikegami, N. (2007) 'Rationale, design and sustainability of long term care in Japan – in retrospect', *Social Policy and Society*, vol 6, no 3, pp 423–34.

Independent Review of the State Pension Age (2016) *Interim report*, London: State Pension Age Independent Review.

Innes, D. and Tetlow G. (2015) *Sharpest cuts to local government spending in poor areas*, Institute for Fiscal Studies press release, 6 March, London: IFS.

IPPR (Institute for Public Policy Research) (2001) *Building better partnerships*, London: IPPR.

Johnson, J., Rolph, S. and Smith, R. (2010) *Residential care transformed: Revisiting the last refuge*, Basingstoke: Macmillan.

Johnson, M. (2012) *Costly and ineffective: Why pension tax reliefs should be reformed*, London: Centre for Policy Studies.

Johnson, M. (2015) *Pensions are finished*, London: Centre for Policy Studies.

Judge, K. and Matthews, J. (1980) *Charging for social care: A study of consumer charges and the personal social services*, London: Allen and Unwin.

Kaldor, N. (1955) *An expenditure tax*, London: Allen and Unwin.

Kangas, O. (2010) 'Work accident and sickness benefits', in F. Castles, S. Leibfried, J. Lewis, H. Obinger and C. Pierson (eds) *The Oxford handbook of the welfare state*, Oxford: Oxford University Press.

Kendall, J. (2003) *The voluntary sector: Comparative perspectives in the UK*, London: Taylor and Francis.

King, S. (2000) *Poverty and welfare in England 1700–1850: A regional perspective*, Manchester: Manchester University Press.

King's Fund (2014) *A new settlement for health and social care*, London: King's Fund.

King's Fund (2016) *New care models*, London: King's Fund.

Klein, R., Day, P. and Redmayne, S. (1996) *Managing scarcity: Priority setting and rationing in the NHS*, Milton Keynes: Open University Press.

Knapp, M. (2007) 'Social care: choice and control', in J. Hills, J. LeGrand and D. Piachaud (eds) *Making social policy work*, Bristol: The Policy Press, pp 147–72.

Kremer, M. and Glennerster, R. (2011) 'Improving health in developing countries: evidence from randomised evaluations', in M.V. Pauly, T.G. Mcguire and P.P. Barros (eds) *Handbook of health economics vol 2*, Amsterdam: Elsevier.

Laing, W. (2014) 'Strategic Commissioning of Long Term Care for Older People: Can we get more for less?'. Available at: www.laingbuisson.co.uk

Lampman, R. (1971) *Ends and means of reducing income poverty*, Chicago, IL: Markam.

Layard, R., Nickell, S. and Jackman, R. (1991) *Unemployment*, Oxford: Oxford University Press.

Le Grand, J. (1991) 'The theory of government failure', *British Journal of Political Science*, vol 21, pp 423–42.

Le Grand, J. (2003) *Motivation, agency and public policy: Of knights and knaves, pawns and queens*, Oxford: Oxford University Press.

Le Grand, J. (2007) *The other invisible hand: Delivering public services through choice and competition*, Princeton, NJ: Princeton University Press.

Le Grand, J. and Bartlett, W. (eds) (1993) *Quasi-markets and social policy*, London: Macmillan.

Leibenstein, H. (1966) 'Allocative efficiency versus X efficiency', *American Economic Review*, vol 56, pp 392–415.

Levi-Strauss, C. (1969) *The elementary structures of kinship* (2nd edn), London: Eyre and Spotiswood.

Lewis, J. (2001) 'The decline of the male breadwinner model: implications for work and care', *Social Politics*, Summer, pp 152–69.

Lewis, J. and Glennerster, H. (1996) *Implementing the new community care*, Buckingham: Open University Press.

Lewis, J. and Meredith, B. (1988) *Daughters caring for mothers at home*, London: Routledge.

Licchetta, M. and Stelmach, M. (2016) *Fiscal sustainability and public spending on health*, London: Office for Budget Responsibility.

Lindbeck, A. (1995) 'Welfare state disincentives with endogenous habits and norms', *Scandinavian Journal of Economics*, vol 97, no 4, pp 477–94.

Lindbom, A. (2014) 'Fiscal squeeze in Sweden, 1990–1997: the causes, the measures, and their short and long run effects', in C. Hood, D. Heald and R. Himaz (eds) *When the party's over: The politics of fiscal squeeze in perspective*, Oxford: Oxford University Press for the British Academy.

Lindert, P.H. (2004) *Growing public: Social spending and economic growth since the eighteenth century*, Cambridge: Cambridge University Press.

Lipsky, M. (1980) *Street-level bureaucracy: Dilemmas of the individual in public services*, New York, NY: Russell Sage Foundation.

Lodge, G. and Trench, A. (2014) *Devo more and welfare: Devolving benefits and policy for a stronger union*, London: Institute for Public Policy Research.

Lowe, R. (1989) 'Resignation at the Treasury: the Social Services Committee and the failure to reform the welfare state 1955–7', *Journal of Social Policy*, vol 18, no 4, pp 505–26.

Lowe, R. (1997a) 'Milestone or millstone?: The 1959 -61 Plowden Committee and its impact on British welfare policy,' *Historical Journal*, vol 40, no 2, pp 463–91.

Lowe, R. (1997b) 'The core executive, modernisation and the creation of PESC 1960-64,' *Public Administration*, vol 75, pp 601–15.

Lupton, R., Thomson, S. and Obolenskaya, P. (2016) 'Schools' in R. Lupton, T. Burchardt, J. Hlills, K. Stewart and P. Vizard, (eds) Social policy in a cold climate: Policies and their consequences since the crisis, Bristol: Policy Press.

Maclennan, D. (1982) *Housing economics: An applied approach*, London: Longman.

Macnicol, J. (1980) *The movement for family allowances, 1918–45: A study in social policy development*, London: Heinemann.

Macnicol, J. (1998) *The politics of retirement in Britain 1878–1948*, Cambridge: Cambridge University Press.

Macnicol, J. (2015) *Neoliberalising old age*, Cambridge: Cambridge University Press.

Maher, J. and Green, H. (2002) *Carers 2000*, London: The Stationery Office.

Mayhew, L., Smith, D. and O'Leary, D. (2016) *Paying for care costs in later life using the value of people's homes*, Geneva Papers, London: The Pensions Institute, pp 1–23.

Maynard, A. (1975) *Experiment with choice in education*, London: Institute for Economic Affairs.

Mazzucato, M. (2013) *The entrepreneurial state: Debunking public versus private sector myths*, London: Anthem.

Merrett, S. (1979) *State housing in Britain*, London: Routledge and Kegan Paul.

Mill, J.S. (1970 [1848]) *Principles of political economy*, Harmondsworth: Penguin Books.

Miller, J. and Bennett, F. (2016) 'Universal Credit: assumptions, contradictions and virtual reality', *Social Policy and Society* (forthcoming).

Ministry of Health (1963) *Health and welfare: The development of Community Care*, Cmnd 1973, London: HMSO.

Mirrlees, J. (1971) 'The theory of optimal income taxation', *Review of Economic Studies*, vol 38, pp 175–208.

Mirrlees Review (2011) *Tax by design: The Mirrlees Review*, Oxford: Oxford University Press and Institute for Fiscal Studies.

Molloy, C. (2014) 'We already own NHS'. Available at: www.opendemocracy. net/ournhs

Murphy, R. (2015) *The joy of tax: How a fair tax system can create a better society*, London: Bantham Press.

National Assembly for Wales, Health and Social Services Committee (2001) *Targeting poor health*, Cardiff: National Assembly for Wales.

National Audit Office (2015) *Tackling tax fraud: How HMRC responds to tax evasion, the hidden economy and criminal attacks*, H.C. 610 Session 2015–16, London: The Stationery Office. Available at: www.nao.org.uk

National Audit Office (2016) *Financial Sustainablity of the NHS HC 784, Session 2016-17*, London: Stationery Office. Available at www.nao.org.uk

NCVO (National Council for Voluntary Organisations) (2015) *UK civil society almanac 2015*, London: NCVO.

Nevitt, A.A. (1966) *Housing taxation and subsidies*, London: Nelson.

Newcastle Commission (1861) *The state of popular education*, London: Education and Charity Commissioners (archives available at Kew Public Records).

Newhouse, J.P. (1993) *Free for all? Lessons from the RAND health experiment*, Cambridge, MA: Harvard University Press.

NHS England (2013) *NHS belongs to you: A call to Action – The technical annex*, London: NHS England.

NHS England (2014) *Five year forward view*, London: NHS England.

Niskanen, W. (1971) *Bureaucracy and representative government*, Chicago, IL: Chicago University Press.

Norton, A. (2016) 'Equity and markets', in A. Harvey, C. Burnheim and B. Matthews (eds) *Student equity in Australian higher education: Twenty-five years of a fair chance for all*, New York, NY: Springer.

Nozick, R. (1974) *Anarchy, state and utopia*, Oxford: Blackwell.

Nuffield Trust, Health Foundation and King's Fund (2015) *The Spending Review: What does it mean for health and social care?*, London: Nuffield Trust.

Oberlander, J. (2015) 'Medicare', in D. Bleland, C. Howard and K. Morgan (eds) *The Oxford handbook of US social policy*, Oxford: Oxford University Press.

Obolenskaya, P. and Burchardt, T. (2016) *Trends in public and private welfare 1979/80 to 2013/14*, CASEpaper 193, London: CASE, London School of Economics.

OBR (Office of Budget Responsibility) (2015) *Spending Review and Autumn Statement 2015*, London: The Stationery Office.

OBR (2017) *Fiscal Sustainability Report, January 2017*, London: The Stationery Office.

OECD (Organisation for Economic Co-operation and Development) (1994) *Jobs study: Facts, analysis strategies*, Paris: OECD.

OECD (2011) *Help wanted? Providing and paying for long term care*, Paris: OECD.

OECD (2014) *Education at a glance 2014*, Paris: OECD.

OECD (2015a) *Revenue statistics*, Paris: OECD.

OECD (2015b) *Pensions at a glance*, Paris: OECD.

OECD (2015c) *Education at a glance*, Paris: OECD.

OECD (2015d) *Health statistics*, Paris: OECD.

OECD (2016a) *Social expenditure data*, Paris: OECD.

OECD (2016b) *Education at a glance*, Paris: OECD.

OECD (2016c) *Health statistics*, Paris: OECD.

Offe, C. (1984) *Contradictions of the welfare state*, London: Hutchinson.

Okun, A.M. (1975) *Equality and efficiency: The big trade off*, Washington, DC: Brookings Institution.

ONS (Office for National Statistics) (2013) *Full story: The gender gap in unpaid care provision: Is there an impact on health and economic position*, London: Office of National Statistics.

ONS (2015a) *The effects of taxes and benefits on household income: Financial year ending 2014*, London: Office for National Statistics.

ONS (2015b) *Life expectancy at the age of 65 by local areas in the UK 2006-08*, London: ONS.

ONS (2016a) *Dwelling stock estimates by country and tenure*, London: The Stationery Office.

ONS (2016b) *House building statistics*, London: The Stationery Office.

ONS (2016c) *Family spending 2014*, London: The Stationery Office.

O'Sullivan, T. and Gibb, K. (eds) (2003) *Housing economics and public policy: Essays in honour of Duncan Maclennan*, Oxford: Blackwell.

Overton, L. and O'Mahony, L.F. (2017) 'Understanding attitudes to paying for care amongst Equity Release Consumers: Citizenship, solidarity and the "hardworking homeowner"', *Journal of Social Policy*, vol 46, part 1, pp 49–67.

Paine, T. (1969 [1791/92]) *Rights of man*, Harmondsworth: Penguin.

Palacios, M. (2003) *Financing human capital: A capital markets approach to student funding*, Cambridge: Cambridge University Press.

Parker, G. (1990) *With due care and attention* (2nd edn), London: Family Policy Studies Centre.

Parker, G. and Lawton, D. (1994) *Different types of Carer: Evidence from the General Household Survey*, London: HMSO.

Paton, C. (2014) 'Garbage can policy making meets neo-liberal ideology: twenty five years of redundant reform of the English NHS', *Social Policy and Administration*, vol 48, no 3, pp 319–42.

Pauly, M.V. (1974) 'Over insurance and the public provision of insurance: the roles of moral hazard and adverse selection', *Quarterly Journal of Economics*, vol 88, pp 44–62.

Peacock, A.T. and Wiseman, J. (1961) *The growth of public expenditure in the United Kingdom*, London: Allen and Unwin.

Peacock, A.T. and Wiseman, J. (1962) 'The economics of higher education', Higher Education Evidence Part Two, Cmnd 2154-xii, pp 129–38.

Pensions Commission (2004) *Pensions: Challenges and choices: The first report of the Pensions Commission*, London: The Stationery Office.

Pensions Commission (2005) *A new pensions settlement for the twenty-first century. The second report of the Pensions Commission*, London: The Stationery Office.

Pension Policy Institute (2013) *Automatic Enrolement Report 1: What level of pension contribution is neded to obtain an adequate retirement income?*, London: Pension Policy Institute.

Piachaud, D. (1971) 'Poverty and taxation', *Political Quarterly*, vol 42, no 1, pp 31–44.

Piachaud, D. (2016) 'Citizens income rights and wrongs', CASEpaper.

Piketty, T. (2014) *Capital in the twenty-first century*, Cambridge, MA: Harvard University Press.

Plant, R. (2012) *The neo-liberal state*, Oxford: Oxford University Press.

Pollock, A., Macfarlane, A., Kirkwood, G. Majeed, A., Greener, I. and Marelli, C. (2011) 'No evidence that patient choice in the NHS saves lives', *Lancet*, vol 378, pp 2057–60.

Powell, M. (2007) *Understanding the mixed economy of welfare*, Bristol: The Policy Press.

Powell, M. and Miller, R. (2014) 'Framing privatisation in the English National Health Service', *Journal of Social Policy*, vol 43, no 3, pp 575–94.

Power, A. (1987) *Property before people: The management of twentieth century council housing*, London: Allen and Unwin.

Power, A. (1993) *Hovels to high rise: State housing in Europe since 1850*, London: Routledge.

Prest, A. (1962) 'The finance of university education in the Great Britain', Higher Education: Evidence – Part Two, Documentary Evidence, Cmnd 2154-XII, pp 139–59.

Productivity Commission (2011) *Caring for older Australians*, Melbourne, Australia: Productivity Commission.

Propper, C. (2001) 'Expenditure on health care in the UK: a review of the issues', *Fiscal Studies*, vol 22, no 2, pp 151–83.

Propper, C. (2012) 'Competition, incentives and the English NHS', *Health Economics*, vol 21, pp 33–40.

Public Schools Commission (1968) *First report*, London: HMSO.

RAND Corporation (2016) 'The health insurance experiment: a classic RAND study speaks to the current health care reform debate', Research Brief. Available at: www.rand.org

Rawls, J. (1988) 'The priority of right and ideas of the good', *Philosophy and Public Affairs*, vol 17, no 4, pp 251–76.

Richards, E., Wilsdon, T. and Lyons, S. (1996) *Paying for long term care*, London: IPPR.

Riley, J.G. (2001) 'Silver signals; twenty five years of screening and signalling', *Journal of Economic Literature*, vol 39, no 2, pp 432–78.

Robbins Committee (1963) *Higher education*, Cmnd 2154, London: HMSO.

Robertson, R., Gregory, S. and Jabbel, J. (2014) *The social care and health systems of 9 countries. Commission on the Future of Health and Social Care in England, background paper*, London: King's Fund.

Rogers, R. and Power, A. (2000) *Cities for a small country*, London: Faber.

Royal Commission on Long Term Care (1999) *With respect to old age*, Cm 4192, London: The Stationery Office.

Ruane, S. and Byrne, D. (2014) 'The political economy of taxation in the 21st century UK', in K. Farnsworth, Z. Irving and M. Fenger (eds) *Social policy review, 2014*, Bristol: The Policy Press.

Sainsbury, R. and Stanley, K. (2007) *One for all: Active welfare and the single working age benefit*, London: Institute for Public Policy Research.

Salamon, L. (1987) 'Partners in public service: voluntary failure and third party government: towards a theory of government non-profit relations', in W.W. Powell (ed) *The non-profit sector: A research handbook*, New Haven, CT: Yale University Press.

Sandel, M. (2012) *What money can't buy: The moral limits to markets*, London: Allen Lane.

Savas, E.S. (1977) 'Policy analysis for local government: public versus private refuse collection', *Policy Analysis*, vol 3, pp 44–74.

Savas, E.S. (1982) *Privatising the public sector: How to shrink government*, Chatham, NJ: Chatham House.

Schokkaert, E. and Van de Voorde, C. (2011) 'User charges', in S. Glied and P.C. Smith (eds) *The Oxford handbook of health economics*, Oxford: Oxford University Press.

Schultz, T.W. (1960) 'Capital formation by education', *Journal of Political Economy*, December, pp 571–84.

Schultz, T.W. (1961) 'Investment in human capital', *American Economic Review*, March, pp 1–17.

Scottish Government (2000) *Fair shares for all. Final report*, Edinburgh: Scottish Government.

Sen, A.K. (1985) 'Rights and capabilities', in A.K. Sen (ed) *Resources, values and development*, Oxford: Blackwell.

Sen, A.K. (1993) 'Capability and wellbeing', in M. Nussbaum and A.K. Sen (eds) *The quality of life*, Oxford: Oxford University Press.

Sjoberg, O., Palme, J. and Carrol, E. (2010) 'Unemployment insurance', in F. Castles, S. Leibrfied, J. Lewis, H. Obinger and C. Pierson (eds) *The Oxford handbook of the welfare state*, Oxford: Oxford University Press.

Smith, A. (1974 [1776]) *The wealth of nations*, Harmondsworth: Penguin Books.

Smith Commission (2014) *Report of the Smith Commission for further devolution of powers to the Scottish Parliament*, Edinburgh: Smith Commission.

Smyth, P. and Deeming, C. (2016) 'The "social investment perspective" in social policy: a longue duree perspective', *Social Policy and Administration*, vol 50, issue 6, pp 673–90.

Somerset Webb, M. (2016) 'Pension schemes need a holiday', *Financial Times*, Money section p 20, 9 July 2016.

Spicker, P. (2013) 'Introducing Universal Credit', in G. Ramia, K. Farnsworth and Z. Irving (eds) *Social policy review 25: Analysis and debate in social policy, 2013*, Bristol: The Policy Press.

Srblin, D.-R. (ed) (2015) *Tax for our times: How the Left can re-invent taxation*, London: Fabian Society.

Stedman Jones, D. (2012) *Masters of the universe: Hayek, Friedman, and the birth of neoliberal politics*, Princeton, NJ, and Oxford: Princeton University Press.

Stone, D.A. (1984) *The disabled state*, Philadelphia: Temple University Press.

Streeck, W. (2016) *How will capitalism end? Essays on a failing system*, London: Verso.

Streeck, W. and Mertens, D. (2013) 'Public finance and the decline of state capacity in democratic capitalism', in A. Schafer and W. Streeck (eds) *Politics in the age of austerity*, Cambridge: Polity Press.

Streeck, W. and Thelen, K. (2005) *Beyond continuity: Institutional change in advanced political economies*, Oxford: Oxford University Press.

Sutherland, G. (1973) *Policy making in elementary education 1870–1895*, Oxford: Oxford University Press.

Tanzi, V. (2011) *Government versus markets: The changing economic role of the state*, Cambridge: Cambridge University Press.

Tetlow, G. (2015) 'Pensions tax relief: time for a TEE-brake?', Chartered Insurance Institute, Thinkpiece 120. Available at: www.ifs.org.uk

Thain, C. and Wright, M. (1995) *The Treasury and Whitehall: The planning and control of public expenditure 1976–1993*, Oxford: Oxford University Press.

Thaler, R.H. and Sunstein, C.R. (2008) *Nudge: Improving decisions about health, wealth and happiness*, New Haven, CT: Yale University Press.

Thane, P. (2005) *The long history of old age*, London: Thames and Hudson.

Thane, P. (2006) 'The history of retirement', in Clark, G.L., Munnell, A.H. and Orszag, J.M. (eds) *The Oxford history of pensions and retirement income*, Oxford: Oxford University Press.

Tiebout, C. (1956) 'A pure theory of public expenditure', *Journal of Political Economy*, vol 64, no 5, pp 416–24.

Titmuss, R.M. (1958) *Essays on the 'welfare state'*, London: Allen and Unwin.

Titmuss, R.M. (1962) *Income distribution and social change*, London: Allen and Unwin.

Titmuss, R.M. (1970) *The gift relationship*, London: Allen and Unwin.

Tobin, J. (1978) 'A proposal for international monetary reform', *Easter Economic Journal*, vol 4, pp 153–9.

Tomlinson, D. and Corlett, A. (2017) *A tough gig: The nature of self employment in 21st century Britain and policy implications*, London: Resolution Foundation.

Tooley, J. (2008) *E.G. West; economic liberalism and the role of government in education*, London: Bloomsbury Academic.

Townsend, P. (1962) *The last refuge: A survey of residential institutions and homes for the aged in England and Wales*, London: Routledge and Kegan Paul.

Travers, T. (2000) 'The development of educational needs formulae 1958 to 1990', in H. Glennerster, J. Hills and T. Travers (eds) *Paying for health education and housing: How does the centre pull the purse strings?*, Oxford: Oxford University Press.

Travers, T. (2015) 'A hyper-centralised anomaly', in D.-R. Srblin (ed) *Tax for our times: How the Left can reinvent taxation*, London: Fabian Society.

Tullock, G. (1976) *The vote motive*, London: Institute of Economic Affairs.

Universities and Colleges Admissions Service (UCAS) (2017) *Application Rates by the January deadline, 2017 cycle*. Cheltenhan: UCAS (available on the UCAS website; ucas.com).

Vandenberghe, V. (1996) *Functioning and regulation of educational quasi-markets*, Louvain-la-Neuve: Catholic University.

Vandenberghe, V. (1998) 'Education quasi-markets: the Belgian experience', in W. Bartlett, J. Roberts and J. Le Grand (eds) *A revolution in social policy: Quasi-market reforms in the 1990s*, Bristol: The Policy Press, pp 79–94.

Van de Ven, W.P.M.M. and Schut, F.T. (2008) 'Universal mandatory health insurance: a model for the United States?', *Health Affairs*, vol 27, no 3, pp 771–81.

Van Parijs, P. (1991) 'Why surfers should be fed: The liberal case for an unconditional basic income', *Philosophy and Public Affairs*, vol 20, no 2, pp 101–31.

Viet-Wilson, J. (1994) 'Condemned to deprivation? Beveridge's responsibility for the invisibility of poverty', in J. Hills, J. Ditch and H. Glennerster (eds) *Beveridge and social security: An international retrospective*, Oxford: Oxford University Press.

Vizard, P. (2006) *Poverty and human rights: Sen's 'capability perspective' explored*, Oxford: Oxford University Press.

Walker, A. (2010) (ed) 'Disability', *The Peter Townsend Reader*, Bristol: Policy Press, pp 488–94.

Walker, A. and Townsend, P. (1980) 'Compensation for disability: The wrong course', in M. Brown and S. Baldwin (eds) *The year book of social policy in Britain 1978*, London: Routledge, pp 57–80.

Webster, C. (1988) *The health services since the war. Volume 1. Problems of health care. The National Health Service before 1957*, London: HMSO.

Weisbrod, B. (1986) 'Towards a theory of the voluntary non-profit sector in a three sector economy', in S. Rose-Ackerman (ed) *The economics of non-profit institutions*, Oxford: Oxford University Press.

Welsh Government (2016) *Local government finance report No 1, 2016-17*, Cardiff: Welsh Government.

West, A. (2016) *Education policy and governance under the Coalition government (2010–16): Academies, the pupil premium and free early education*, London: London Review of Education.

West, A., Pennell, H., West, R. and Travers, T. (2000) 'Financing school based education in England: Principles and problems', in M. Coleman and L. Anderson (eds) *Managing finance and resource in education*, London: Paul Chapman.

West, E.G. (1975) *Education and the Industrial Revolution*, London: Batisford.

Wiener, J. (2003) 'The role of informal support in long term care', in J. Brodsky, J. Habib and J. Hirschfield (eds) *Key policy issues in long term care*, Geneva: World Health Organisation.

Williams, P. and Whitehead, C. (2015) 'Financing affordable social housing in the UK: building on success?', *Housing Finance International*, pp 14–19. Available at: http://eprints.lse.ac.uk/63399/

Wittenberg, R. and Hu, B. (2015) *Projections of demand for and costs of social care for older people and younger adults in England 2015–35*, PSSRU Working Paper 2900, London: LSE.

Wolfe Report (2011) 'Review of Vocational Education'. Available at: www.gov.uk

Zweifel, P. (2011) 'Voluntary private health insurance', in G. Glied and P. Smith (eds) *The Oxford handbook of health economics*, Oxford: Oxford University Press.

Index

References to tables and figures are in *italics*

Printed in Poland
by Amazon Fulfillment
Poland Sp. z o.o., Wrocław